D0787902

The Final Leap

The publisher gratefully acknowledges the generous support of the General Endowment Fund of the University of California Press Foundation.

The Final Leap

Suicide on the Golden Gate Bridge

John Bateson

UNIVERSITY OF CALIFORNIA PRESS

Berkeley   Los Angeles   London

University of California Press, one of the most distinguished university
presses in the United States, enriches lives around the world by advancing
scholarship in the humanities, social sciences, and natural sciences. Its
activities are supported by the UC Press Foundation and by philanthropic
contributions from individuals and institutions. For more information, visit
www.ucpress.edu.

University of California Press
Berkeley and Los Angeles, California

University of California Press, Ltd.
London, England

Library of Congress Cataloging-in-Publication Data
Bateson, John, 1951–
    The final leap : suicide on the Golden Gate Bridge / John Bateson.
        p.   cm.
    Includes bibliographical references and index.
    ISBN 978-0-520-27240-8 (alk. paper)
    1. Suicide victims—California—San Francisco.
    2. Suicide—California—San Francisco.   3. Golden Gate Bridge (San Francisco,
 Calif.)   I. Title.
    HV6548.U52S36   2012
    362.2809794'61—dc23

                                                                    2011038983

Manufactured in the United States of America

20   19   18   17   16   15   14   13   12   11
10   9   8   7   6   5   4   3   2   1

To everyone who has lost a loved one
to the Golden Gate Bridge

To William~

On the occasion of your
(early) birthday. A book about
one of the most iconic and
tortured structures, right in
our backyard. I hope you
enjoy it as much as I did.
Shed some tears, too. Happiest
of birthdays, my dear, dear
friend.

Love
As always
Stacy

CONTENTS

ACKNOWLEDGMENTS

First and foremost, I want to thank the family members and friends of Golden Gate Bridge jumpers who shared their stories with me. Some didn't want to be identified or have their stories told so they're not mentioned. Regardless, my heart goes out to them, and I'm sorry for their loss.

A few family members have been public with their grief, knowing that it's necessary to influence decision makers and ultimately end suicides from the bridge. It has taken tremendous courage, and it has made a difference. I thank John and Erika Brooks, Dave Hull, Dayna Whitmer, and Mary Zablotny in particular for telling their stories to me and to others.

When friends and colleagues learned that I was writing this book, many wondered how I could sleep at night immersed in so much tragedy. Even tragedies have heroes, I replied, people who refused to be silent, who have stood up for what's right despite being criticized. This book has heroes, too, three in particular. I'm speaking of California Assemblyman and former Bridge District board member Tom Ammiano, bridge jump survivor Kevin

Hines, and recently retired Marin County coroner Ken Holmes. They will deserve much of the credit when suicides from the Golden Gate Bridge end.

A number of mental health professionals have advocated strenuously over the years in support of a suicide barrier. I thank Mel Blaustein, Anne Fleming, Margaret Hallett, Eve Meyer, Jerry Motto, Richard Seiden, Ron Tauber, and many others for this. In addition to their advocacy, Blaustein and Tauber amassed extensive files of press clippings, meeting minutes, reports, and correspondence regarding suicides from the Golden Gate Bridge, and shared them with me.

Also deserving thanks are Linda Allen, Ken Baldwin, Robert Bea, John Draper, Lorrie Goldin, Eric Hall, Patrick Hines, Thomas Joiner, Dave Kahler, Paul Muller, Nancy Salamy, Eric Steel, Janice Tagart, and Janet Wilson. At various times they served as sources of information and expertise.

I'm grateful, too, for the cooperation I received from Golden Gate Bridge District officials. Denis Mulligan, the CEO and general manager, and Mary Currie, the public affairs director, answered every question I asked, as well as provided background information. Kary Witt, the bridge manager, and Lisa Locati, the captain of bridge security, freely answered questions as well.

So did representatives of the U.S. Coast Guard. Leanne Lusk, the sector San Francisco command center chief, and Mark Allstott, commanding officer of Station Golden Gate, made themselves available to talk with me about their work as it pertains to Golden Gate Bridge suicides.

One person I did not interview but who merits acknowledgment nonetheless is Tad Friend. His 2003 article in the *New Yorker* focused attention on Golden Gate Bridge suicides in a way that hadn't happened before. In some respects he was able to report in 5,000 words what has taken me 70,000.

Locally, the *San Francisco Chronicle*'s seven-part series in 2005 about Golden Gate Bridge suicides was among the most in-depth pieces of reporting the paper has ever done. Much of the information is still relevant today, and some of the photos that are reprinted here, with permission, appeared first in the *Chronicle*.

The staff and board of the Contra Costa Crisis Center also have my gratitude. They provided encouragement and valuable advice throughout the development of this book.

In all likelihood, the final draft would be much different if it had been handled by anyone other than Naomi Schneider and her talented team at the University of California Press. When I decided that there was enough material for a book, and put together a proposal, UC Press was my first choice to publish it.

Writing a book, for the most part, is a solitary process. Other than conducting interviews, the work—from research to writing to revising of various drafts—takes place alone. If one has a family, it means that others have to understand and be supportive. No one could receive more understanding or support than I have from Suzan and our four adult children—Sara, Cassidy, Chloé, and Trevor. You have my love and my thanks.

Prologue

It's a little after 6 A.M. on Tuesday, January 29, 2008. A lone figure walks head down on the Golden Gate Bridge. She is seventeen years old, pretty, with shoulder-length brown hair. In five
months she's supposed to graduate from Redwood High School
in Marin County, one of the top-rated high schools in California.
In the fall, her friends will be heading off to college. She could be
heading off to college, too; she has a 3.7 grade point average and
has been accepted at Bennington College in Vermont, her first
choice. Bennington is a long way from home, which is part of its
attraction. Also, it's a small college—another attraction. She liked
the campus when she visited it with her parents, thinking that she
would study environmental science and journalism. Now, though,
she's on the Golden Gate Bridge, early in the morning on a school
day, and has a different plan.

Near the midpoint of the span she stops. No one is around. At
this hour of the day, in the middle of winter, it is cold and still
mostly dark. The pedestrian walkway is deserted. There's no
one to see her, no one to stop her. She climbs over the railing

onto the chord, the 32-inch-wide girder on the other side of the railing. She's in good shape from playing soccer and lacrosse; however, the railing is only four feet high so being in shape doesn't matter. Almost anyone can climb over it. Between the chord and the dark water of the bay far below is salt air, thick and beckoning.

At nearly the same time, her father is up as usual in the family's Tiburon home, seven miles north of the Golden Gate Bridge. He is an executive in San Francisco and commutes every day across the bridge to work. This morning, as on many mornings, he goes into his daughter's bedroom to wake her up. On the wall above her bed a poster from the movie *Trainspotting* proclaims "Choose Life" in bold letters. He doesn't see the poster, though. What he notices immediately is that his daughter's bed is made and the keys to the family's red Saab are missing. A few days earlier there had been an argument and his daughter had been grounded, denied use of the car.

On the bed is a note. "The Saab is parked at the Golden Gate Bridge. I'm sorry."

His daughter, Casey, has suffered from emotional problems since infancy. She was born prematurely, in Poland, to a mother who abandoned her. There had been a twin sister who was stillborn, but Casey's adoptive parents, John and Erika Brooks, had not told Casey about her, wanting to wait until Casey was a little older, a little better able to handle the news.

Casey was fourteen months old when the Brookses adopted her from a Polish orphanage. She had the developmental capacity of a six-month-old. She couldn't stand, sit, talk, or feed herself. Doctors told the Brookses that best case, Casey was under stimulated and suffered from learning disabilities. For five weeks, while the Brookses were in Poland waiting for Casey's visa to be approved, Casey showed rapid progress. By the time they left the country, Casey was able to sit up and walk.

She continued to progress, and in many respects seemed "normal." She was a talented writer, did well in school, and was popular with classmates. The trauma Casey suffered during infancy had a lasting effect, however. As she got older, her father says, "She was unable to soothe herself. She had periodic temper tantrums and crying fits, would lock herself in her room, and scream it out." He speculates that she suffered from an attachment disorder and "had a lot of self-loathing." At the same time, "She put on a great game face, not letting people see what she was fighting."

Starting in middle school, the Brookses took Casey to a succession of therapists. It wasn't easy; in fact, Casey fought therapy vigorously and her parents almost literally had to drag her to sessions. "She had demons inside her and didn't want anyone to touch them," her father says. Eventually, they gave up, deciding that it wasn't productive. Moreover, Casey made it known that she wouldn't take any medications that were prescribed for her. "Seventy-five percent of the time she was delightful," John Brooks says. "Twenty-five percent of the time she was a nightmare." It was hard to know whether this was common or atypical. The Brookses had no parenting experience to draw on; besides, every child is different, and adolescence is a time of emotional angst.

To an outside observer, Casey Brooks led a life of privilege. An only child, she grew up in one of the wealthiest communities in the United States. The median price of a home in Tiburon is $2 million, and many homes cost more than $10 million. Views are spectacular—panoramic and breathtaking. Houses are oriented to the water, to San Francisco Bay and the Golden Gate Bridge.

Being an orphan from Eastern Europe, abandoned at birth and developmentally delayed due to a lack of attention, and now living in one of the most beautiful places in the world, Casey had trouble believing that she fit in. Her entire life could have been spent in the orphanage or on a Polish farm, yet she was living in luxury. Her guilt was reflected in a poem she wrote for English class a week before her thirteenth birthday, titled "Don't Stereotype Me."

Just because I live in Tiburon, I'm not a billionaire, I'm not
 conceited, I don't gossip, and I'm not stuck up.
Just because I live in Tiburon, I don't own a $200,000 Bently
 [sic], I don't live in a mansion, I don't go to an expensive
 private school, and I don't get whatever I want.
Just because I live in Tiburon, I haven't my own basketball
 team, it doesn't mean I'll get a Mercedes on my 16th
 birthday, it doesn't mean I go to fancy spas every day, and
 it doesn't mean I'm any better or worse than you.
Just because I live in Tiburon, why should it matter anyway?
 Why do you judge me? You don't even know who I am.
 What does it matter, I'm no different from you. What
 counts is your personality, not your possessions.
Just because I live in Tiburon, don't stereotype me."

One reason Casey wanted to go to college far away was to escape the prejudices of people who thought, in her mind, that she must be full of herself since she grew up in affluence. That's not how she saw herself; it wasn't who she was. "If I had one word to describe Casey," her father says, "it would be 'authentic' or 'genuine.' She hated phonies."

Despite periods of depression, Casey never exhibited any obvious signs of suicidal behavior, her father says. Death was not a theme in any of her writing, and she did not talk about dying, let her appearance go, withdraw from others, give away prized possessions, or exhibit any risk-taking behavior other than sneaking an occasional cigarette. Now, though, she was on the bridge.

His heart pounding, John Brooks calls 911. The dispatcher contacts the California Highway Patrol, which in turn contacts the Bridge Patrol and the Coast Guard. It's a regular occurrence for the Golden Gate Bridge security force to receive a B.O.L. (be on the lookout) report either by phone or e-mail from a parent whose child may be heading to the bridge to jump. The red Saab is found, abandoned, near the bridge. There's no sign of Casey, though, either on the bridge or in the water.

A few months earlier, Casey and a friend were driving across the Golden Gate Bridge. They talked casually about a number of things, and the subject of suicide came up. Both agreed that the only way to do it was to jump off the Golden Gate. The friend asked Casey, hypothetically, which side she'd jump from. Casey answered without hesitation—the east side, the side facing San Francisco.

On Sunday night, just two days earlier, Casey had snuck out of the house and driven to the bridge. She didn't know until she got there that the gate to the pedestrian walkway is locked from 6 P.M. to 5 A.M., November to March (the rest of the year it's open until 9 P.M.). Few people—and no tourists—are interested in walking on the bridge after dark. Frustrated, Casey had returned home. The next morning, on a message board to her friends, she wrote, "I had a really, really bad scare last night. In reality it was so close between life and death and at least right now, I'm still not sure if I made the right decision. I'm just so tired, tired of life and tired of everything in it. I hope [I] never, ever even think of doing, or almost doing, such a thing again."

Monday night she stayed up past midnight doing homework. She carried a heavy academic load, including three Advanced Placement classes. Her last communication was with a friend via computer. They talked about reincarnation. Casey wrote, "I think if I was reincarnated as anything in my next life it would probably be really shitty because I've been so lucky in this life."

After making the 911 call, John and Erika Brooks drive to the bridge in a state of high anxiety. They hope desperately that it's all a mistake, that even though the Saab is at the bridge, Casey has run off somewhere. Police officers try to prepare them for the worst. It is not unusual for them to find an abandoned car near the bridge that eventually is linked to a suicide.

One of the officers reviews videotape from bridge cameras taken early that morning, then shares the information with the Brookses. Even though it is semi-dark, a young woman matching the description of Casey Brooks is clearly visible on film. She's dressed like a jogger, walking alone on the pedestrian path, smoking a cigarette. After surmounting the railing on the east side, the side facing San Francisco, she stands motionless on the chord for ten seconds. Then she jumps.

The world of John and Erika Brooks will never be the same.

ONE

Beauty and Death

The couple that held hands and jumped from the
Golden Gate Bridge after a last kiss Saturday
was identified yesterday.

—*San Francisco Chronicle*, October 4, 1977

I've been thinking about suicide for a long time. In fact, it has
occupied my daily life for the last fifteen years. That's how long
I have directed the Contra Costa Crisis Center, a twenty-four-
hour crisis intervention and suicide prevention center in Contra
Costa County, California.

Contra Costa has a population of 1.1 million people. It is
directly east of San Francisco, across the bay from the city. This
fact isn't particularly notable except that it's a short ride by car
or bus from many parts of the county to the Golden Gate Bridge.
After San Francisco and Marin, the two counties that are joined
by the world's most famous span, Contra Costa is the county
with the highest number of Golden Gate Bridge suicides. On our
crisis lines we talk down people who intend to jump from the
bridge, and in our grief counseling program we console family
members and friends of bridge jumpers.

One of my first lessons at the crisis center concerned the Golden Gate Bridge. A local artists' guild brought new paintings every month to display in the agency's offices. As soon as they went up, staff went around and made sure that none of them included an image of the bridge. If they did, the paintings came down. We didn't want to hurt or offend anyone whose loved one might have jumped.

Over the years, I've written periodic articles and opinion pieces about Golden Gate Bridge suicides. When published, they have elicited shock and disbelief. People, especially local people, are stunned to learn that the bridge is the top suicide site in the world. Since it opened in 1937, there have been more than fifteen hundred confirmed suicides, although the actual number is believed to be well over two thousand. That's because the bodies of many jumpers aren't ever found, they're washed out to sea. Other times the body is found, but far enough away that the death cannot be attributed with certainty to the bridge. Police need evidence to verify a death, and if a body isn't recovered or a jump isn't witnessed, there can't be confirmation, even if personal effects and a suicide note are found.

The same people who are shocked when they hear the extent of the problem, a problem that is rarely publicized (no book has been written about it before), are surprised to learn that the Golden Gate Bridge is the only international landmark without a suicide barrier. The Eiffel Tower, the Empire State Building, St. Peter's Basilica, the Duomo, and Sydney Harbor Bridge—to name just a few—have had suicide barriers added to prevent a procession of tragic and unnecessary deaths. The Golden Gate Bridge, so far, has not. It stands today as the location where more people go to kill themselves than anywhere else. The bridge's easily surmountable, four-foot-high railing, year-round pedestrian access, fame, and beauty make it alluring to anyone who's fighting inner demons and looking for a quick way out.

In this book I offer a perspective that is gleaned from my many years of work in the field of suicide prevention. In addition to directing the crisis center, I was appointed by the governor of California to a blue-ribbon committee that developed the state's suicide prevention strategy. I also helped draft the legislation that resulted in the creation of California's Office of Suicide Prevention. In addition, I served four years on the steering committee of the National Suicide Prevention Lifeline, based in New York City, which operates America's three suicide hotlines (800-273-TALK, 800-SUICIDE, and 888-628-9454, the latter for Spanish-speaking callers). It is my belief—and I'm certainly not alone in this—that suicide, in most instances, is preventable. In fact, it's the most preventable form of death. Moreover, one of the surest ways to prevent suicide, as many studies have proven, is to restrict access to lethal means. That's where the Golden Gate Bridge comes in; it's about the most lethal means there is. The odds of surviving a jump from the bridge are roughly the same as surviving a gunshot to your head. The major differences are that with jumping one doesn't have to obtain or handle a weapon, and there's no messy cleanup for loved ones to deal with afterward. A person just has to get to the bridge and jump.

For many people, the Golden Gate Bridge represents hope and a fresh beginning—the pot of gold at the end of the rainbow, the chance to start a new life in one of the most glamorous, beautiful, and tolerant cities in the world. For others, the bridge represents an altogether different destination—the end of the trail. They throw themselves off it with such regularity and so little fanfare that the public forgets that the problem exists. Certainly no one is reminded how often it occurs. Most people see only the splendor of the bridge; not the deaths linked to it.

That used to be the case with me. Although I've lived in the San Francisco Bay Area my entire life, I never gave much thought to the issue of suicides from the Golden Gate Bridge or the need for a suicide barrier. No one I knew well had ever jumped from the bridge, seriously considered jumping, or lost a family member or friend that way. Never in my infrequent walks across the bridge had I seen someone jump or attempt to jump.

After I started at the crisis center, everything changed. I learned facts about the bridge that astonished me, mainly because I felt that I should have known them already. Then I realized that most of the people I knew or came into contact with didn't know them either. That was the genesis for this book.

For instance, most people don't know that the vast majority of individuals who jump from the Golden Gate Bridge live relatively close to it. Only a small number of those who use the bridge to attempt or complete suicide come from other states, an even smaller number come from other countries. Despite the myth that the bridge serves as a mecca for troubled and depressed souls around the world, in actuality its attraction is largely local.

Most people don't know that it's not just single men suffering from mental illness who jump. More than 10 percent of Golden Gate Bridge jumpers are adolescents. Adult jumpers, meanwhile, include virtually every profession. Many are married with children. Some live in affluence.

Most people don't know that because of the short railing, at least three young children have been thrown over the side by parents who jumped after them. In another case, a five-year-old girl was told to jump by her father, and complied.

Most people don't know that it's not unusual for jumpers to survive the fall. Upon hitting the water their bones shatter, their body organs burst, they plunge deep beneath the surface, and ultimately they drown. Far from being a fast and painless way to die, jumping from the bridge can produce final minutes that are excruciating and terrifying.

Most people don't know that the original design for the bridge called for a higher railing specifically to protect against suicides. In a last-minute design decision, however, this safety feature was sacrificed for the view.

Most people don't know that at one time the Golden Gate Bridge actually had a safety net. It was installed during construction at a cost of $130,000 (the equivalent of $2 million today), ran the length of the span, and was designed to protect bridge workers. At various times, nineteen men fell into the net and were saved. When the bridge was completed, the net was removed.

Most people don't know that one section of the bridge has had a barrier for many years. There is an eight-foot-high, 350-foot-long chain-link fence on the San Francisco side, before the toll booths. It's not pretty, but then it's not intended to be. It's also not there to prevent suicides. Its purpose is to prevent garbage from being thrown onto visitors walking below, at Fort Point.

Most people don't know that the reason why the Golden Gate Bridge has surveillance equipment and motion sensors has nothing to do with suicide prevention. Yes, the equipment is used to spot would-be jumpers and direct rescue workers to the location as quickly as possibly. And yes, Bridge District officials promote the system as evidence that they are concerned about suicides and have procedures in place to prevent them. But the reason why surveillance equipment was originally installed was to monitor traffic conditions on the bridge and in the toll plaza area. The reason why it has been beefed up substantially in recent years is to fight terrorism. Because it's an international landmark, the Golden Gate Bridge is considered a primary target for terrorists. Closely monitoring the goings-on of motorists and pedestrians is deemed critical to the safety of millions of residents.

The most important thing that people don't know about the bridge is how big the suicide problem is. To hear that more than fifteen hundred people have died jumping off the Golden Gate Bridge is hard to believe. To hear that the deaths continue at a rate of two to three per month—with virtually no public outcry—is even harder to accept. To hear that no other site in the world is close to the Golden Gate Bridge when it comes to suicide leaves one feeling numb and of the opinion that this problem can't continue, it has to end.

That's the reason for this book. It's intended to educate readers about Golden Gate Bridge suicides with the hope that more people will realize that this deplorable situation must be remedied at once, without further delay. And it can be. A taller railing or a well-designed net underneath will solve the problem immediately and effectively. Of course, there are people who object to any changes because the bridge is such an icon. As a centerpiece, conduit, and symbol it reigns supreme, not only for the city of San Francisco but for California and the West. Yet doing nothing only adds to the death toll.

In the following chapters I provide a wide-ranging examination of the most popular suicide site on earth. I explore the bridge's celebrated history; it's unfortunate appeal to people who want to die; the dark stories of the suicides themselves; how the few survivors of Golden Gate Bridge jumps view their near-deaths; the roles of the police, Coast Guard, coroner, Bridge District, and mental health community; and the simple change that would without a doubt prevent these tragedies in the future.

The story of Golden Gate Bridge suicides started mere weeks after the bridge opened in May 1937 when a World War I veteran became the first official casualty, and it has continued ever since. One reason why it continues is because people don't want to believe or, perhaps, prefer to ignore that the extraordinary, spell-binding, one-of-a-kind bridge is blemished. That might damage San Francisco's thriving tourism industry, which supports thousands of businesses as well as enhances government coffers. It also would give pause to artists, photographers, moviemakers, and poets who craft paeans to the bridge. Most importantly, it would mean confronting a problem that's unpleasant to consider, that some people are so distressed they want to end their lives.

Another reason why Golden Gate Bridge jumps continue is because the subject of suicide remains taboo. Society as a whole and people individually don't want to talk about it. Some individuals believe that if you talk about suicide, you plant the thought in someone's mind when it wasn't there before. Curiously, this same fear isn't raised in regards to public awareness campaigns to reduce drunk driving, drug use, domestic violence, cigarette smoking, or unprotected sex. In those instances, acknowledging and talking about the problem are considered important first steps in addressing it, leading to a clearer understanding of the issues while simultaneously dispelling misperceptions. Suicide though, is different. It is still concealed and largely unknown, on a par only with incest, perhaps, in terms of public avoidance. Because of the shame and stigma associated with suicide, many people want to keep it that way, including people who have been directly impacted, who have lost a loved one to suicide.

In chapter 2 I examine the much-touted history of the Golden Gate Bridge. Not only was it the longest single suspension span in the world at the time it was built, but it was the first bridge to be erected at the mouth of a major harbor. This is important because in addition to all the engineering challenges, such as high winds, deep water, strong currents, and close proximity to the San Andreas fault, which nearly leveled the city of San Francisco in the 1906 earthquake, the bridge had to be tall enough to accommodate large ships passing underneath.

The height of the Golden Gate Bridge is a key reason why it attracts suicidal people. The roadbed is 220 feet above the water, far higher than most other bridges. Jumping off it, a person is virtually certain to die—especially if he or she lands any way other than feet first. An even bigger reason for the bridge's fatal attraction, however, is the railing. It's only four feet high. When people walk on the bridge for the first time, they're always surprised at how low the railing is. If you're young, it's easy to hurtle; if you're older, it's easy to climb over.

Irving Morrow is the person who created the bridge's distinctive Art Deco style. He's also the person credited with making the last-minute design change that has led to so many deaths. By lowering the railing, his intention was to achieve even greater beauty, primarily for pedestrians and motorists on the bridge. He accomplished this goal; however, success came with a steep price. The bridge became a shrine for suicide.

In chapter 3 I relate the impact of bridge suicides on the lives of others. Each suicide has multiple victims. There's the person who dies, and there's everyone else who is left to mourn. The stories of Golden Gate Bridge victims put a face on the problem. There's the championship wrestler, the esteemed physician, and the one-time football star. There's the respected minister, the decorated

Marine, and the former debutante. There's the fourteen-year-old, straight-A student who took a $150 cab ride to the bridge because she was too young to drive. There's the overweight, seventy-five-year-old matron who had no trouble climbing over the railing. There's Roy Raymond, the founder of Victoria's Secret; Duane Garrett, a personal advisor to Al Gore; and Marc Salinger, whose father, Pierre, was the press secretary for presidents John F. Kennedy and Lyndon B. Johnson. Their deaths and the deaths of hundreds of others, young and old, have torn the hearts out of everyone who loved them.

The role of the Marin County coroner is described in chapter 4. In addition to conducting the autopsies of Golden Gate Bridge jumpers, the coroner's office handles the death notifications. As gruesome as the autopsies are, notifying next of kin is worse. It takes what might otherwise be an ordinary day in someone's life and turns it into the worst day he or she may ever have. At one time coroner Ken Holmes believed that Golden Gate Bridge suicides shouldn't be publicized because that exposure might lead to even more deaths. It was better to keep the problem hidden, he reasoned, to discourage imitative behavior. He changed his mind when he realized that silence wasn't working; the number of jumps wasn't declining. In fact, in 2007 it reached a ten-year high. That's when Holmes decided to become vocal. He began providing data to the media about bridge suicides without prompting. He's the only person who has.

In chapter 5 I explore the attitudes, experiences, and opinions (pre and post) of an ultra-select group—the thirty-two people who are known to have survived a jump from the Golden Gate Bridge. Nearly all were young when they made their attempt, in their teens and twenties. All entered the water feet first, at a slight angle. All had their jumps witnessed and were picked up quickly by boaters or the Coast Guard. All suffered injuries that required hospitalization and, in many instances, permanent treatment. Of particular interest, most survivors of a Golden Gate Bridge jump say that as soon as they let go of the railing, they wanted to live. One survivor, Kevin Hines, had the presence of mind to flip himself midair to avoid hitting the water head first. Another survivor, Ken Baldwin, divides his life in halves—the half before August 1985, when he jumped from the bridge, and the half afterward.

When asked why they jumped, survivors have provided a two-part answer. First, they sought relief from their emotional pain. Death—the great unknown—was more attractive than life, which was both known and unbearable. Second, no planning was needed. One didn't need to procure a gun, hoard pills, cut themselves, breathe carbon monoxide, or wonder whether the rope would hold. One also didn't need to worry about leaving a messy death scene. All that was required was a short trip to the bridge and a second or two to surmount the railing. After that the height, the fall, and the dark waters below took care of everything.

The fact that the Golden Gate Bridge is both an engineering marvel and a work of unparalleled artistry adds to the allure. As the most famous bridge and largest Art Deco sculpture on the planet, it holds a special place in people's minds. If someone's life seems filled with despair, there's always the possibility, one imagines, of a glorious exit.

The work of helpers and responders is described in chapter 6. Helpers range from mental health professionals to highly trained volunteers, from bedside clinicians to hotline counselors. They provide therapy and support to people who are suicidal, as well as to the few individuals who survive bridge jumps and to the loved ones of all those who do not. Helpers know firsthand the magnitude of the problem. They know that nearly twice as many people in the United States die by suicide as homicide. They know the enormous toll that suicide takes on the families of victims. They know the deadly mystique of the Golden Gate Bridge. They also know that suicide is preventable if society is committed to ending it.

Responders consist of police officers in the Golden Gate Bridge Patrol and the California Highway Patrol, as well as U.S. Coast Guard crew members. The former talk down suicidal people from the bridge, something they receive minimal training to do. Mostly it's learned on the job. Successful interventions can take hours and leave officers emotionally exhausted, while failures haunt their minds. The latter recover the bodies of bridge jumpers. It's not something they signed up for; they joined the Coast Guard to save lives. There are more search and rescue cases in San Francisco Bay than anywhere else in the country, in part because the job includes retrieving the bodies of Golden Gate Bridge jumpers.

In chapter 7, I examine the unique role of the Golden Gate Bridge, Highway, and Transportation District (known as the Bridge District). The Golden Gate Bridge is the only bridge in California with its own governing authority. All other bridges fall under the purview of the state Department of Transportation, commonly known as Caltrans. Since it opened, the Golden Gate Bridge has been governed by an independent, stand-alone entity. Bridge District board members set tolls, supervise maintenance projects, approve special events, and decide whether there should be any kind of suicide deterrent on the bridge. Over the years they have studied barrier options, assessed the potential impact of a barrier on wind resistance, and touted the effectiveness of bridge surveillance and monitoring efforts—the latter in an attempt to defuse blame and downplay the problem of bridge suicides. To their dismay, not only have people continued to throw themselves off the bridge, but in recent years the problem has become better known.

A large part of this is due to Eric Steel, a New York City filmmaker. In 2005 he released a documentary movie about suicides from the Golden Gate Bridge. The movie probably did more to bring bridge suicides out of the shadows than anything else. Rarely is the sight of real people dying real deaths shown to mainstream audiences. Steel deceived local officials in order to get permission to place cameras on the bridge for a year, and captured on film people jumping off. When the movie came out, Bridge District officials were incensed. Not only did they dislike being misled, they blamed Steel for contributing to the problem by making it public. Nevertheless, three years later the Bridge District board voted in favor of a suicide deterrent on the bridge. Specifically, directors approved the addition of a rigid steel net strung twenty feet below the span. The net will cost $50 million and they will not allow bridge tolls to pay for any of it, so where the money will come from is unknown. Thus, the actual end to the problem is still years away.

The suicide barrier controversy is discussed in depth in chapter 8. The issue of a suicide barrier on the Golden Gate Bridge has been debated for years, ever since Harold Wobber leaped over the side soon after the bridge opened (Wobber's body was never recovered, in part because no one had planned for that possibility). Although numerous studies have been commissioned and designs proposed, anyone can still walk on the bridge today, climb over the side in seconds, and jump to a near-certain death. The logical question to ask is, why? Why doesn't the bridge have a barrier?

The nominal reasons are easy to name: because a barrier would be expensive; because it would impact bridge aesthetics; and because many people believe that it would not make a difference (their argument being that someone intent on suicide would go somewhere else to jump or, being thwarted, choose another lethal means). Even if those reasons were true—and there's substantial evidence that they're not—they don't answer the question. Every other architectural wonder in the world that once was a site of frequent suicide attempts now has a barrier even though at one time the same arguments were voiced against it. Why did people in Paris, New York, Rome, Florence, Sydney, and elsewhere ignore those arguments and erect suicide barriers— sometimes after fewer than a dozen deaths—while citizens of San Francisco, to date, have not? Is it because local residents, famous for their tolerance, choose to accept deaths from their international icon and perhaps even derive perverse enjoyment from the macabre nature of the bridge? Is it because San Franciscans don't care, because they reason that it's only a few dozen people per year who are dying and many of them are marginalized by mental illness so, from a societal point of view, it's not worth worrying about? Or is it because most residents haven't even thought about it, that despite living in the shadow of the bridge they are oblivious to the siren call it emits?

If two to three people died every month in a cable car accident, it's a good bet that the cable cars would stop running until the problem was fixed. If a baseball fan died every ten days at AT&T Park—home of the San Francisco Giants—because of batted balls, shattered bats, or an accidental fall over the second-deck railing, preventative measures would be implemented. If an intersection in the city was the site of frequent fatal accidents because vehicle traffic was unregulated, a stoplight or stop signs would be installed immediately. Public pressure would demand it. Yet suicides continue from the Golden Gate Bridge in greater number than anywhere else and relatively few people, including local people, know it or seem bothered by it.

In the epilogue I touch on a recent, related problem—suicides at various train crossings in the Bay Area. I also describe steps being taken to implement suicide barriers on a number of bridges elsewhere, including the Aurora Bridge in Seattle, which for many years was the number two suicide site in the United States after the Golden Gate Bridge, with 250 deaths. Finally, I note that the new section of the Bay Bridge that links Oakland with San Francisco is being modeled after the Golden Gate Bridge with a high roadway, pedestrian access (to date pedestrians haven't been allowed on the Bay Bridge), and only a fifty-four-inch railing. The new section is scheduled for completion in 2013, and already U.S. Coast Guard crews, mental health professionals, and others are bracing for the possibility of another major suicide magnet in the area. The Bay Bridge already has several suicides per year, and the number is sure to increase once there is pedestrian access.

Additional information, including a summary of research on why people kill themselves, is included in the appendices. From the early studies of sociologist Emile Durkheim, who theorized that suicide is caused by social factors such as isolation and lack of connectedness, to psychologist Edwin Shneidman, the father of suicidology, who coined the phrase "psychache" to describe the emotional pain that drives people to take their lives, to psychiatrist Aaron Beck's research on hopelessness and psychologist Thomas Joiner's current studies in which desire and capacity are key elements, the thinking about suicide has changed over the years. We know now that 90 percent of people who die by suicide are clinically depressed, and their actions may be further influenced by drugs or alcohol. Yet many people who suffer from depression never make an attempt. Some researchers believe that suicidal behavior is linked to physiological or genetic factors, but so far this has not been proven conclusively. What has been proven is that most people fixate on one means of death. Eliminate access to that means—whether it's a safety lock on firearms, a blister tab on medications, or a barrier on a bridge—and suicides are reduced.

The appendices also include numbers to call for help and information if you or someone you know is feeling suicidal, as well as the most complete listing to date of people who have killed themselves by jumping off the Golden Gate Bridge. The latter has a table with a year-by-year count of known suicides from the bridge. The total, midway through 2011 is 1,575. The actual number, as noted earlier, is certainly higher.

The Golden Gate Bridge is beautiful, but not to everyone. It's not beautiful to families and friends who have lost loved ones. While others celebrate the splendor, grace, and technological triumph of the bridge, they're reminded of a deep, never-ending hurt. With each new viewing of the span, whether in person, in a movie, in a company logo, or on an article of clothing, the wound is reopened. Few other death scenes embody so much emotion for so many people.

The bridge isn't beautiful to people who are unfortunate enough to witness a jump. Whether that person is a pedestrian on the bridge, a motorist driving by, a sailor on the bay, or a bridge worker, seeing a person hurtle over the railing is traumatizing. You view the bridge differently after that. Beauty and death can't be separated.

The bridge isn't beautiful to many police officers or Coast Guard personnel, either. It represents an unsavory part of their job, something they do only because there's no one else to do it.

This is the story of how one of the world's most famous landmarks became the top destination of people wanting to die. It's also the story of why, so far, the Golden Gate Bridge remains that way. If it takes you a week to read this book, and the Golden Gate Bridge still doesn't have a suicide deterrent, odds are that another tortured soul will have jumped before you finish. And a whole new group of people will be left to mourn.

One day steps will be taken so that suicides from the bridge end, just as they have ended on other famous monuments around the world. When that happens, lives will be saved. Unfortunately, that day isn't here yet. As a result, the deaths continue—tragic, misunderstood, and totally preventable.

TWO

Fatal Decisions

The Golden Gate Bridge is practically suicide proof.
Suicide from the bridge is neither possible nor
probable.

   —Joseph Strauss, chief engineer,
      Golden Gate Bridge, 1936

The issue of suicide has been inextricably linked with the Golden
Gate Bridge since it was built. From the bridge's inauguration in
1937 to the present, the dangers of this iconic landmark have been
ignored, obscured, and dismissed by nearly everyone—especially
public officials and the media. The dark underside of the bridge's
history offers testimony to its Janus-like appeal. While it is a mon-
umental edifice, noted for its beauty, it also serves as the world's
leading site for suicide.

   The building of a bridge, over the shortest point at the mouth of
San Francisco Bay, was deemed impossible during the nineteenth
century due to the high winds and strong currents of the Golden
Gate Strait. This stretch of water, named by Captain John Fremont
several years before gold was discovered in California, intimidated
engineers and city planners for decades. In 1872 business tycoon
Charles Crocker advocated unsuccessfully for a bridge, and forty

years later it was still deemed unfeasible. Nevertheless, Michael O'Shaughnessy, the city engineer of San Francisco, prompted by a local newspaper editor named James Wilkins, who had studied engineering, began sounding out others about ways that it could be accomplished. The population in and around San Francisco was growing, yet the city was surrounded on three sides by water. It had no place to expand. Meanwhile, fifty thousand people were commuting to San Francisco every day on ferryboats. The majority came from Alameda and Contra Costa counties to the east, although some also came from the north, from Marin, Napa, and Sonoma counties. They debarked en masse at the Ferry Building in downtown San Francisco, causing a mad crush of people that worsened as communities in surrounding areas increased in population. The most attractive option was to facilitate automobile access from the north; after all, by the 1920s Henry Ford was mass-producing cars, turning out one every fifteen minutes, at prices that were affordable to many working-class people. The ability to construct a bridge over the treacherous strait of water presented a significant roadblock, however.

The few engineers who said it was possible placed an enormous price tag on it—$100 million or more. That's when Joseph Strauss entered the scene. Strauss had never built a bridge remotely close in size or complexity to what the site demanded. He had graduated from the University of Cincinnati thirteen years before the school conferred engineering degrees, and he never belonged to the American Society of Civil Engineers. Furthermore, his specialty was drawbridges—he had constructed more than four hundred, all of the same basic design. Nevertheless, what he lacked in technological know-how he made up for with persistence, determination, and chutzpah. He told O'Shaughnessy that a bridge could be built across the strait at a cost of $27 million. In 1921 he submitted his design for it.

Resistance to the bridge came from multiple sources. The U.S. War Department, which had jurisdiction over the area, was concerned about possible disruptions to shipping and military traffic in the harbor. The War Department also owned the land on both sides of the strait, where the bridge's approaches would be located, and did not want to be responsible for the cost of maintaining them.

Southern Pacific Railroad opposed the bridge for financial reasons. In addition to railroads which crisscrossed the country, the company owned the ferryboats that transported passengers every day into San Francisco. Its lucrative monopoly was threatened if the city became accessible from the north by car. Company lawyers fought fiercely to protect Southern Pacific's interests; however, a series of court cases ended in rulings that favored the bridge.

Environmentalists also opposed the bridge. They believed that the site was too beautiful to mar with any kind of man-made structure. From bluffs on the Marin Headlands and cliffs on the San Francisco side, hikers had sweeping, unobstructed views of the bay, the hills, and the Pacific Ocean. This was one location where the awe-inspiring views had to be preserved, unblemished, they claimed.

Several counties north of San Francisco—Mendocino, Napa, Lake, and Humbolt—had supported construction of the bridge early on, but backed out as cost estimates rose. In the midst of the Depression, financing a project of this magnitude was considered too daunting even though it would provide much-needed jobs. It didn't help that the nearby Bay Bridge, connecting Oakland and Berkeley to the east with San Francisco, was already under construction, and all available government funding was allocated to it. The Golden Gate Bridge, as a result, had to be financed with bonds that would be paid back by revenues from future tolls.

In 1923 the California State Legislature passed the Golden Gate Bridge and Highway District Act. The act gave San Francisco and five counties north of it the right to form a bridge district, borrow money, issue bonds, build a bridge, and collect tolls. In 1928, the Golden Gate Bridge and Highway District was established, consisting of San Francisco (which is both a city and a county), Marin County, Sonoma County, Del Norte County, and portions of Napa and Mendocino counties. (In 1969, the legislature approved a bill that expanded the district's responsibilities to include bus and ferry service in the area. At that time the word "Transportation" was added to the district's name.)

After the district was formed, Strauss was named chief engineer of the bridge. His main task, early on, was to lobby for a ballot measure that approved construction. Multiple measures went down to defeat, and for awhile it looked like the bridge would never be built. At the same time, another problem emerged. Strauss's original design was part suspension span and part cantilever structure. Its functionality was questionable, and its appearance was far from elegant. According to Golden Gate Bridge historian John van der Zee, it was "a ponderous, ugly structure of mixed parentage, based on erroneous survey information and precious little actual engineering." Most local officials didn't know enough to question the science behind the design. They were disappointed by the look of the bridge, though, and wanted something more inspiring, befitting the sweep of the bay and the international sophistication of San Francisco. Strauss brought in several consultants to help, among them Leon Mois-seiff and Charles Ellis.

Moisseiff was born in Latvia and came to the United States in 1891 at age nineteen. When Strauss began working on designs for the Golden Gate Bridge, Moisseiff was considered one of the best bridge designers in the country, having designed the Manhattan Bridge, among others. It was Moisseiff who determined that it was possible to construct a single span suspension bridge across the Golden Gate Strait even though no bridge had ever been built at the mouth of a major harbor, and no suspension bridge that long had ever been erected.

Unlike other spans, suspension bridges sway in the wind. They also expand in hot weather and contract in cold weather (the cables lengthening and constricting depending on the temperature). The longer the span, the more swaying and variation occurs, much like a clothesline. Given that the Golden Gate Bridge would be longer than any other suspension bridge in the world, it would sway more than any other. Based on the load it was supporting and the temperature, the bridge would deflect one to two feet both longitudinally and sideways, causing the floor of the bridge at mid-span to rise or fall ten feet from its normal elevation.

Charles Ellis was a faculty member in the engineering department at the University of Illinois when Straus contacted him. It was Ellis, the author of *Essentials in the Theory of Framed Structures*—must reading for engineering students at the time—who crunched the numbers upon which calculations for the Golden Gate Bridge were based. The calculations were complex, done with a circular slide rule and an adding machine, and filled eleven volumes. Seven different rivers empty into the Golden Gate Strait, which at its deepest point is 335 feet. In addition, the area is marked by high winds, thick fog, and rough tidal action. Also, the bridge would be built almost on top of the San Andreas Fault, a major fault line in California and the source of the 1906 earthquake that reduced much of San Francisco to rubble.

Many factors are considered in designing a bridge. Some are obvious, such as the length of the span and the terrain to be crossed (water presents different challenges than chasms). Others are more technical, such as height, materials, and the state of technology at the time of construction. Still other factors are considered only by engineers such as live load (the weight of traffic that the bridge will carry), dead load (the weight of materials that the bridge is constructed from), and wind load (the pressures exerted by wind on the bridge). Height was a key factor in the design and construction of the Golden Gate Bridge. Because it was the first bridge in the world to be built at the mouth of a major harbor, it had to be high enough to allow tall ships to pass underneath. As a result, the roadway—with pedestrian access—is considerably higher than the roadways of most other bridges. This height is the main reason why jumping from the bridge is so deadly; it's the equivalent of a twenty-five-story building.

Using Moisseiff's concept of a light-weight, highly calibrated suspension bridge that would sway with the elements, Ellis set to work. What inspired him was that the site for the new bridge was a dramatic meeting place of land and water. Ellis was a classical scholar as well as a civil engineer who translated passages from Greek to English in his spare time. He understood that this was an extraordinary opportunity to meld engineering skills with unparalleled beauty.

Ellis took charge of the test borings for the bridge towers, the surveying, and the location of the footings at both ends. The two steel towers of the bridge would be the largest and tallest ever built at that time, rivaling Manhattan skyscrapers. Their height above the water—746 feet—would be 190 feet greater than the Washington Monument. Each anchorage would require massive excavation and a staggering amount of concrete. Each tower would have a small elevator so that workers could make repairs to the saddles at the top holding the cables (originally, the elevators also would transport visitors to glassed-in observatories; however, this idea was scrapped for financial reasons). The south tower, on the San Francisco side, would be in the open sea, eleven hundred feet from shore. Professional divers were hired to search the ocean floor for an appropriate site, often swimming in near darkness due to alluvial deposits. Once a site was identified, divers cleared it and prepped it for the foundation. This tower required construction of a special pier, too, built like a bowl, set in the water and as long as a football field. Shortly after it was built, the pier was destroyed by a ship that was thrown off course because of heavy fog and crashed into it. It had to be reconstructed.

All of these details—and many others—Ellis calculated and recalculated in precise fashion. He worked twelve- and fourteen-hour days in order to meet Strauss's demanding schedule. Even with the efforts of Moisseiff and Ellis, as well as other engineers, the Golden Gate Bridge wouldn't be what it is today were it not for Irving Morrow. The bridge wouldn't be half as beautiful, half as distinctive, or anywhere near as famous. It also wouldn't be as deadly.

Morrow was a little-known architect who primarily designed houses, as did his wife, Gertrude. Every day he commuted by ferry from his home in Oakland to his office in San Francisco. During these trips he was continually struck by the play of light and shadows on the water at the mouth of the bay. When Strauss entrusted him with the task of making the bridge attractive,

Morrow jumped at the chance. He added the distinctive Art Deco styling for which the bridge is now known. He tapered the enormous twin towers in order to accentuate their height, added vertical, chevron fluting on the tower bracing to pick up and reflect sunlight, and designed the toll plaza and pedestrian walkways. The latter, aimed to provide signature views, enabled people to amble, jog, and bicycle across the bridge. Unfortunately, they also gave individuals an easy avenue to jump.

Morrow chose the bridge's paint color, too—orange vermillion, or "international orange." While Strauss's plans called for carbon black and steel gray, Morrow wanted a color that complimented the green hills of Marin County and the blue sky that often bathed the area, as well as was more visible in heavy fog. Orange vermillion was encouraged by California painter Maynard Dixon, a friend of Morrow's, and supported by a number of local residents, including San Francisco's preeminent artist and sculptor of the day, Benjamin Buffano. Requests by the U.S. Air Force to paint the bridge orange with white horizontal stripes so that it would be more visible to aircraft, and by the U.S. Navy to paint the bridge black with yellow stripes so that it would be more easily identifiable to passing ships, were—thankfully—rejected.

Strauss's original plans included a safety railing on the bridge that was five-and-a-half feet high. It would be, he boasted in the *San Francisco Call-Bulletin*, "practically suicide-proof" because of the way the guard rails were constructed. "Any persons on the pedestrian walk could not get a handhold to climb over them," Strauss said. Shortly before construction began, the railing was reduced to its present four-foot height. Some people have theorized that this change occurred because Strauss himself was short—only five-feet tall—and wanted to be able to see over the side. In fact, Morrow is the person most often credited with the decision to lower the railing because he wanted people to have unobstructed views of the bay. It was another artistic decision.

Strauss submitted final plans for the bridge in August 1930. That November, by a vote of 145,057 to 46,954, citizens in the six counties encompassed by the Bridge District approved a $35 million bond measure to finance construction. At that time the country was in the midst of the Great Depression, however, and no one was buying bonds. Strauss turned to A.P. Giannini for help. Giannini, the son of Italian immigrants, had started a small bank in order to lend money to blue-collar workers, who had a tough time getting loans. Called the Bank of Italy in homage to his ancestors, it grew to become Bank of America. Giannini agreed with Strauss that a bridge spanning the Golden Gate was needed, and his bank bought $6 million worth of bonds. With that, construction could begin.

On January 5, 1933, workers started digging foundations out of hillsides for the anchorages and concrete pylons. In some cases, they had to blast through hard rock to a depth of sixty-five feet below water. Strong tides and heavy swells made excavation on the San Francisco side of the bridge especially difficult. In all, more than three million cubic feet of earth were removed. Meanwhile, sections of the twin steel towers, manufactured by Bethlehem Steel in Pennsylvania, were sent by train to seaports on the East Coast, loaded onto ships, transported through the Panama Canal to San Francisco, and carried by barge to the construction site. There, giant cranes lifted them into place while teams of workers bonded them together with rivets and hot steel. Next came fabricating and installing the thick, heavy rope cable on each side. This guide wire, adjusted to the proper sag, determined the placement of all the vertical wires connecting to the roadway. Each of the two cables would weigh twenty-two million pounds. There was no way to lift cables this heavy so the John A. Roebling & Sons Company, based in New Jersey, spun them on site. Steel saddles were placed on top of the two towers to hold the cables as they were made, and workers traversed catwalks of wire rope and redwood planking to position them. These sixteen-foot-wide catwalks were the first structures to cross the width of the Golden Gate Strait.

It took six months to complete the cabling. After that, the roadway was built. On May 27, 1937, four-and-a-half years from the day that work began, the Golden Gate Bridge was completed. The first day only pedestrians were allowed on the bridge. At 6 A.M., eighteen thousand people were waiting to cross. There weren't any speeches or ribbon cutting. By the end of the day, an estimated two hundred thousand people had walked along the roadway. The following day, President Franklin D. Roosevelt pressed a telegraph key in the White House and announced to the world that the Golden Gate Bridge was open to vehicle traffic. For the rest of the week there were celebrations—fireworks, parades, tournaments, races, and live entertainment.

During construction, eleven workers died. That number would have been higher except Strauss implemented safety precautions that were unprecedented at the time. He commissioned hard hats (actually mining hats made of leather) and insisted that workers wear them. He saw that tinted goggles were issued so that men would not be blinded by the sun's reflection, that steel workers were prescribed special diets to counteract dizziness, and that hand and facial creams were available to protect against the wind. Most significantly, in addition to safety lines, Strauss had a safety net mounted sixty feet below the bridge, running its entire length. He justified the cost ($130,000, equivalent to $2 million today) by saying that the men would be more confident and work faster if they felt more secure. Considering that the bridge was completed on time and within budget, he was right. At various times, nineteen men fell into the net and were saved. They became known, in the sardonic humor of the trade, as the "Halfway-to-Hell Club."

Only one person died during the first four years that the bridge was being built. Three months before completion, however, on February 17, 1937, a section of scaffolding fell through the safety net and ten of the twelve men on it perished (two workers survived the fall, suffering broken bones and massive internal injuries). Strauss had a new net erected immediately, spending $130,000 again. When the bridge was completed, the net was removed.

The names of the eleven workers who died have been preserved for posterity. They appear in Bridge District publications and on the Golden Gate Bridge Web site. In contrast, no such list is maintained by the Bridge District or local historians of all the people who have leaped to their deaths. There's a practical reason for this: mentioning the names of jumpers might appear to glorify them and encourage others to jump. Furthermore, deliberately not naming these individuals serves to protect the commercial interests of the area and the tourism industry that feeds it by suppressing an unseemly problem.

Harold Wobber, a forty-seven-year-old veteran of World War I, is the first known suicide from the Golden Gate Bridge. Two-and-a-half months after the bridge opened, on August 7, 1937, he took a bus to the south end, walked out halfway, told a stranger, "This is as far as I go," and jumped over the side. His body was never found.

The first suicide may have been even earlier, however. Only two weeks after the bridge opened, on June 12, 1937, the body of

Henry Clay Torrence of Richmond, California (Contra Costa County) was recovered on Angel Island in San Francisco Bay. According to two brief articles in the *Oakland Tribune*, Torrence suffered the sort of trauma associated with "having struck the water with a terrific force." There were no apparent witnesses to his death, and no conclusion as to whether he died from an accidental fall, murder, or suicide.

In early 1939, barely eighteen months after the Golden Gate Bridge opened, ten more people were known to have jumped. Representatives from the California Highway Patrol, among others, began to express concerns. A year later, Bridge District officials discussed for the first time installing an "anti-suicide screen" on the bridge. After some debate, it was voted down for aesthetic and financial reasons, as well as for engineering concerns, that it might lessen wind resistance on the bridge.

Over the next twenty-five years, there were repeated failures to address the growing problem of suicide from San Francisco's famous landmark:

- In 1948, the Bridge District commissioned the first full study of a suicide deterrent. It took four years to complete, was referred to a district subcommittee, and ultimately was ignored.

- In 1949, the president of the Bridge District proposed to make it illegal to jump off the bridge. This arose after a Hollywood stuntman jumped from the bridge intending to live. Following his death, there was concern that others would try to survive a jump. The proposal went nowhere after an editorial in the *San Francisco Chronicle* noted that "a person seriously bent on suicide is not going to be deterred by a law that, once he jumps, can never reach him." The state legislature thought there was merit to the idea nevertheless, and the same year passed a law making it a misdemeanor to climb on the rails, cables, or towers of the bridge without permission. That law remains in effect today. Thus, while it's illegal to get into position to jump from the Golden Gate Bridge, and can result in a $10,000 fine for trespassing and a year in jail if convicted, there's no law against actually jumping.

· In 1951, with suicides from the bridge continuing unabated, the general manager of the Bridge District suggested that there be a twenty-four-hour bridge patrol, consisting of five men on motorcycles. He reasoned that the patrol would cost $20,500 annually, which was cheaper than a suicide barrier. One board member commented, "If it saved one life a year, it would be well worth it." Nevertheless, the board took no action. Neither did the board take action on another suggestion, to post signs on the bridge saying "Think Before You Leap."

· In 1953, three engineers who specialized in bridge design were hired by the district to study the issue. They reported that a suicide barrier could be erected for $200,000. The barrier would reduce the number of suicides, they said, but probably wouldn't eliminate them entirely. District officials replied that this wasn't good enough, that they would only consider a barrier that was 100 percent effective.

· In 1954, two plans were proposed by a Bridge District security committee. One plan would extend the current railing two feet; the other would extend it three feet. Neither plan was acted on, although the district approved

$325,000 to widen the southern approach, as well as $3.5 million to add new trusses below the roadway in order to buffet the bridge in high winds.

- In 1960, Bridge District officials voted to close the pedestrian and bicycle paths on the bridge from dusk to dawn every day "in the interest of public safety and security." Their concern did not extend to approving a physical deterrent—it only involved buying four padlocks. The decision was designed to show sympathy for the victims without inconveniencing tourists, who were unlikely to walk on the bridge at night.

- In 1964, the Bridge District created a three-person subcommittee to consider applications from engineering firms to design a suicide barrier. Six years later, no firm had been hired.

By 1968, it became impossible to ignore the four hundred confirmed suicides from the bridge. District officials voted unanimously to take action: they doubled the tolls on the bridge in one direction and eliminated them in the other. The real purpose of this was to improve traffic flow; however, it also would free up half the tollbooth workers who could be reassigned to patrol the bridge. The increased surveillance reduced the number of suicides, but only temporarily. The number dropped from twenty-nine in 1968 to seventeen in 1969; however, it rose to thirty-seven in 1970, thirty-five in 1971, and forty in 1972.

There was enough momentum in late 1969 to convene a symposium on Golden Gate Bridge suicides. Among those speaking were three national suicide experts—psychiatrist Jerome Motto and psychologists Richard Seiden and Edwin Shneidman. Motto noted that the Golden Gate Bridge attracts suicides because it's easily accessible, is simple (no preparation is needed), there's no mess, death is virtually guaranteed, and there's a psychological appeal (jumping from the bridge is dramatic). Seiden recommended that there be an epidemiological investigation in order to provide an overview of the problem as well as answer questions such as who jumps, when, where on the bridge, and why. Shneidman suggested that an aerodynamically-approved barrier be temporarily bolted onto the entire length for three months, then removed for three months, then restored and taken down in alternating three-month intervals over the course of three years, with subsequent studies done to determine the effectiveness of the barrier. (He noted the moral dilemma if, during the first three months, there were no suicides whether authorities had the right to take down the barrier, making suicide possible again, and said public opinion would have to determine that.) Bridge District board members said that they would study the proposals, but ended up taking no action.

A year later, the district commissioned the firm Anshen & Allen Architects to develop several designs for a suicide barrier. The designs included barbed wire fencing, safety netting, plexiglas screening, horizontal tension cables, vertical tension rods, U-shaped spikes on top of the rail, low-voltage electricity, and high-voltage laser beams. Many of the designs were deemed unattractive, and since the electric fence and laser beams might burn pedestrians and bridge workers, they were removed from consideration.

Three designs looked promising, and Anshen & Allen was hired to draft preliminary drawings. The designs, labeled 11, 16, and 17, consisted of thin, vertical steel rods eight feet high and six inches apart. Eventually, design 11 was eliminated because its curved spikes at the top were out of keeping with the rest of the bridge, and number 17 was eliminated due to its $3.5 million-plus price tag. The remaining design, number 16, held interest for three reasons. First, at $750,000 it was relatively affordable. Second, by replacing the current, solid bridge rails with thin steel rods, it would reduce the weight of the bridge by forty pounds per square foot, which in turn would lower the cost of bridge insurance because the insurance was based on weight per linear foot. Third, the slim steel rods (painted orange to match the rest of the structure) would provide everyone who used the bridge—motorcyclists, cyclists, and pedestrians—with fuller views of San Francisco Bay and the shorelines.

According to a Bridge District report, there were 102 suicides and 386 thwarted attempts on the bridge from 1970 to 1972, when the Anshen & Allen study was being reviewed—more than in any three-year period in the bridge's history to that point (there were actually 112 confirmed suicides during this time according to other sources). Even so, Bridge District directors determined that none of the Anshen & Allen designs was acceptable. No specific reasons were given, but one thing that was clear was that money was not a factor. Instead of a suicide deterrent, Bridge District officials allocated $15 million of the $17.5 million they had in reserves for upgrading ferries and the ferry terminal, and replaced some of the bridge's vertical steel cables.

In his book *November of the Soul: The Enigma of Suicide*, George Howe Colt describes driving down a restricted road just south of the Golden Gate Bridge toll plaza with Dr. Richard Seiden. There, in a meadow piled high with broken window casings, old ladders, chicken wire, and other detritus, Seiden showed Howe a steel fence. Writes Howe: "It was painted the same russet red as the Golden Gate Bridge. Its pencil-thin spires rose about eight feet into the air. On one-half of the fence the spires pointed toward the sky; on the other half they curved gently inward at the top, like the fingers of a cupped hand." The two of them looked at the sculpture wordlessly for several seconds. Then Seiden said softly, "Winning design number 16. It's been sitting there for years."

In 1973 Seiden, a Berkeley professor, wrote a paper published by the School of Public Health describing the magnetic attraction of certain suicide sites. Citing H. R. Fedden's book *Suicide: A Social and Historical Study*, Seiden recounted that at *Les Invalides* in France there had not been a suicide for the two years prior to 1792. Then a soldier hanged himself from a beam in one of the corridors. Within weeks, twelve other soldiers hanged themselves from the same beam. When the governor closed the corridor, the suicides ended. Similarly, in 1813, in the Swiss village of Saint Pierre Monjau, a woman hanged herself from a large tree. It wasn't long before other women died in the same way from the same branch. Seiden explained that the reasons why certain places develop a reputation for suicide are complex, but "an important component appears to be the fact that a person achieves the kind of notoriety and attention in death that he may not have received in a lifetime of loneliness and depression." He went on to note that "particular methods or suicide plans have a deep personal significance, and are not capriciously transferred to another time or location." Such is the case, he concluded, with the Golden Gate Bridge. It had developed a fatal lure. Seiden also cited examples—and several years later conducted his own research (described in chapter 8) to confirm—that if people are stopped from jumping off the Golden Gate Bridge, they won't go somewhere else to kill themselves. For this reason, a suicide deterrent would be effective.

In 1976, the Bridge District considered closing the span to pedestrians on weekdays. According to the board president,

Edwin M. Fraser, "This would stop 90 percent of the suicides off the bridge." Tourists could still walk the bridge on weekends, and the bike lane on the west side would remain open to cyclists. The proposal ignited much debate—people didn't want to be denied access to the bridge—and eventually was defeated.

The same year, the district installed a fence on the southern section of the Golden Gate Bridge. It was chain link, eight feet high, 350 feet long, and not at all in keeping with the design of the bridge. While the aesthetic impact of a suicide barrier on the bridge was of great concern to many people, no one complained about this fence. Its purpose was not to save lives; it was put up to stop litter. People were dropping rocks, bottles, beer cans, and even a bowling ball onto the grounds of Fort Point below, which often had visitors, and board members felt that they needed to be protected. "It has been a continuous problem," Dale Luehring, the bridge general manager, said at the time. Warning signs were posted on the bridge telling people that if they willingly dropped or threw an object from the bridge, it would be a misdemeanor and they would be prosecuted.

May 27, 1977, was the fortieth anniversary of the opening of the Golden Gate Bridge. It also was the day that the parents of a nineteen-year-old jumper, Kenneth Pattison, filed a claim against the Bridge District alleging that the board was negligent in not providing a suicide barrier. The claim—the first of its kind—was a prerequisite before the district could be sued. The Pattisons said that their son wasn't under psychiatric care, had never attempted suicide to the best of their knowledge, and would be alive today if a barrier was in place. They didn't seek a monetary award; they sought a safe bridge. To date, there had been seven hundred confirmed deaths.

"The Bridge District has already admitted and recognized they have a responsibility to do something about suicides," said Gene Rosenberg, the Pattison's attorney. "They've trained toll collectors and security guards to recognize and restrain potential suicides, and even installed TV monitors. Legally, once they have embarked on trying to prevent suicides, they are obligated to complete the task in a careful and diligent manner. But they've failed to do this; time and again, the Bridge District has refused to put in the one simple, effective measure to stop suicides—a suicide prevention barrier."

Attorneys for the Bridge District rejected the claim, and the Pattisons did not take it further. In the ensuing years the mothers of two other jumpers would, though. Meanwhile, the issue of a bridge barrier was revisited because the existing railing was scheduled to be removed, sandblasted, and repainted. In what has to be considered the most ironic moment in the history of suicide prevention, a rally in favor of a barrier was organized on Memorial Day, March 31, 1977, by three religious leaders. One of the three was the Reverend Jim Jones, who called suicide victims "casualties of society" and the lack of a suicide barrier on the bridge a "symbol of social failure." (Eighteen months later, Jones induced more than nine hundred of his Peoples Temple followers to swallow Kool Aid laced with cyanide in the jungles of Guyana.) The appeal for a suicide barrier went nowhere.

Twenty years after Bridge District board members decided that none of the barrier designs in the Anshen & Allen study was viable, the suicide barrier had became a forgotten subject, at least by the general public. The jumps, of course, continued as always, observed by innocent witnesses while Coast Guard crews continued to retrieve the bodies as loved ones mourned the deaths. Nevertheless, a feeling arose among suicide prevention advocates that publicizing the problem might be making it worse, resulting in imitative behavior. Clearly it was in the Bridge District's best interests that the media not report bridge suicides; however, possibly it was in the best interests of those most at risk that suicides go unnoticed, too. Mental health professionals collectively approached local media and asked them to refrain from reporting Golden Gate Bridge jumps when possible. Local media, for the most part, agreed, and for two decades most bridge jumps weren't covered.

In 1995 there were forty-five confirmed suicides from the bridge—up from thirty-nine the year before and the highest one-year total in history. Clearly, silence wasn't working. According to Bridge District engineer Mervin C. Giacomini, writing in a report to the board, "The statistics show that the majority of suicides were pedestrians (83 percent), most jumped from the east side of the Bridge (82 percent), and most occurred during daylight hours (77 percent)." Giacomini did not note—but a subsequent report did—that 76 percent of jumpers were men. In addition, 77 percent were under the age of fifty, and 24 percent were under the age of thirty, evidence that Golden Gate Bridge jumpers tended to be considerably younger than suicide victims in general. About two-thirds of all jumps were witnessed.

Despite the record number of deaths, the Bridge District board accepted the recommendation of its building and operating committee not to erect a suicide barrier on the bridge. Instead, directors voted to start foot and scooter patrols, allocating $76,736 for four temporary, part-time security officers who would be paid $14.50 per hour. The patrols, which began in April 1996, followed by two years the installation of thirteen emergency telephones on the bridge. The day the phones were installed, church bells rang throughout San Francisco and Mayor George Christopher proclaimed that they would save lives. Meanwhile, work began on a $402 million seismic retrofit of the bridge.

The patrols proved effective in that they stopped one person per week from jumping. They didn't stop everyone—twenty-three people jumped in 1996, and thirty-three in 1997. Still, with an annual budget of $93.8 million and a profit of $2.6 million in 1996, board members considered the patrols a good investment and voted to continue them; now at a cost of $110,000.

A new push took place in 1998 after the total number of deaths exceeded twelve hundred. Bridge District officials approved testing of a high-tension, flexible wire fence stretching six feet above the current railing. Thin, vertical "z-clips" that were virtually impossible to separate would keep the fence in place. The criteria used in the Anshen & Allen study in 1970 hadn't changed, however. In other words, the manufacturer had to design, develop, and test a prototype that "cannot cause safety or nuisance hazard to pedestrians or bridge personnel, must be totally effective as a barrier, cannot bar pedestrian traffic, weight cannot be beyond established allowable limits, cannot cause excessive maintenance problems, and aerodynamics cannot be beyond established allowable limits."

Z-Clip International Fencing Systems of Danville, California, was hired to create a prototype. The results, when unveiled, were unsatisfactory. On the plus side, the fence was lightweight yet also hard to cut. Simple wire cutters wouldn't do it; a suicidal person would have to prepare in advance to carry bolt cutters. Also, it was designed so that the top wires were looser and curved back toward the walkway, making it difficult to surmount. On the negative side, many people considered the fence ugly and out of keeping with the bridge's design. When a 125-foot-long test section was displayed near the toll plaza, critics complained that it looked like "the chicken-wire fences that enclose concentration camps." An architectural review committee labeled it hideous, and an editorial in the *San Francisco Chronicle* said that installing the fence "would be an act of vandalism.... To add such a jerry-rigged monstrosity to the graceful span would be a grave insult to San Francisco's landmark masterpiece."

From April to September 1998, the Bridge District received twenty-seven items of public correspondence about the fence. Sixteen were in favor. Martha Killebrew, whose daughter, Jane, jumped from the bridge in 1972, expressed the view of many victims' families who said that any kind of barrier, regardless of appearance, was better than nothing. "To me, these wires are no more obtrusive than rear-window defrost lines in cars," Killebrew said. "One just doesn't think about them."

Eleven writers opposed the fence. One woman said that she moved from New York to California because New York "destroyed much of what was worthwhile" by having too many rules. "It is ironic that such a barrier intended to save lives actually makes life a little less worth living," she concluded. Another woman wrote, "If and when I decide to die, I would prefer the bridge as an exit point, and I don't want to be kept from it by a high, jail-like railing."

A man whose brother jumped four years earlier said that the bridge provided a useful service. His brother, he said, "had a clean death, involving no one else, unlike, for instance, stepping in front of a train," and "I did not have to discover his body hanging from a chandelier or with open veins in the bathtub."

A retired, twenty-eight-year-veteran in the California Highway Patrol expressed a similar opinion. "Not long ago," he wrote, "a man jumped from a high floor in a hotel in San Francisco in the interior of the building, almost striking several doctors attending a function that was being held there. This is an example of what can happen if you make it impossible for them to jump from the bridge."

A second problem with the z-clip fence, at least from the Bridge District's point of view, was that it wasn't foolproof. Five of fourteen people chosen to test the fence were able to climb over it. Those who succeeded were "mostly young and in good physical condition," according to the bridge engineer's report. Four were males ages 27, 32, 36, and 41, all weighing under 190 pounds. One was female, age twenty-five, weighing 120 pounds. Adjustments were made, the space between fasteners was shortened from six to five feet, after which only one of the fourteen (the 120-pound woman) was successful. This didn't meet the district's requirement of 100 percent effectiveness, however. No one reported a curious fact about the testing, which was that in order to ensure everyone's safety, bridge personnel placed large airbags under each tester to cushion the person if he or she fell. The airbags alone gave each participant a two-foot advantage in reaching the railing. Also, no one noted that when the distance between fasteners was reduced to four feet, none of the participants was able to scale the fence.

A final problem with the z-clip fence was the price: $3 million. In addition to concerns about appearance and effectiveness, board members considered the cost prohibitive. This was before any wind tunnel tests were commissioned to determine whether the fence would affect aerodynamics. Yet board members did approve plans for a movable, median barrier on the bridge at an estimated cost of $15 million. The barrier would prevent crossover collisions, which had killed thirty-six people in the past twenty-eight years (an average of 1.3 fatalities per year).

In the fall of 2001, foot and motor patrols on the Golden Gate Bridge were increased. The reason wasn't because of suicides, it was because of 9/11. Just as the original surveillance equipment on the bridge was designed to monitor vehicle and pedestrian traffic, so were the added patrols intended to keep the bridge safe from terrorists. Suicide prevention was an afterthought.

Only with new funding in 2005 from the federal Metropolitan Transportation Commission did the Bridge District approve a $2 million study to once again consider the feasibility of a suicide barrier on the Golden Gate Bridge. There was one major difference this time: the requirement that the barrier had to be 100 percent effective was dropped. There were two reasons for this. One was because it was a requirement that was proving to be virtually impossible for any manufacturer to meet. While restricting access to lethal means can prevent most people from killing themselves, someone who is truly intent on dying will go to extraordinary lengths sometimes, taking actions that others don't expect and can't plan for. The more compelling reason, though, was because promoting a barrier as being 100 percent effective exposed the Bridge District to liability if there was a death. It was better to have a barrier that was 95 percent effective than risk a future lawsuit by claiming that it was foolproof.

The Bridge District also tested the wind performance of taller railings on the Golden Gate Bridge. In 2007, Jon Raggett, the owner of West Wind Laboratory, set up a five-foot scale model representing the middle section of the Golden Gate Bridge, which is the section most vulnerable to high winds. The railings on the model were proportionate to the four-foot-high railings that actually existed on the bridge. Raggett gave the model a gentle push, then turned on a fan that was next to it, producing the equivalent of a seventy-one-mile-per-hour wind. The model rocked slowly side to side, then faster and wouldn't stop. "At this rate, pieces would start falling off the bridge," Raggett told onlookers. "Then we would see catastrophic failure."

Turning off the fan and stopping the swaying of his model, Raggett added small, flat sheets above the railing as if the whole railing had been raised several feet, as proposed by various anti-suicide designs. He gave the model a slight push and turned on the fan again. The bridge came to a complete stop, even when the fan was cranked up to approximate wind speeds of 130 miles per hour. Raggett determined that if the Golden Gate Bridge had a fourteen-foot-tall suicide barrier, it was possible for the bridge to withstand westerly winds of one hundred miles per hour—an event considered likely to occur only once every ten thousand years. As it is, the bridge is closed when winds exceed seventy miles per hour, something that has happened three times (in 1951, 1982, and 1983).

Raggett was hired for his technical expertise, but he also had a personal interest in the project. A friend of his had driven to the Golden Gate Bridge planning to jump. The only reason he didn't was because he couldn't find a parking space. That alone was enough of a deterrent. Imagine if there was a real deterrent, Raggett believed, one that was intentionally designed. Lives would be saved.

Because the Golden Gate Bridge is considered to be one of the greatest engineering feats in the world, any structural changes to it, such as a suicide barrier, are viewed first and foremost from an engineering perspective. Wind resistance is part of it. The bridge is designed so that wind moves through it, which is why the bridge's walkways can't be walled in with clear fiberglass. That would create vortex shedding or "unstable flutter"—the colloquial term—leading a suspension bridge to lurch uncontrollably. Instead, wind needs to be able to move freely through the structure.

According to Denis Mulligan, for many years the chief engineer of the Golden Gate Bridge who was promoted to chief executive and general manager in September 2010, it's possible to think of a cross section of the bridge as the wing of an airplane. If you change the flap, you change the way that the wing responds to wind. The same is true, he says, of the bridge. Thus, even the handrails that were added in 2003 to the barrier that separates the pedestrian and bike lanes from vehicle traffic had to be carefully considered. Current bridge architect Donald MacDonald designed them to be as thin as possible so that they would not impede wind flow.

Add to the issue of wind resistance the issue of aesthetics, which is paramount for many people, and engineering becomes more challenging. While a suicide barrier doesn't need to enhance the design of the bridge, it's widely believed that it can't detract from it. In addition, a barrier can't be too heavy, can't interfere with regular bridge operations, and can't be too difficult to maintain. Practically speaking, it shouldn't require more attention than any other element of the bridge. The only difference a barrier should make is to stop people from jumping.

Twice in the past fifteen years, engineering students at the University of California, Berkeley have designed a suicide barrier on the Golden Gate Bridge as a class project. Their professor, Robert Bea, requires students to select a real-life challenge with social implications, then incorporate actual constraints—cost, environmental regulations, and politics—into their engineering designs. Bea gained prominence in 2010 as an expert in the design and construction of oil rigs who explained to national audiences how the Deepwater Horizon oil spill occurred, laying the blame squarely on BP. Previously he consulted on the Exxon Valdez oil spill, Hurricane Katrina, and other tragedies, earning the nickname "Dr. Disaster" from his students.

For his class, Civil Engineering 180: Design of Enhanced Structures, Bea divides students into teams of four so that they learn how to approach challenges collectively. This is how the real world functions; people don't design and build things in a vacuum. He tells the teams that they can work on any project that interests them as long as it's practical and has social value. His goal, he tells me, "is to educate young engineers that there's such a thing as public service."

Four students in Bea's 1997 class chose a suicide barrier on the Golden Gate Bridge as their project. They based their design on the top-rated Anshen & Allen option in 1970. Anshen & Allen's recommendation was rejected because the barrier wasn't 100 percent effective; several people were able to climb over it. The Berkeley students—Walt Aldrich, Casey Bowden, Lori Dunn, and Serena Volpp—added thin, vertical cables spaced six inches apart so that they would be too small to squeeze through. "Not only would it be more effective," Bowden said at the time, "but our design weighs less than the current rail and is less affected by the wind. It shows that a suicide barrier is not so much an engineering problem as a political problem."

The students readily admitted that their design had limitations. Primarily, it would be difficult and expensive to construct, but other, more experienced engineers could deal with that. The goal of the students was to show that a suicide barrier could be effective and also aesthetically pleasing. "We think a safe and attractive suicide barrier can be built," Dunn told a reporter.

"With our report and model, we hope to bring more attention to the need for a suicide barrier."

Each team of engineering students presented their final projects, including engineering reports and physical models, to a panel of judges recruited by Bea. In 1997, the team that designed the Golden Gate Bridge suicide barrier won top honors. Bea called their project "real professional" and said that, in his opinion, "the bridge looks better rather than worse. I was amazed."

In 2005, another team of Bea's students revisited the idea of designing a suicide barrier for the Golden Gate Bridge. This time, instead of modifying a previous concept, they started from scratch. The team—Danielle Hutchings, Robert Simpson, Ryan Stauffer, and Douglas Wahl—designed three different barriers, each one taking into account engineering challenges and aesthetic concerns. Of the four, Wahl had a special interest in the project. His cousin had died by suicide four years earlier.

"She didn't jump from the bridge," he was quoted as saying, "but that experience prompted me to think about what goes through people's minds when they're thinking about killing themselves.... If we can take away the means to easily complete the act, such as creating a barrier on a bridge, we can often get people past that suicidal state."

In creating their designs, the 2005 team drew on the expertise of people in realms far different than their own. This included psychiatrists, psychologists, and officers in the Oakland Police Department who intervened in suicide attempts. The 1997 team also consulted on the 2005 project. Eight years into professional careers, each was happy to assist the next generation of engineers.

As in the past, each team's final project was presented to a panel of judges for review. This time one of the judges was Denis

Mulligan, a Berkeley graduate who was the Bridge District's chief engineer. In recounting the experience, Mulligan told me that all of the students were "very passionate, young engineers" whose concepts were solid. The suicide barrier team didn't have access to data for wind dynamics on bridges specifically; nevertheless, they created workable designs. The 2005 team, like the 1997 team, was awarded first place.

"One of the things we are so proud of," Hutchings told a *San Francisco Chronicle* reporter, "is that these designs keep the aesthetics of the bridge in addition to saving 20 lives a year."

On the occasion of the sixty-eighth anniversary of the opening of the Golden Gate Bridge, in 2005, the Psychiatric Foundation of Northern California sponsored the presentation of the students' three designs to Tom Ammiano and Cynthia Murray, the two Bridge District board members who were the strongest supporters of a barrier. Ammiano and Murray said that the designs were well conceived and in keeping with the bridge's architecture. Joseph Strauss, the chief engineer who presided over construction, probably would have approved.

As it was, Strauss didn't live long enough to see his creation turn into the world's number one suicide site. He died in May 1938 of a heart attack, eleven days before the first anniversary of the bridge's opening. It is commonly believed that his death was induced by the stress of the project. At one point during construction, he suffered a breakdown and was absent from the site for six months. Only when the Bridge District threatened to fire him did he return to work. Still, his health may have been affected as much by the stress of knowing what he had created as by the creation itself. At the time of his death, six people had jumped, and Strauss probably had a good idea about what the bridge was becoming. *New Yorker* writer Tad Friend reported that at the dedication ceremony, A.R. O'Brien, the bridge's director, said that Strauss "put everything he had" into the bridge "and out of its completion he go so little.... The Golden Gate Bridge, for my dead friend, turned out to be a mute monument of misery."

Leon Moisseiff, the engineer who believed that it was possible to span the Golden Gate Strait with what turned out to be the longest suspension bridge in the world at the time, went on to be the lead designer of a suspension bridge in Washington State. The bridge, built in 1940 on the same theory as the Golden Gate Bridge, and crossing the Tacoma Narrows in Puget Sound, was nicknamed "The Galloping Gertie" because of the way it moved in the wind. With no small measure of pride, Moisseiff called it the "most beautiful bridge in the world," even more beautiful than the Golden Gate Bridge. Shortly after it was completed, however, it twisted apart in a forty-two mile-per-hour wind, forever damaging Moisseiff's reputation. He died three years later of a heart attack. The collapse of the Tacoma Narrows Bridge sent a chill up the backs of Golden Gate Bridge District officials. They feared that any structural change to their world-famous span, such as a higher railing, might produce a similar effect.

Meanwhile, Charles Ellis, the engineer whose voluminous mathematical computations were the basis for the Golden Gate Bridge's construction, was not fully acknowledged for his contributions until well after his death. Strauss fired Ellis before actual construction began, saying that "The structure was nothing unusual and did not require all the time, study, and expense which [Ellis] thought necessary for it." Then Strauss turned the job over to Clifford Paine, an Ellis protégé, who used Ellis's design, making only minor changes to it. Ellis's colleagues believed that the real reason for the firing was because Strauss was jealous. He didn't like it that Bridge District directors were going to Ellis for information rather than coming to him.

Ellis retired from the faculty at Purdue University in 1947 at age seventy-two, and died two years later. He's remembered as a self-effacing man, uninterested in the limelight. He didn't spend a lot of time bemoaning his dismissal, and it's not known whether he ever saw the Golden Gate Bridge in person after it was completed. Nevertheless, he kept a picture of the bridge over his desk at work and was known to say, if anyone brought it up, "I designed every stick of steel on that bridge."

The archives at Purdue contain Ellis's papers, letters, and engineering drawings with his signature on them, plus telegrams and photographs. Once they were unearthed, it was suggested to the Golden Gate Bridge District that Ellis receive some sort of tribute as the true designer. Since a statue of Joseph Strauss was erected near the bridge, perhaps a portion of the span could be named in Ellis's honor. The matter was referred to a historical research committee of the American Association of Civil Engineers. The committee confirmed Ellis's work, but the drive to see that Ellis receive proper credit lost momentum. With the passage of time, and all of the key players deceased, no one really cared who did what. All that mattered was that the bridge was built, and that it was an architectural and engineering triumph. The person who made, perhaps, the single greatest contribution to the construction of one of the modern wonders of the world became a mere footnote in history.

As for Irving Morrow, the man who designed the pedestrian walkways and in all likelihood made the decision to lower the railing on the bridge, thereby creating the opportunity for virtually anyone of any age to jump, he returned to his architectural business, designing residential and commercial buildings with his wife. If he had any regrets about the bridge, he didn't express them publicly. Morrow died in 1952 at the age of sixty-eight. At that time, the official number of bridge suicides was under 150. In the coming years it would escalate dramatically.

While preventative measures were being implemented at other sites that were developing reputations as suicide magnets, business continued as usual on the Golden Gate Bridge. Commuters crossed daily, tolls were collected, tourists took snapshots, the bravery of bridge workers was extolled, and people everywhere continued to marvel at the beauty of it all.

What also continued were bridge suicides. "Why do they make it so easy?" one jumper lamented in a suicide note.

For the families of the victims, whose numbers increased every month, it wasn't business as usual. Instead, it was the beginning of their worst nightmare, a nightmare that, try as they might, they could never fully wake from.

THREE

Endless Ripple

Everyone is better off without this fat, disgusting,
boring girl.
　　—Suicide note of Marissa Imrie, age 14,
　　　who jumped in 2001

It is widely believed that each suicide directly affects at least six
people, family members and close friends. Since there are more
than 35,000 suicides every year, on average, in the United States,
roughly 200,000 Americans lose a loved one to suicide annually.
Over ten years, that's two million people, all of them grieving
a new, inexplicable, and often preventable death.

The dark trail of suicides on the Golden Gate Bridge over
decades has left thousands of people to mourn. In uncovering
the personal stories of victims and their families, one learns how
silence and stigma have conspired to mask the depth and breadth
of the social costs of these suicides.

Renee Milligan's fourteen-year-old daughter, Marissa Imrie,
jumped from the bridge on December 17, 2001. Marissa was a
straight-A student at Santa Rosa High School, the same high
school her mother graduated from. Ironically, Milligan had chosen the Golden Gate Bridge as the subject of a senior class report.

Although she was afraid of heights, Milligan had walked across the bridge as part of her research. She was awed by the immense towers and steel cables, and chilled by the sight of the water far below. Little did she know that many years later her first-born daughter would become a bridge casualty.

Marissa's good grades were a source of pride to her divorced parents, but not to Marissa. She was more concerned with how she looked than how she scored in school. Like many teenagers, she considered being popular more important than being smart. In her mind she was overweight and unattractive, even though in photos she appears pretty and athletic (she was on the school's cross-country track team).

Santa Rosa is fifty miles north of San Francisco. Because she was too young to drive, Marissa collected all her money and took a $150 cab ride to the bridge. The cab driver asked her why she wasn't in school. Marissa replied that she was eighteen and attended junior college. On the bridge, Marissa passed a maintenance worker. He looked at her and said hello. She didn't reply, just continued walking. Near a lamppost she placed her wallet on the ground. Then she climbed the bridge's short railing and without any apparent hesitation she jumped.

After Marissa died, her mother examined files on Marissa's computer and discovered that her daughter had visited suicide Web sites. One site recommended jumping from heights of 250 feet above water if a person wanted to be virtually certain of dying.

Renee Milligan was so devastated by Marissa's suicide that she considered jumping off the bridge, too. Only the presence of her other daughter, age five, stopped her. Over time, with the help of therapy and a support group of mothers whose children had killed themselves, Milligan's thoughts of suicide faded. She began working with troubled teenagers at the high school, talking with them about suicide and about healthier ways to deal with stress. She also established the Marissa Imrie Scholarship Fund with proceeds coming from an annual dinner that Milligan hosts at the school.

Milligan did one more thing: she filed a wrongful-death lawsuit against the Golden Gate Bridge District. It was the second suit filed against the district in ten years. Milligan didn't seek financial restitution; she sought a suicide barrier. "Through their acts and omissions," Milligan's suit charged, "Defendants have authorized, encouraged, and condoned government-assisted suicide."

The response of district officials made their position clear. "Plaintiff's injuries, if any, were the result of Plaintiff's own actions (contributory negligence)," they alleged. In other words, if Milligan suffered personally or emotionally from Marissa's death—and the district wasn't admitting that she did—she herself was to blame for neglecting her daughter's needs and failing to monitor her daughter's movements. Moreover, Bridge District lawyers said, "Plaintiff cannot show that Ms. Imrie used the property with due care for the purpose it was designed." Bridges are made for traveling across, the district claimed, not jumping from, regardless of how easy it is to do the latter.

Similar arguments have been made—usually successfully—defending gun shops that sell firearms used in homicides and suicides. Milligan's suit, like the Pattison's claim before it (discussed in chapter 2), was dismissed without cause. Several years after Marissa's death, her father hanged himself. In the note he left, Tom Imrie said that it was too painful for him to live without his daughter.

Dave and Jean Hull's daughter jumped from the bridge on October 26, 2003. Kathy Hull, twenty-six, a student at the University of California at Santa Cruz, filled the gas tank of her white Honda Accord, drove an hour-and-a-half to San Francisco, crossed the Golden Gate Bridge at twilight, and parked at Vista Point. From there she began walking across the bridge. Midway, she laid down her purse, climbed over the railing, and stood on the chord. Before anyone could stop her, she placed her cell phone on the girder and jumped. A bridge worker found the phone and pressed the home number on it. When Dave Hull answered, the bridge worker asked him if he'd lost his cell phone on the Golden Gate Bridge. The bridge worker also told Dave that Kathy Hull's purse was found on the bridge. Hull and his wife sat in stunned silence. A short time later, a police officer called. Kathy's car had been found in the parking lot at Vista Point, on the Marin side of the bridge. That night, the Hulls were notified that their daughter's body had been retrieved by the Coast Guard after someone on the bridge had seen and reported it.

Dave Hull's world stopped. For weeks he didn't shave, get haircuts, tend to his garden, or report to work. He ate because he was told to, showered and brushed his teeth mindlessly, and didn't want the world to go on. "It was as if I could be closer to her if nothing changed," he says. "It was Joan Didion's magical thinking; just a few hours separated me from Kathy alive. That's not much. Isn't there something I could do that would change that?"

The year before Kathy died, Dave walked 120 miles on the Pacific Crest Trail, from the high desert to Mt. Whitney, the same path conservationist John Muir had followed. Dave planned to walk another section of the trail the following summer, and Kathy had asked to come along. He doesn't know if he'll ever make the trip now. "The Japanese have a saying," he says. "'White hair should go before black hair.'" In other words, grandparents should die before parents, and parents should die before children. "Losing a parent is shocking," he says. "Losing a child is unspeakable." His voice chokes on the words.

Following Kathy's death, Dave and his wife took eight weeks off work, spending much of the time walking through the redwood park above their home. "We 'walked in beauty,' as the Navajos say," he says, "and every glimpse sliced and ached because Kathy loved the outdoors, the natural world, the plants and animals. Each glimpse of beauty, Kathy would never see." Dave remembers trying to trick himself: "Well, Kathy won't see this," he'd say, "so I'll have to enjoy it twice as much, for her.'"

After eight weeks, Dave returned to work. He was employed by the National Park Service as the principal librarian at the San Francisco Maritime National Historic Park. It was a position he held for 38 years, until he retired in December 2010. From his office window he could see the Golden Gate Bridge. "I hated the words, 'move on,'" he says. "It felt like a denial of Kathy, a forgetting of her, an erasure. I hated the words, the concept, the world's evidence." Instead, he ruminated over memories he had of her, agonizing over things he believed he should have done, but didn't. The recriminations were so brutal that he contemplated suicide himself, believing—as many people do who have lost loved ones this way—that he was partly to blame. By not protecting his daughter, he was in some degree responsible for her death.

"Of course I did not kill my daughter," he says today. "Kathy jumped off the bridge. But in those first few weeks I conducted an excruciating accounting, attempting even to put percentages of responsibility upon everyone." He ticks them off: upon himself and his wife; upon the mental health clinic at school where Kathy, four days before she jumped, sat for three hours waiting to see a particular therapist, but finally had to leave for class without seeing him; upon Kathy's roommates and friends who might have heard "Kathy's last muted announcements of intent;" upon the board of the Golden Gate Bridge District who for seventy years took no meaningful action to prevent bridge suicides; upon the general public who preferred the views to a taller railing; and, of course, to Kathy herself, who "bears the largest single assignment of responsibility," Hull says. "It was she who made and carried out the decision. Whether all the percentages of responsibility that the rest of us bear amount to more than 50 percent, I could never decide, but it is possible that all of us together could have prevented it [Kathy's death]."

One reason why Dave Hull didn't follow through on his thoughts of suicide was because, like Reneé Milligan, he had another child. It was bad enough that his son had lost a sibling, Dave reasoned, he couldn't lose a parent, too. At the same time, Dave remembers how close he came. "Suicide is contagious," he says. "It puts everyone else at risk." In time, Dave resumed elements of his life. He wrote poetry about Kathy. He returned to the Park Service. He disposed of Kathy's possessions, including her car. He also began talking about the need for a suicide barrier on the Golden Gate Bridge.

"It had nothing to do with a resolution to produce something positive out of an awful event," he tells me. "It was rage and a sense of rightness that drove me to involvement.... The bridge exerts a powerful, even mythical allure. If you don't believe me, walk alone to the middle of the bridge and look over the railing at the water below. That bridge fosters the myth of the perfect death, the gold standard of suicide. Those in pain are in great danger on the bridge. Don't go near it when you're having a bad day. The barrier is too late for Kathy, but it's not too late for me.

It's not too late for you. It's not too late for your child. It's not too late for our children."

The lack of a suicide deterrent consigned Jonathan Zablotny to an early death as well. A high school senior, Jonathan, while bright, was plagued by chronic procrastination. He turned in papers late and missed deadlines, including the deadline to apply for the University of California system. His parents tried to prod him gently, but that just seemed to make things worse. When a teacher warned his mother that Jonathan might not pass senior year history unless he turned in a paper on the Challenger space shuttle explosion—a topic Jonathan chose—his chances of getting into Reed College in Oregon, his first choice, were jeopardized.

The morning of February 1, 2005, he threw his backpack over his shoulder and set off on foot for the six-block walk from his home in San Francisco to school. He didn't make it. No one knows what time he arrived at the Golden Gate Bridge, but pedestrians saw his body floating in the water at 4:45 P.M., nine hours after he left home. He was still wearing his backpack. A few days later, his aunt found a note on his computer. "I'm a coward" the note read. "I'm taking the coward's way out and it should be honestly said what has happened, I have struggled with the same problem for 6 years and it is painfully obvious to me that I cannot overcome it for any length of time and be happy. jonathan zablotny."

In Mary and Ray Zablotny's Queen Anne Victorian home, Mary shows me photos of Jonathan, including his high school graduation photo—the last photo taken of him. There are also photos of Jonathan's older brother, Dave. Dave worked as an auto mechanic for a long time, Mary says, until recently, when he went back to school. "Dave gave himself the time he needed to figure life out," Mary says wistfully. "Jonathan didn't. He lost faith in himself."

The night before Jonathan died, his mother was unnerved. She remembers thinking that he had a look in his eyes she hadn't seen before. "I didn't understand it at the time," she says. "It's called the 1,000-yard stare. I thought he was upset about the paper, but I think now he was staring his own death in the face." It was Monday, and Jonathan had done all of the research for the Challenger paper that was due Friday, so there should have been enough time, Mary says. But Jonathan was running lights and sound for the school play, which had dress rehearsals every night that week. "I told him, 'Come home. I'll help you on the paper as much as I can,' " Mary says.

Jonathan didn't seem any different the next morning. He wasn't sullen or withdrawn following the fight he'd had with his parents over the Challenger paper. He also wasn't buoyant as some suicidal people are once they develop a plan and feel like they've taken control of their life. When Mary told Jonathan that she loved him and wanted him to be happy, he just nodded, picked up his backpack, and headed out the door.

Tuesday night, when he hadn't come home, she called his friends and was told that Jonathan never went to school. In all likelihood he wandered around the city. A short time later she received the news that no parent ever wants to hear.

"Do you think Jonathan would be alive today if the bridge had a barrier?" I ask.

Her eyes flash and she answers immediately, "Yes, he'd be alive—especially after everything I've learned about suicide. You fixate on a particular method, and if it's not available to you, you back off, you don't do it."

"Has opposition to a barrier surprised you?"

Again, she's quick to reply. "The ignorance surprises me. Opponents keep coming up with fact-less arguments. As soon as one argument is proven false, they raise another one, equally fact-less."

Anyone who thinks that mental health professionals, by virtue of their education, training, and experience can always discern suicidal intentions in their progeny will be surprised to learn that Jonathan's father was chief of psychiatry at a Kaiser hospital. His son's death not only rocked his private life, but caused Ray Zablotny to question his professional competencies. Ray's mother suffered from clinical depression. He'd treated suicidal patients. He was on the hospital's suicide death review committee (a position he resigned from after Jonathan died). He knew the warning signs of suicide, and his son had not exhibited them. "The thing about Jonathan's death," says Mary, "is that there was practically no warning. He didn't seem unhappy—in fact, just the opposite. There were no major conflicts at home. The only thing lacking in his life was his ability to buckle down with his studies."

Several weeks after Jonathan jumped, students at his school showed up at the Bridge District board room. Jonathan's best friend, Patrick Fitzgerald, wrote a tender, articulate op-ed piece about suicide, Jonathan's death, and the Golden Gate Bridge. He followed it up with a letter and petitions that he presented to the Bridge District in which he said that the effort to get a suicide barrier on the bridge had become his expression of grief. "These words are my tears," he wrote in the letter.

"If an 18-year-old can do that," Mary says, "talk about losing someone he loves, I decided that that must be a good route to take." It's why she and her husband have been public with their grief.

Mary is an artist, and one of her passions is making labyrinths out of beads. She shows me the labyrinth she designed, made, and always has with her since Jonathan's death. "It's a walking meditation," she says. Unlike mazes, labyrinths have only one path leading to the center and the same path or a different one that takes you out. There are no wrong turns or dead ends. She sketches the labyrinth first, using special ink that's water and fade resistant.

I ask her how she'll celebrate personally when the bridge has a barrier. She says that she'll make a beautiful and original bicursal labyrinth (the kind with one way in and another way out). As we're talking, she says, "I need to think of the symbolism." She's silent for just a minute, then says, "The entrance will be when the bridge was built, and farther in the suicides mount. The center will be when the Bridge District no longer can ignore the people, their will and the publicity. The path out is the path to a suicide barrier. When you come out, the barrier is there."

Most people can't imagine anything worse than discovering that your child, parent, spouse, partner, sibling, or friend killed themselves, especially if they were young or in the prime of life. There is, however, something that's even worse. It's when your loved one dies by suicide and the death is never confirmed. This leaves all sorts of questions unanswered. When do you start grieving? How long do you hold out hope? What's the appropriate time to have a memorial service? Also, with no remains to bury or cremate, where do you go to place flowers or otherwise pay your respects?

If the body of a Golden Gate Bridge jumper isn't recovered and the leap isn't witnessed, the victim's family is placed in limbo. The death cannot be legally verified. There have been a number of instances in which a person made it appear that he or she jumped from the bridge to escape legal, financial, or family problems, then turned up later, in another part of the country or the world, quite healthy and living under an assumed identity. For this reason, the official status of persons who are suspected of jumping but the jump can't be confirmed is "missing." This creates further hardships for the family.

There is little doubt that twenty-year-old Matthew Whitmer jumped from the Golden Gate Bridge on November 15, 2007. After playing video games at home with his younger brother until 1 A.M., he got up five hours later, drove to the bridge, left his car in the south-end parking lot, walked out on the span, and leaped over the side at light pole number ninety-seven. That afternoon his parents were contacted by the California Highway Patrol. A young man had been seen jumping from the bridge at 6:25 A.M. Matthew's car, with his identification in it, was found abandoned in the parking lot.

Matthew didn't leave a suicide note, and his body was never found. Since his death can't be confirmed, he is legally considered "missing" even though a later investigation of his computer revealed his intent. The last online search he did was to look up whether there was a suicide barrier on the Golden Gate Bridge. After he learned there wasn't, he got driving directions. At 6:23 A.M. he sent a text message to a friend: "Peace Out," it said. It is, according to his mother, Dayna, the way he said good-bye.

At 8 A.M. the Coast Guard had stopped searching for his body. That started his parents' worst nightmare. "It was incredibly difficult to spend hours calling all the local hospitals for Matthew or 'John Doe,' because he left his I.D. in the car," says Dayna, a medical technician with the Department of Veterans Affairs in Martinez. "More difficult was placing monthly calls to multiple coroner's officers looking for 'John Doe' or, worse yet, 'partial remains.'"

When a person is missing, the family must file a report with the local authority. In California, this information is entered into the state's missing persons database. Families need to provide dental records, as well as items that may be used for DNA matching such as toothbrushes and hair brushes. Parental DNA also may be requested. It can take five years, under California law, before a person is declared dead if his or her body isn't recovered. It's possible to have the declaration made sooner if the family petitions the probate court and provides enough evidence, even if the evidence is circumstantial. Dayna and Mark Whitmer have done that, and as of fall 2011 they are still waiting. The whole process "can be incredibly difficult both emotionally and financially for families," says Dayna, "especially families with young children who lose a parent off the bridge."

In 2008, to celebrate what would have been Matthew's twenty-first birthday, Dayna did what she says her son might have done: she got drunk and got a tattoo. The tattoo, just above her heart, has Matthew's name over a green Celtic cross (shortly before his death Matthew had showed interest in his Irish heritage).

Dayna also became an active member of the Bridge Rail Foundation. Founded by Dave Hull after his daughter's death, the all-volunteer organization has one mission—to end suicides from the Golden Gate Bridge. Several times in recent years it has staged what is referred to as the "Whose Shoes" exhibit to commemorate everyone who has jumped from the bridge since it was erected. Hundreds of pairs of shoes are displayed—"worn oxfords, floral flip-flops, inline skates, sparkly high heels, fuzzy blue slippers," as the *San Francisco Chronicle* described it—topped by a pair of World War I boots representing Harold Wobber, the World War I veteran who was the bridge's first reported suicide. The shoes, many of them contributed by family members of jumpers, are stacked neatly and form a large, silent monument in memory of everyone who has died.

In the wake of her son's death, Dayna also put together a booklet to help families deal with the trauma of having a loved one officially declared "missing." The booklet explains what the authorities will do, what loved ones should do within the first four hours, first twenty-four hours, and next two to three days, and what to tell children. It also provides tips on taking care of yourself, as well as contact information for crisis centers in the Bay Area. Some California Highway Patrol officers as well as the Marin County coroner keep copies of Dayna's booklet on hand to give to grieving families. More recently, Dayna launched the Web site http://goldengatebridgesuicides.org. The site, which is dedicated to her son, has an electronic version of her booklet. It also has the most complete listing of suicides from the Golden Gate Bridge to be found. This list was created in consultation with coroner Ken Holmes, and is printed, with permission, in appendix C of this book.

Maria Martinez, a political organizer who once worked for Nancy Pelosi, knows full well the trauma of losing a loved one whose death is not confirmed. In 1988, Leonard Branzuela, Maria's son, was one match away from making the U.S. Olympic wrestling team. Five years later, at age thirty-two, he was a wrestling coach at Lowell High School in San Francisco. On a hot day in June 1993 he got a haircut, then went to his mother's apartment. Her son hadn't told her that he was coming, and Maria was out when he arrived. Leonard waited awhile, then took a bus to the Golden Gate Bridge.

For a week afterward, Maria didn't hear from Leonard, which was unusual. She left messages, but they weren't returned. In July she filed a missing person's report. The following day she received a form letter from the California Highway Patrol (CHP). It was addressed to Leonard and had been forwarded to her from one of his previous addresses. It said that the highway patrol had his wallet and was holding it.

Maria and her grown daughter, Anna—Leonard's sister— drove across the Golden Gate Bridge to retrieve Leonard's wallet and find out what had happened. Maria was handed a CHP report that was dated three weeks earlier. It suggested the possibility of suicide. Although Leonard's body wasn't recovered, a witness described seeing a man in the water below the bridge, and Leonard's wallet was found on the walkway. According to the report, attempts to notify his family were not successful— this despite the fact that Maria's business card and the phone numbers of other family members were in Leonard's wallet. Maria stared at the CHP report in disbelief. She hadn't known that her son might be dead, much less that he probably killed himself. According to the *San Francisco Chronicle*, Anna Branzuela "led her wailing mother to the car, and in stunned silence they drove home, across the Golden Gate Bridge."

The following week, mother and sister rented a helicopter to look for Leonard's body, feeling that they had to do something. It was for naught, however. His remains have never been found. "We never had closure," Maria Martinez said. "It's not like we can go visit his grave. Where am I going to go—the bridge?"

Feeling helpless and filled with grief, Maria did what the parents of nineteen-year-old Kenneth Pattison had done two decades earlier and what the mother of Marissa Imrie did several years later. She filed a claim for general damages against the Bridge

District for "failure to protect the public from access to dangerous and unprotected bridge rails" and "failure to provide suicide prevention barriers." The suit was dismissed in Superior Court because, under California law, if a person is hurt or killed on state property, plaintiffs can sue only if they are able to prove that the victim used the property "with due care."

"There's no question that deliberately jumping off a bridge that's over 200 feet from the water is not exercising due care," said a Bridge District attorney. He added, "The fact that suicides have occurred in the past on the bridge and that, therefore, you could argue, further ones are foreseeable, does not mean we are liable."

Martia appealed the ruling because it failed to address whether "a mentally ill person bent on suicide is capable of acting with due care." Citing various court cases, her attorney said that the state legislature surely never intended to absolve a governmental entity from liability in situations where it knew or had reason to know that its property was being used by mentally unstable individuals to kill themselves, yet took no reasonable measures to prevent it.

At the same time that Maria Martinez's suit was being considered, public officials expressed concern that the district might be opening itself to liability if it erected a suicide barrier and someone jumped anyway. Taking precautions to reduce the likelihood of suicide could backfire, they said, if it meant the Bridge District had a duty to prevent suicides and wasn't 100 percent successful in this regard.

In both instances, the prevailing opinion was upheld. Maria's appeal was turned down, and no case law was found to support the position that a public entity is liable if it builds a suicide barrier on property it controls and someone still dies by suicide.

Regarding the latter, the Bridge District's own attorney said, "The construction of a suicide deterrent will not subject the District to any greater exposure than it now faces without such a structure."

An interesting sidebar to all this is that several years later, the Bridge District approved $5 million for a barrier separating bicycle traffic from vehicle traffic on the bridge. As odd as it sounds, the reason why this barrier was erected wasn't to protect bicyclists. After all, no bicyclist had ever been killed on the bridge. And it wasn't erected to protect motorists since they weren't endangered by people riding on the bike path. No, the reason why the bike barrier was approved was because it protected the Bridge District. Bicyclists, you see, *were* using the bridge for the purpose it was designed, and if a bicyclist was hurt or killed because the bridge lacked a safety barrier, then the district would be liable. Thus, one of many ironies concerning the Golden Gate Bridge is that while Maria Martinez's suit didn't result in a suicide barrier, it did contribute, in a roundabout way, to the construction of a bicycle barrier on the bridge.

Even though the body of their daughter, seventeen-year-old Casey Brooks, whose jump is described in the prologue of this book, was never found, John and Erika Brooks were spared the uncertainty that the Whitmers, Maria Martinez, and others have experienced. Because Casey's leap was captured on bridge cameras, the Brookses know what happened—or at least they're pretty sure they do. John Brooks says now that there's a small part of him that wonders whether the girl seen on film actually was Casey or another girl who happened to look like her. Maybe Casey is still alive, he says, "in Brazil or somewhere." He knows that that's just the hope of a despairing parent, and that the truth is she's dead, so he forces it from his mind.

He and his wife haven't filed a missing persons report because they don't see a reason to. They did decide to get tattoos, though, like Dayna Whitmer, to honor Casey. Each made the decision before informing the other, and both were surprised to find that they shared the same thought. "The attraction of a tattoo," Erika tells me, "is that it's permanent and always with me. Unlike a necklace that can break or a T-shirt with Casey's picture on it that wears out over time, her tattoo is part of me forever, even after I die."

Deciding to get a tattoo was only the first step. John and Erika had to decide what it would be of, where it would be on their body, and who would do it. They went to several tattoo parlors, but left almost immediately, dismayed by the conditions. Coincidentally, a few weeks later they traveled to Los Angeles so that John could be interviewed on the *Dr. Phil Show* about the Golden Gate Bridge and Casey's death. They met a tattoo artist backstage and felt that he was the right person. He ended up being so moved by Casey's story that after he created the design on paper, cut it out, and put it in place so that they could see what it would look like, he did the actual tattoo work in their home.

Erika's tattoo is on the back of her right hand, where she can always see it. It's of a flowering lupine plant with nine leaves, representing nine levels of wisdom. Above it, on her right ring finger, is a mission blue butterfly, actual size, which is only about half an inch. It's an endangered species native to the California north coast, feeds off of lupine, and was a favorite of Casey's. John's tattoo consists of the words "I Love Casey" on each bicep, one in Chinese and the other in Sanskrit.

The Brookses readily admit that after Casey died, their lives lost all meaning. Nothing mattered anymore. No one could hurt them worse than they had been hurt already. At one point Ken Holmes, the Marin County coroner whose office does the autopsies of Golden Gate bridge jumpers and notifies next of kin, feared that John Brooks would kill himself. Brooks was so raw, so brittle, so devastated. Holmes asked Brooks if he ever thought of suicide.

"Every day," Brooks replied.

"You know you can't," Holmes said. Too many other people needed him.

"I know I shouldn't," Brooks said.

What has helped John and Erika Brooks the most is the support they've received from Casey's friends, who continue to stay in touch with them, as well as the support they've been able to provide to these young and impressionable youths. Together, they're helping each other cope with a tragedy that shouldn't have ever happened.

Since Casey jumped, hundreds of poignant messages have been posted on her Facebook remembrance page.

"I had this mad intense dream about you last night, it was sweet. it made me think a lot. nobody is like you, and it's not fair. but I woke up happy even though I missed you more than usual."

"I put a 'I heart Casey' on my window on the driver's side. [Casey's parents had these made and gave them to her friends.] Now folks think I have a boyfriend. Seriously, I think I'm going to post those bumper stickers on every stop sign around SF's Civic Center. You will always be remembered!'

"It was a beautiful day out today. The sun was shining, and
there was a glimmer of hope. That made me think of you."
"You might not be here, physically, but I feel as if part of you
is always with me."

John and Erika Brooks continue to read the postings, learning things that shed a small amount of light on Casey's death.
For instance, a year before she jumped, when Casey was working as a clerk at a Williams Sonoma store, another employee
leaped off the Golden Gate Bridge.

Roxanne Makoff was Casey's best friend. In September 2008
she testified before the Bridge District board of directors. "If
you have ever thought about killing yourself, please raise your
hand," she began, then paused. "If you did not just raise your
hand, you are lying," she said. Casey "did not think through the
consequences of her actions, and I'll be the first to tell you that
what she did was selfish and thoughtless, but I am also telling
you today that with a barrier, she would still be among us. Casey
had issues, don't get me wrong, but her issues only became life
or death when she realized the accessibility of the Golden Gate
Bridge." Makoff challenged the belief that someone who's determined to die will resort to any possible means:

Casey would have never slit her wrists, hanged herself, or overdosed on pills to kill herself.... Her only method of suicide was the
Golden Gate Bridge. I have proof of this because just three weeks
before her death, I was riding in her car with her across the Golden
Gate Bridge when I casually asked her, "If you were to kill yourself,
how would you do it?" Call me stupid, call me messed up, call me
whatever you want, but in this day and age, a question like this one
isn't uncommon. Casey's response: "The Golden Gate Bridge, of
course. So beautiful, so easy, so clean." I agreed.... The night of
Casey's death, she completed all of her homework, studied for all

of her tests, and carried on normal conversation with us, her friends. Somehow after all of this normality, Casey decided her life wasn't worth living anymore. It was early in the morning, a lack of sleep had gotten the best of her, and the cold weather dampened her spirits and somehow in her mind she decided it was time to end her life.... Build a suicide barrier. It is imperative. The loss of a life to suicide does not affect only the family and the close friends. It affects an entire community.... Save our loved ones who are similar to Casey Brooks.

Sarah Barr grew up with Casey, and lived on the same street. She said that she was opposed to a suicide barrier before Casey Brooks died and now felt that one was critical to prevent other deaths. In her testimony, she stated,

> This is just wrong. Casey should have graduated, she should have gone to college, she should be moving into her dorm right now, but she is not.... We live in an affluent area, and there are pressures to dress well, get good grades, excel at something—whether it be sports, art, debating—it has to be something. We all feel like escaping that pressure at times. That the bridge is so easy to jump from is just wrong. I'm 17, and I've known three people who have jumped. There is something wrong with that.... I want a barrier so that every teenager has the opportunity to see what there is to live for."

Bridge District officials had heard heartfelt testimony before. Families and loved ones of victims had testified. Responders and helpers had testified. Coroner Ken Holmes had testified, as had Kevin Hines, a bridge jump survivor. All spoke articulately and passionately about the need for a suicide barrier. None had quite the same impact as the testimony of Casey Brooks's friends, however. According to Tom Ammiano, a member of the Golden Gate Bridge District board for twelve years, "When the young people came out, everybody was moved." Even Gavin Newsom, the mayor of San Francisco at the time (now lieutenant governor of California), who previously had made public statements opposing a suicide barrier, changed his mind after hearing Casey's friends speak.

"The strange thing about the bridge," says filmmaker Eric Steel, whose 2005 documentary movie *The Bridge* focused on Golden Gate Bridge suicides (and is discussed in detail in chapter 7), "is that when someone dies there, there's this big splash and within minutes it's like nothing ever happened. All the ripples go away. And the traffic keeps moving and the pedestrians are walking and the water's going under the bridge. But for the families, that ripple keeps going forever."

That's as good a description of the impact of suicide in general and Golden Gate Bridge suicides in particular as I've ever heard. When a loved one dies by any means, there's a hole in your heart that can only be mended by time and a strong support system. With suicide, the hole is bigger, the pain tends to be greater, and the recovery period usually is much longer. With the Golden Gate Bridge, there's the added dimension that society seems to be condoning the death by doing nothing to stop it.

Four days after his father, Charles Gallagher Sr., a successful businessman, jumped off the Golden Gate Bridge, his son followed him. The younger Gallagher, twenty-four, was a premed student at UCLA. He drove his father's car to the bridge and jumped from nearly the identical spot. His suicide note was short: "I am sorry... I want to keep Dad company."

Stories of victims underline the immeasurable human potential that disappears with each suicide. Vince Mulroy, who jumped in 2009, was the starting wide receiver for Stanford in the Bluebonnet Bowl thirty years earlier, after being a star decathlete and football player at Newport Harbor High School in southern California. Mulroy also was a first-team Academic All-American, recipient of the university's prestigious J. Walter Sterling Award, and a finalist for a Rhodes scholarship. Bill Walsh was his coach. After attaining an MBA from Harvard Business School, Mulroy had a successful career in real estate. He also was an active volunteer with two youth groups. At age fifty-two, suffering from depression and chronic back pain, the latter due to football injuries and a later car accident, he jumped from the bridge, leaving a wife and two teenage children.

Roy Raymond was another casualty. A self-made millionaire, Raymond started Victoria's Secret, the lingerie company, after being embarrassed to buy his wife a slip in a regular department store. When he sold the company, he invested in a high-end children's toy store that failed, then in a children's bookstore that also lost money. Although friends said that Raymond was eternally optimistic and unfazed by business failures, he must have been more depressed than they knew. In August 1993, he drove his Toyota to the middle of the Golden Gate Bridge, wrote notes for his wife and their children, then jumped.

Duane Garrett jumped, too. A longtime Democratic Party fundraiser and personal friend of former Vice President Al Gore, Garrett managed political campaigns for Walter Mondale, Bruce Babbitt, Barbara Boxer, and Dianne Feinstein. He also was a political analyst at a television station in San Francisco. Mere hours before he jumped, he left a message at the station saying that he couldn't do the next day's show. His car was found in a parking lot near the toll plaza. His body was found floating underneath the Golden Gate Bridge after it was spotted from above.

Dr. Phil Holsten was valedictorian of his high school class in Modesto, graduated from the University of California San Francisco Medical School, completed his residency at Stanford, and was a doctor at California Pacific Medical Center. An avid bicyclist, Holsten told Sarah Cherny, his fiancée and a fellow physician, that he was going to ride in the Marin Headlands on his day off. Instead, according to two witnesses, around 11 A.M. he stopped halfway across the bridge, dismounted, leaned his bike against the railing, placed his helmet over the handlebars, and jumped without any hesitation. It was 2004; he was thirty-three years old.

A year later, Cherny testified before the Bridge District board. As reported by *San Francisco Chronicle* reporter Joan Ryan, Cherny told board members that Holsten gave no warning signs. "He had already paid for a trip to Guatemala that he was taking with me and my parents," she said. "I found out later he had been planning a surprise birthday party for me in two weeks.... If there was a barrier, I would have seen him at home that night instead of on a metal gurney after his autopsy."

Cherny's father also testified. "You may think it can never happen to you," Robert Cherny told Bridge District board members. "I am here to tell you that it can." The elder Cherny taught history at San Francisco State University and was on the San Francisco Landmarks Preservation Advisory Board. He referred to the latter capacity in appealing for a suicide barrier on the bridge. "I sometimes get to vote on saving buildings," he said. "You get to vote on saving lives."

Sarah Cherny noted that two of the primary arguments against a suicide barrier—that it will cost too much and that it will ruin the view—were the same arguments that were raised seventy years earlier when people objected to building the bridge itself. Eventually those arguments were overcome—or at least cast aside—by a stronger, prevailing opinion that the cost was worth it and the view would be preserved.

Today, no one questions the cost of the Golden Gate Bridge, although commuters do question the cost of rising bridge tolls, which subsidize the Bridge District's bus and ferry service (the bridge itself was paid off in 1971). And the view continues to be breathtaking, among the most spectacular in the world. In hindsight it's easy to see that concerns about the cost and the view were unfounded.

The same will be true when a suicide deterrent is erected on the Golden Gate Bridge. The lives that are saved will be worth the price, and the view won't be affected in any significant way.

It's a rare occurence to hear someone say that a suicide deterrent mars the appearance or views of the Eiffel Tower, Empire State Building, or other architectural wonders of the world. People are so used to them that they hardly even notice their presence or if they do notice they don't bemoan the fact that they're there. The barrier is accepted as part of the structure— unfortunate perhaps, but necessary. Tourism isn't affected.

The same can't be said about the Golden Gate Bridge, at least not yet. Each month produces more jumps, more witnesses to jumps, and more loved ones who are left to mourn. Each month also produces more attempted jumps, more police interventions, and more people who are escorted off the bridge for their personal safety. Simultaneously, there are many reasons why someone who's suicidal chooses to jump from the Golden Gate Bridge. There's the allure of the bridge, the mystique, and the romanticism. There's the belief that death will be quick and painless. And there's the easy access.

Several years ago, Patricia Dunn was interviewed on TV's *60 Minutes* about her controversial ouster as president of the board of computer giant Hewitt-Packard. Dunn's professional life was in shambles, her integrity was attacked, her health was declining, and she was reeling emotionally. Leslie Stahl, the *60 Minutes* reporter, asked Dunn how she was dealing with everything when the story was so public and she was receiving so little support from former colleagues. Dunn paused, started to answer, couldn't find the words, then said softly, "Well, there's always the Golden Gate Bridge."

Dunn wasn't at a point where she was seriously contemplating suicide. Still, she was voicing the thought that many local people have if things get really bad: with the bridge so close and omnipresent, it's always an option. Moreover, loved ones are spared the physical shock of a person's death—there's no horrifying sight to discover, no room that's forever associated with a tragic act, no gruesome cleanup. Once you're over the side, it's the problem of trained professionals—Coast Guard crew members and coroner's investigators. That is, if your body is found. If it's not found, so much the better; you just disappear.

The only thing that's left is a ripple—a ripple that may be felt for generations.

FOUR

Opening Up

Early on, I was indifferent to suicides from the
bridge. After being here, though, and talking with
families of the victims, it swung me completely over
to the other side.

—Ken Holmes, coroner of Marin County

With Golden Gate Bridge suicides, it's often the coroner who
uncovers the complexity and pain inherent in the act of jumping. The stories conveyed by this public servant illuminate a
mesh of psychological and physical suffering.

Most suicides are planned. When Diane Hansen, thirty, of
Sausalito jumped from the bridge, it was two weeks after her
mother died and was cremated. As Hansen fell, narrowly missing a Harbor Queen cruise ship filled with tourists, she held
onto a 10-by-10-inch white box that contained her mother's ashes.
Stephen Hoag, twenty-six, of San Francisco, left a suicide note
that said, "Do not notify my mother. She has a heart condition."
There was no need to notify his mother, however—she saw it on
the evening news. Hoag was the five hundredth official suicide
from the bridge.

Even when the act is planned, however, the moment of action may remain in doubt. On April 24, 1998, for example, two women ages twenty-two and fifty-one who did not know each other ended up at the same spot on the bridge at the same time with the same intention of killing themselves. They sat on the chord, on the other side of the railing, talking to each other. A Bridge Patrol officer noticed them and tried to talk them back to safety; instead, one woman stood up and stepped backward off the bridge. The other woman then followed her.

A few suicides appear almost fanciful. John Thomas Doyle, forty-nine, of San Francisco died leaving a suicide note that read, "Absolutely no reason except I have a toothache." Eilert Johnson, seventy, of Oakland held a hat on his head with both hands the whole way down as if he was afraid it would blow away.

The majority of deaths resulting from Golden Gate Bridge jumps are investigated by the Marin County coroner's office. Prior to 1991, the bodies of Golden Gate Bridge jumpers were delivered to Letterman Hospital, an Army hospital in the Presidio at San Francisco. When the Coast Guard station in San Francisco was relocated to Marin County in 1991, however, the coroner's office in Marin began receiving the corpses.

Ken Holmes worked in the Marin County coroner's office for thirty-five years, starting as an investigator in 1975. In 1998 he was elected coroner, and he held that position until December 31, 2010, when the office was merged with the sheriff's department and Holmes retired. In 2005 he was asked by a reporter about the physical impact on a body from jumping off the Golden Gate Bridge. "Some people seem to think that jumping off the bridge is a light, airy way to end your life," Holmes said, "like going to join the angels. I'd like to dispel that myth. When you jump off the bridge, you hit the water hard. It's not a pretty death."

A jumper's body travels at a speed of seventy-five miles per hour. Upon impact the outer body stops but the internal organs keep going, tearing loose from their connections. Sternums, clavicles, and pelvises shatter. Aortas, livers, and spleens are lacerated. Skulls, ribs, and vertebra are fractured. The result is similar to that of a pedestrian who's struck by a car going seventy-five miles per hour. In many cases, jagged rib bones puncture the heart, lungs, or major arteries, causing the brain to shut down immediately for lack of oxygen-bearing blood.

If a person does not die right away, he or she dies by drowning. Bodies plunge deep into the frigid waters of San Francisco Bay and breathe it in. In rare cases, jumpers not only survive the fall but are able to swim to the surface despite suffering massive internal injuries. They flail away in the water hoping to be rescued, their bodies broken, every breath painful. Overall, about 5 percent of Golden Gate Bridge jumpers drown according to a report in the *Western Journal of Medicine*, based on a study of 169 Golden Gate Bridge jumpers. The 2 percent who survive the fall hit the water feet first and at a slight angle so that their body arcs back to the surface. Those who land perfectly straight end up diving too deep and drown, while those who land any other way tend to die on impact, with deep bruises on their torso, back, buttocks, and the underside of their arms.

One woman was so intent on killing herself, and so worried about the pain if she survived the fall, that she carried a gun with her to the bridge and shot herself in the head on the way down. She left a note for her roommate saying that she didn't want to feel the impact of hitting the water or take a chance that she might live.

One Coast Guard officer described the effect of a bridge jump this way: "It's as if someone took an eggbeater to the organs of the body and ground everything up."

Over the years, Holmes and his staff have witnessed many gruesome sights. They are largely inured to it; after all, if you do autopsies you'd better be comfortable around mutilated bodies. Still, when people hit the water face first, it obliterates features and opens up gaping holes. Other jumpers land on rocks, usually on the north end of the bridge, and their body just comes apart. In some instances only partial remains are found after a body has been in the water for days or even weeks. Nothing is as bad, though, as receiving the body of a child.

In January 1993, a thirty-two-year-old man drove his three-year-old daughter to the bridge, threw her over the side, and followed her. Pam Carter is a senior coroner's investigator in Marin County. At the time, she was working as a nurse at Marin General Hospital. The daughter, named Kellie, was brought into the hospital's emergency room, still alive. Doctors worked frantically for ninety minutes trying to save her, but there was nothing they could do. Afterward, Carter was told to take Kellie's body to the hospital morgue. The thought of leaving the child on a cold slab was abhorrent to her so she borrowed a crib, took it to the morgue, and laid the girl inside. "That had to be the worst," Carter told a *San Francisco Chronicle* reporter. "This little thing, taken like that by her father, the person she loved and looked up to. It was awful." Even after that incident, which was well publicized, many people opposed a suicide barrier. The *San Francisco Examiner* conducted a poll and 54 percent of respondents said they were against it.

There have been at least two other instances where a parent has thrown a child over the railing, then followed them to their deaths. In 1964, a forty-five-year-old airplane mechanic jumped with his four-year-old son. In November 1993—the same year that little Kellie was hurled over the side—a thirty-seven-year-old man jumped with his two-year-old son.

One of the arguments against a suicide barrier is that people who choose to kill themselves don't deserve society's protection. Yet these three children didn't have a choice, and they did deserve protection.

Marilyn DeMont wasn't officially murdered, but she might as well have been. She's considered the bridge's youngest suicide. In 1945, five-year-old Marilyn was on the bridge with her father. He told her to climb over the railing and stand on the girder on the other side. As Allen Brown describes it in his book *Golden Gate*, "The wind blew through her blond hair as she silently looked back at her father for instructions. He commanded her to jump. Then August DeMont, a thirty-seven-year-old elevator installation foreman from San Francisco, gracefully dived after his daughter." A note found later in August DeMont's car didn't explain the two deaths, it merely said, "I and my daughter have committed suicide."[1]

When the Bridge Patrol or California Highway Patrol receive a call that a person has jumped off the Golden Gate Bridge, an officer is sent to the location of the jump as determined by the light pole number. There, the officer drops a nineteen-inch-long marine location marker, also known as a Mark-25 or "smoke float," into the water. The marker emits both smoke and a flare for up to

---

1. Suicide prevention advocates discourage use of the phrase "committed suicide." It implies that suicide is against the law when it's not. No one says that a person "committed cancer." Instead, the person died by cancer and that's the way suicide deaths should be referred to; thus, "the person died by suicide." It is also acceptable to say that a person killed himself or herself, or that there was a "completed suicide."

thirty minutes. Supplied by the Coast Guard and stored on the bridge for easy access (they're not reusable), the marker is weighted and indicates which way the tide is moving, enabling the Coast Guard to develop search patterns. On the bridge, officers follow the marker with binoculars and maintain radio communication with the Coast Guard. The current is so strong and variable in the straits that the bodies of bridge jumpers have washed out to the Farallon Islands, nearly thirty miles away, then washed back in under the bridge.

When the Coast Guard lifeboat arrives and the jumper is located, two members of the four-person crew, wearing protective body suits, retrieve the jumper and perform CPR. If the person is alive, he or she is taken to shore in San Francisco or Marin County (whichever side is closest), loaded onto a waiting ambulance, and transported to San Francisco General or Marin General hospital. If the person is dead, the body is delivered to the Marin County coroner. If a body isn't recovered by the Coast Guard, which spends two to three hours searching, and subsequently washes up further down the coast, the coroner in that county performs the autopsy. Whatever happens, when a jump or potential jump from the Golden Gate Bridge is reported, the California Highway Patrol (CHP) handles the investigation. The CHP is responsible for all incidents, accidents, and deaths that occur on California freeways, including highways 1 and 101, which join to cross the Golden Gate Bridge.

There's a solemn ritual when the body of a Golden Gate Bridge jumper is delivered to the coroner. Coast Guard crews bring the body to shore at Fort Baker in a long, shallow container that's covered with a tarp. Placed on top of the tarp or alongside it are the person's belongings, if there are any. The container is set on a dock, awaiting the arrival of a coroner's investigator. According to international maritime law, the Coast Guard's jurisdiction ends when a body touches land, although sailors stand guard over it until there's a proper handoff.

When the coroner's investigator arrives, he or she meets first with the CHP officer handling the case. The officer relates any information about the jumper, including whether the jump was witnessed. Then the coroner's investigator goes to work. The coroner's office has four responsibilities: identify the deceased, notify next of kin, conduct an autopsy to determine the cause of death, and file a death notice. With the exception of the death notice, which is easily handled once the facts of the case are known, a bridge suicide can be a lot of work, depending on the circumstances.

If a wallet is found on the body, identification is easy to confirm. The investigator checks records with the Department of Motor Vehicles (DMV) to determine whether the person owned a car, then goes to the bridge parking lots to see if the car is there. If the deceased's body is found with car keys, the inspector will try them on all matching makes of cars. "It's a lot easier today," Ken Holmes says, "because most cars come with remotes. You just stand in the parking lot and press the button. If the car is there, the lights will flash." Sometimes a jumper leaves a suicide note in the car. Other times he or she mails a good-bye letter to people, making sure to time it so that the letter arrives after the person jumps.

If there is no identification, then "a long and expensive process begins," according to Holmes, to determine who has died, where he or she was living, and next of kin. First, the investigator checks fingerprints of the deceased against California DMV records. If there's no match, the investigator checks against the Federal Bureau of Investigation database maintained by the Department of Homeland Security. The investigator also charts the deceased's teeth to match against possible dental records, as well as notes the person's jewelry, piercings, and clothing labels. Eighty percent of the time, Holmes says, the person is identified within one month. The other 20 percent, more legwork is required.

Recently, a person's remains were found high up on a small beach near the north tower of the Golden Gate Bridge. Depending on the tides, the beach is often underwater and not visible. A kayaker went up into the rocks (probably to go to the bathroom, Holmes speculates) and found the skull and upper torso of a male that had been there six or seven years. Scavengers had picked the skull clean, but the torso was still clothed. In addition, there was a Sony Walkman nearby. The coroner's investigator ran a check of the Walkman's batteries and determined that they were made in March 2002. A subsequent check of the jacket the man was wearing revealed that it was first sold in 2004, so that established the earliest he could have died. To date, the coroner's office has put in sixty man-hours on the case, with more to come. The condition of the body indicates a considerable fall, consistent with a jump from the bridge, although the person could have fallen accidentally or been pushed. As a result, the death is unlikely to be recorded as a suicide unless the body is identified and writings are found indicating the person's intent.

Identifying a body isn't as simple as one might think. In the first place, many people jump with no identification on them. They leave their wallet or purse on the bridge or in their car. Second, a person's absence may not be noticed and a missing persons report most likely has not been filed yet so investigators don't have a lot to go on. Third, bodies disintegrate the longer they're in seawater. Only pieces of a body may be found, and then sometimes a considerable distance from the bridge. If the cavity is breached, then the gases that are caused by decay, which normally keep a body afloat, leak out and the body sinks. The result is that the person's remains probably never will be recovered, meaning that no autopsy can be conducted and no one will know with certainty what happened.

A recent success was the identification of a woman whose body washed up on Angel Island after being in the water two to three weeks. Because water softens the skin, there were no fingerprints and no facial features. ("Soft things are eaten," Holmes says.) She was five-foot-two, 110 to 120 pounds. Her lungs were lacerated, her ribs were broken, there was extensive bruising, and her skull was fractured, indicating that she fell from a great height and probably landed on her head. The coroner's office issued a "found unidentified report," which is the opposite of a missing person's report. It notes that a body has been found with no identification. People who are looking for a missing person go through these reports, of which there are thousands, to see if there's a match. In this case, a private investigator in Los Angeles contacted the Marin County coroner's office. He was searching for a woman meeting that general description who had eight siblings, including sisters in Los Angeles, San Jose, and San Francisco. The woman told her family that she was going to live with her sister in San Jose, but never showed up. That's when the family hired the private investigator. The coroner asked the sisters to send photos of their sister, particularly photos that showed jewelry she was wearing. The body that was found had unusual jewelry—three-hoop interlocking earrings, matching rings and necklaces, and a bracelet with tiny skulls. Dental records wouldn't help because the deceased had had considerable dental work done in recent years, and there was no possibility of using DNA (even though the coroner could collect DNA from the body, there was nothing to compare it to—no hair follicles on a brush or saliva on a toothpaste). In the photos that Holmes's office received, the woman was wearing the exact same jewelry. When the investigator asked if the deceased always wore this jewelry, her sisters replied that she never took it off. A positive identification was established in only five weeks. When asked, one sister said that her sibling was depressed. Unless stronger evidence turns up, however, this death won't be attributed to the bridge.

Once a victim is identified, investigators attempt to determine his or her next of kin. This is done by searching marriage records and other public documents. If the victim lived in an apartment, the landlord is asked whether the person provided emergency contact information. If the person's employer is identified, emergency contact information is requested from the human resources department.

Contacting next of kin is the hardest part of the job. "Death notifications are the most difficult, most heart wrenching, most heartbreaking thing we do," Holmes says. "We change somebody's life forever. We ruin some part of it." Whenever possible, notification is done in person. As bad as it is to be told that a loved one has died, it's worse to receive the information over the phone. Even if the family member lives in another state, Holmes and his staff make arrangements for the person to be told face-to-face. "If next of kin live in Tuscaloosa," Holmes tells me, "we contact the police department there, ask them to contact the individual in person, tell them that Joe has passed away in Marin County, and give them our number. We also ask officers to wait with the person until he or she calls us. We advise the police officer to suggest to the person that they go get a neighbor or contact their pastor, too—anything so that they're not alone."

When the person calls, Holmes and his staff give the truth as softly as possible. Their aim is to be factual, but not sound bureaucratic. "It appears that Joe has taken his own life. He was found floating in water underneath the Golden Gate Bridge. People saw him climb over the rail and jump." If there's a note and it's addressed to a specific individual, the coroner shares the contents only with that person or with someone the person authorizes. If it's a general note, along the lines of "Good-bye world," then it's shared with next of kin.

Through experience, coroner's investigators have learned not to answer a deceased person's phone if it rings after they have taken possession of it. It might be the person's parent or spouse, and lead to questions. "This is Joe's mother. Who are you? Why are you answering my son's phone?" Then the investigator has to explain what happened, a situation that Holmes tries to avoid until it can be done in person.

Marin County doesn't have a morgue. A "body removal" company picks up the deceased in a van and delivers the remains, on a rotating basis, to one of three mortuaries. At the mortuary, a pathologist performs the autopsy. Everyone—transport company, mortuary, and pathologist—is on contract with the Marin County coroner's office.

Determining the cause of death tends to be relatively straightforward. There's a checklist that medical examiners go though. While there may not be much visible external damage for a bridge jump—just scrapes where the Coast Guard pulled the body from the water or large, purple bruises covering areas that took the brunt of the impact—invariably there's massive internal bleeding that's consistent with falling from a great height. Still, the body is checked for signs of foul play—just in case—as well as for needle marks and evidence of drug use, which may be important factors.

If there's a suicide note or the jump was witnessed either by people on the bridge or by bridge cameras, then suicide as the cause of death is fairly obvious. Without a note and without witnesses, however, a ruling of suicide is speculative. In general, the higher the fall the greater the trauma to the body and the more likely that suicide is the cause. Fatal falls that are caused by accidents and homicide tend to be from lower heights.

It's common for family members to pressure coroners not to rule questionable deaths as suicides, primarily because of the shame associated with it but also because it may result in the denial of a life insurance claim. If a person is determined to have died by suicide within two years of a policy becoming effective, payment can be contested (beyond two years, life insurance is paid regardless of how the person died). In the absence of compelling evidence, a coroner may conclude that death occurred from a fall and leave it at that, not assessing whether it was a suicide and not connecting the death to the bridge at all.

The San Francisco coroner doesn't have a category for bridge jumps, only "falls from great heights," according to Holmes, which can be from a bridge, tall building, or cliff. Holmes believes that this is deliberate, based on pressure from the San Francisco Board of Supervisors. Because of "pattern injuries," Holmes says, the chief medical examiner can tell whether the person jumped from the bridge, but by not classifying it that way there's no recorded connection.

The word *autopsy* means "see for yourself." Following a loved one's death, the family can ask the hospital to perform an autopsy. In cases where the cause of death is unknown or there's reason to believe that it could be homicide, suicide, or an accident, autopsies are required by law and don't require the consent of family members. Such is the case with Golden Gate Bridge jumpers.

The coroner's office receives the body of a bridge jumper in a body bag. A new bag is used for each person so that only evidence pertaining to that individual is contained in the bag. Before the body is removed from the bag, the investigator examines it. Usually, it's easy to tell if a jumper drowned—there's bubbly mucus coming out of the person's nose (in addition, water is found in the lungs during the autopsy). The investigator also looks for visible signs of trauma, such as deep or massive bruising, and the condition of clothing, which may be shredded or lost on impact.

After the initial assessment, the pathologist removes the body from the body bag and conducts an external examination. The deceased's gender, ethnicity, age, hair color, eye color, and other distinguishing characteristics such as birthmarks, moles, and old scar tissue are recorded. Following this, the body is undressed, cleaned up, weighed, and measured, and any visible wounds are analyzed as potential clues in the person's death. Next comes the internal examination; this is where the impact of death due to multiple blunt-force injuries is most visible. When someone jumps from the Golden Gate Bridge, regardless of the angle that the person hits the water, ribs are fractured and organs are lacerated.

Coroners recognize how different their relationship is to the deceased than that of other people. They never knew the person while he or she was alive; they only know the person after death. It's to the credit of Holmes and his staff that they make an effort to glean information from family members about what the person was like, as well as refer loved ones to grief counseling and other services.

Shortly after Casey Brooks jumped, for example, a community forum was held at Redwood High School—Casey's school—to talk about teen suicide. Holmes attended and stayed in the back of the room, silently observing. Half the people who attended were parents and half were students. He noticed a couple sitting near the front of the room, to his left. The man asked several matter-of-fact questions in a flat voice while the woman cried continuously. Afterward, Holmes approached them, introduced himself as the coroner of Marin County, and said that judging by their emotions they must have lost someone recently. It was John and Erika Brooks. Holmes has remained in close contact with them ever since; in fact, he e-mails Erika every few weeks to check in with her.

I asked Holmes what it is about Golden Gate Bridge suicides that resonate so strongly with him. He replied that it's the fact that they can be prevented: "I've never been an advocate before, but I'm an advocate about this [the suicide barrier]. Bridge District officials have to stop pretending that suicides are not happening."

Holmes isn't one to mince words, and when he testified before the Bridge District board he was direct. "There are 25 to 30 confirmed suicides per year," he told board members, "another 6 to 12 that aren't confirmed, and 80 people are taken off the bridge before they jump. That's 120 people per year planning to kill themselves by jumping off the bridge—not an insignificant number. Are you proud of that, or not? Are you willing to end it, or not?"

For a long time Holmes was opposed to media stories about bridge suicides. He thought that if the problem wasn't publicized, suicidal people wouldn't be encouraged to go to the bridge. Over the years, however, the number of deaths didn't go down despite the lack of media attention. In fact, there were more bridge suicides in 2007—thirty-nine—than in any of the previous ten years (also in 2007, more people were stopped from jumping off the bridge—ninety—than in any of the previous ten years, according to Bridge District records). Limiting media coverage wasn't doing anything to save lives; all it was doing was hiding the problem. Holmes decided that it was time to try a different tact. If silence wasn't working, maybe being vocal would.

In 2007, Holmes, in partnership with the nonprofit Bridge Rail Foundation, issued a report that summarized data pertaining to Golden Gate Bridge suicides over the previous ten years. The release date coincided with the seventieth anniversary of both the completion of the bridge and the bridge's first suicide. As much as anything, the report renewed the debate regarding a suicide barrier on the bridge and contributed to the Golden Gate Bridge District's decision in 2008 to add a deterrent. For that, and because Holmes has been the only person to maintain records of Golden Gate Bridge suicides and disseminate the information to the public, the American Association of Suicidology honored him at the organization's 2008 annual conference, which happened to be held in San Francisco. A modest man, Holmes accepted the award while minimizing his contribution. He preferred that the spotlight be focused on bridge suicides and what can be done to prevent them, not his personal role.

Holmes issued a second, even more comprehensive report two years later. There was still no suicide deterrent on the bridge, nor was one imminent. While Bridge District directors had approved a net—the first time in history that the board voted in favor of a physical deterrent on the bridge—the board had done next to nothing to see that one was erected. No money had been raised for construction, nor did the board develop any plans to identify potential funding sources. Indeed, it seemed to be business as usual, with the deaths continuing unabated.

Both reports provide a clear picture of Golden Gate Bridge jumpers—where they live; their age, gender, race, and marital status; whether their jump is witnessed; and their last-known profession or occupation. The reports also refute some common myths. For instance, most people who jump from the bridge don't come from far away—certainly not from all over the world. They live locally. According to Holmes, 93 percent of Golden Gate Bridge jumpers are from California, 90 percent are from northern California, and 80 percent are from the San Francisco Bay Area. Only 6 percent are from elsewhere in the United States, and fewer than 1 percent are from another country.

Holmes's report contained more data. Eighty percent of jumpers were white, nearly three-fourths were male, and the median age was forty—considerably younger than people who suicide by other means. The youngest victim in Holmes's reports was fourteen (Marissa Imrie, the girl who took a $150 cab ride to the bridge), the oldest was eighty-five. As for marital status, 56 percent of Golden Gate Bridge jumpers had never married, 19 percent were divorced, 5 percent were widowed or their status was unknown, and 19 percent were married. Nearly three-fourths of Golden Gate Bridge jumps had been witnessed.

One element that Holmes didn't address in his reports was the myth that everyone who jumps does it from the east side, the side facing San Francisco. This was because in 2005 the *San Francisco Chronicle* published a map showing the locations of 833 jumpers whose leaps were witnessed. The locations corresponded to the bridge's 128 light poles, which were added in 1972 and have numbers painted on them. The poles are spaced evenly from the parking lot at Vista Point in Marin County to just before the toll plaza leading into San Francisco. The even-numbered poles are on the west side, illuminating the bike lane, while the odd-numbered poles are on the east side, lighting the pedestrian walkway. The reason why the poles are numbered is because it helps the district track maintenance projects on the bridge. A side benefit is that it assists police officers who respond to the scene of potential jumps. According to the map, the most popular jumping spot by far is light pole number sixty-nine, in the center of the bridge, midway between the two towers, on the east side facing San Francisco. A total of fifty-six people jumped from there. Second most is the light pole next to it, number seventy-one. Thirty-six people chose that point to jump. In total, 713 people whose jumps were witnessed did so from the east side, the San Francisco side. Still, 120 people (14.4 percent) chose the west side, the side facing the Pacific Ocean. The most popular spot on the west side was light pole number sixty-eight, in the center.

Another myth is that everyone jumps from the center of the span, yet a number of individuals hardly ventured out onto the bridge to jump. After they parked their cars at either end, or took a bus or taxi to the bridge, three people jumped from the first light pole on either side, eight more from the second. Based on the map, eighty people jumped close enough to shore that they landed on rocks rather than water. This may have been their intention, or maybe it was a surprise. Intended or not, it was probably a sight that any tourists and other passersby who came along at just that moment have had trouble erasing from their memory. It's not just memories of the jump and of the landing that are hard to forget, but memories of the aftermath, of a body lying broken below. Observing a bridge jump is traumatic enough, but at least within seconds the person disappears from view, swallowed up by the waters of San Francisco Bay, leaving no visible evidence. It's harder, though, to deny the reality of a jump when the person takes off close to shore, strikes solid ground, and lies there for minutes, until a Coast Guard crew arrives and removes the body. The lingering image—and what it means—are difficult to dismiss.

Several years ago a Girl Scout troop from southern California was on the Golden Gate Bridge for a "bridging" ceremony. This is a common event where girls celebrate their transition from Brownies to Junior Girl Scouts. It's almost always held on a bridge, frequently the Golden Gate. During this particular ceremony, a man jumped over the railing right in front of the girls. The ceremony promptly ended, and troop leaders scurried to find counseling services for the witnesses, many of whom were still shaking hours later.

When Holmes's reports were picked up by local media, he was criticized by Bridge District board members and staff. They said that by publicizing Golden Gate Bridge suicides, Holmes was making the problem worse. It was the same thing that Bridge District officials said whenever a story—or when the movie *The Bridge*—came out about the bridge's dark secret.

"The bridge folks don't like it," Holmes said at the time. "They say I'm ruining the reputation of their bridge. But it's not me. It's the high number of suicides."

That number is conveyed effectively in Holmes's second report. Instead of names, he listed the dead based on their last-known occupation. The list is mesmerizing in its simplicity. Virtually every profession is represented: accountant, administrator, architect, art director, artist, attorney, auto painter, bank teller, bartender, bell man, bus driver, business owner, card dealer, caregiver, carpenter, cartographer, cashier, chef, child psychologist, chiropractor, clerk, computer engineer, computer programmer, construction worker, cook, counselor, custodian, dentist, driver, editor, educator, electrical engineer, electrician, engineer, factory worker, fashion designer, film animator, financial analyst, firefighter, florist, forklift operator, frame maker, funeral director, gardener, general contractor, glazier, grant administrator, handyman, homemaker, hotel valet, housekeeper, investor, journalist, laborer, landscaper, librarian, loan officer, machinist, maintenance worker, mechanic, metal worker, military personnel, molecular biologist, mortgage broker, musician, nurse, optometrist, painter, paralegal, park supervisor, photographer, physical therapist, physician, plumber, political consultant, postal clerk, printer, probation officer, proofreader, psychiatrist, psychologist, radio talk show host, real estate agent, receptionist, restaurant manager, sales representative, security guard, singer, social worker, software engineer, student, taxi driver, teacher, telemarketer, translator, tree trimmer, tutor, waiter, web designer, welder, and writer. Tellingly, since Golden Gate Bridge jumpers are younger, on average, than people who kill themselves other ways, the most common occupation was student. There were twenty-seven. The second-most common occupation was teacher, at nine.

Looking at the list, one senses that a person could choose any period in the Golden Gate Bridge's history and the result would be the same—a broad cross-section of society. One also senses the impact of each death. In addition to the personal tragedy felt by loved ones, there is the loss that all of us experience when someone dies who had professional skills or the promise of developing them, who was an artist or entertainer and graced us with exhibitions of talent, or who was a service worker, caregiver, or homemaker that others depended on.

The same year that Holmes's second report was released, the Psychiatric Foundation of Northern California began listing on its Web site similar details about some Golden Gate Bridge jumpers, gleaned from media sources:

"...president of the Oakland Real Estate board."

"...was known not only for his professionalism...but also...for incisive comments laced with laconic British wit."

"...pastor of Ebenezer Lutheran Church."

"...prominent attorney from Richmond."

"...former Deb."

"...a senior member of the American Federation for Clinical Research...served as president of the San Mateo Medical Society."

"...the eldest son of former White House press secretary Pierre Salinger."

"...in his pockets were two dollars, a San Francisco Public Library card, two keys, and a bank savings account book with almost no balance."

Obviously, it is impossible to summarize a human life in just a sentence or two. In obituaries and on tombstones we record the date someone was born and the date that he or she died. What really matters, though, as the poem titled "The Dash" by Linda Ellis notes, is the short line between the two. It is the dash that represents everything the person did, thought, believed in, and stood for during his or her lifetime.

The dash is measured in years. In reading or hearing about someone's death, one's first inclination is to determine the person's age by subtracting the year of birth from the year of death. If the person was substantially older than us, death doesn't seem so bad. His or her time had come, we think. If the person was roughly the same age, we feel a little nervous. We're aware of our own mortality. If the person was substantially younger, it is upsetting even if he or she was a stranger. The natural order of the universe is altered in ways that don't seem right.

Only family members and close friends know fully what a person's dash represents. For the rest of us, it is just a number.

When individuals die prematurely, especially by their own hand, the hardest part for loved ones is knowing that the number could have been higher. There could have been—should have been much more to the dash. That's the case with people who jump off the Golden Gate Bridge. Their lives are cut short by the bridge's magnetic pull, short railing, pedestrian access, and lack of a suicide deterrent.

A few individuals have been lucky—incredibly lucky—to survive a jump from the bridge. Their insights and experiences inform the rest of us about what it's like to be so desperate, and how it feels to be given a second chance at life. You'll meet several of them in the next chapter.

FIVE

Surviving the Fall

As soon as I jumped, I wanted to live.
—Kevin Hines, survivor of a
Golden Gate Bridge jump

If you jump from the Golden Gate Bridge, there's little chance that you'll survive. Statistically, the odds are one in fifty that you'll hit the water at exactly the right angle to live and tell about it. In the stories of the few survivors, one gleans two main themes: first, that suicide is often preventable; second, that a suicide attempt doesn't foretell a future filled with misery and despair. In fact, survivors seem to live fully and sometimes make it their life's work to keep others from making the same mistake. In their minds, and in those of the experts who treat them, suicides can be prevented if doing so becomes a public health priority.

As of 2011, thirty-two people are known to have survived a jump from the Golden Gate Bridge. That's a small number considering the much larger number of people who have died. Most members of this ultra-select group suffered serious injuries that required emergency room treatment and resulted in permanent disabilities. What's telling is that only three survivors have subsequently died by suicide (this includes Sarah Birnbaum, an eighteen-year-old who is the only person known to have jumped from the bridge a second time). The rest have chosen to live. In a number of cases, the survivors say that this decision was made the instant they let go of the railing.

The first known survivor, Cornelia Van Ireland, jumped in 1941, four years after the bridge opened. She was twenty-two, a clerk in the state Department of Employment. She also was engaged to be married. As reported by Allen Brown in *Golden Gate*, painters heard her scream and notified the police, who in turn contacted the Coast Guard. As they approached her, hooks ready to snag the body of another bridge jumper, officers on board were astonished to hear her crying faintly for help. While her clothes were shredded by the force of the impact and she had suffered major injuries, including two broken arms, broken vertebrae, and a broken neck, she was still alive.

Afterward she said, "I don't know what happened. I had an irresistible impulse to jump, and suddenly I clambered over the railing and fell into space. I had no particular sensation going down. I know I prayed, but I had no feeling of pressure against me, no sensation of falling. I don't remember when I hit the water, but I know I was conscious. I was conscious every moment." Doctors thought the big coat she was wearing aided her survival. It ballooned out like a parachute, slowing her descent. Weeks later she was released from the hospital, wearing heavy braces on both arms and a rigid cast on her back. Shortly thereafter she married her fiancée as planned.

Tom Tawzer, age sixteen, is the second known person to survive a jump from the Golden Gate Bridge. A runaway from Livermore High School (California), Tawzer was living with a friend in Oakland until the friend decided to leave town—alone. In a coffee shop Tawzer wrote a letter to his mother saying that he knew his parents were looking for him, but he couldn't return home and hoped they would understand. Then he asked an elderly woman which bus he should take to the Golden Gate Bridge. He had never been to the bridge before and didn't know what bridge security was like. He walked toward the center of the span, ever alert to the possibility of being caught. After saying a short prayer, he stepped over the rail and felt briefly like he was flying, wind lifting his arms over his head. He doesn't remember hitting the water, and almost was run over by a massive cargo ship before a Coast Guard crew rescued him. Outside his room at Letterman Hospital, the hallway was filled with reporters who were eager for an interview. Tawzer told Nora Gallagher, a freelance writer, that when he saw them the realization suddenly hit him: "I thought, oh my God, I'm going to live. Now what?"

Gene Robens, James Layton, and Thomas C. Baker III survived attempts in the 1960s, and there were ten more bridge jump survivors in the 1970s (five males and five females), seven in the 1980s (four males and three females), and ten in the past 20 years (seven males, one female, and two unidentified). Nearly all were in their teens or early twenties when they jumped, and their youth probably aided their chances of survival.

"Dying was not the issue," James Layton told Gallagher, who profiled him, Tom Tawzer, and a third, unidentified bridge jump survivor in *San Francisco* magazine. "It was really living." When Layton was twelve, his father jumped out of a five-story building, dying two days later. In high school, Layton realized that he was different from his classmates. For one thing, he was small and frail-looking. For another thing, he was gay. The day before he jumped, in 1969 at age twenty, a medium visited his classroom. Layton wrote on a piece of paper, "Will I make it through the Golden Doors and will I be united with my soul mate?" The medium answered, "Yes." Layton jumped by 1 P.M. the next day.

John Adams, a twenty-one-year-old student at Stanford, jumped in 1976. Of the survivors, he's the only one who fell on land—the area of sand and rocks below the north tower known as Lime Point. When a Bridge Patrol lieutenant arrived at the scene, he was astonished to see that Adams was alive. The fact that Adams was wearing a ski jacket when he jumped may have helped by filling with air and reducing his speed. Also, he had consumed eleven tablets of a depressant and was heavily drugged so his body probably was relaxed. His only injuries were two collarbone separations.

In 1975 David Rosen, a psychiatrist at the University of California San Francisco Medical School, published a study in the *Western Journal of Medicine* based on in-depth interviews with six of the eight people known to have survived a jump from the Golden Gate Bridge, including Van Ireland, Tawzer, Robens, and Layton. He also interviewed one of the two people to have survived a jump from the San Francisco-Oakland Bay Bridge. Rosen hoped to find out why Golden Gate Bridge jumpers chose that location, why they wanted to die, whether their life flashed before their eyes as they fell, whether they lost consciousness, how they handled the experience afterward, and what the long-term effect of the jump was on their life.

Of the eight survivors of Golden Gate Bridge jumps, seven were male and one was female. They ranged in age from sixteen to thirty-six, with an average age of twenty-four. Six were single, one was married, and one was divorced. Three were receiving psychiatric treatment at the time Rosen interviewed them (Rosen sought and received permission from each person's psychiatrist to do the interviews). All six of the Golden Gate Bridge survivors

Rosen talked to said that their suicide plan involved only the Golden Gate Bridge. They didn't have an alternate plan such as jumping from another location, shooting themselves, ingesting poison, or hanging. As one survivor put it, "It was the Golden Gate Bridge or nothing."

Another survivor said that he chose the bridge because of "an affinity between me, the Golden Gate Bridge, and death. There is a kind of form to it, a certain grace and beauty." A third survivor said that jumping from the bridge was "a romantic thing to do." In addition, it promised "certain death in a painless way." The symbolic association of the bridge with beauty and death was cited by every survivor. So was the bridge's easy access.

As for why they jumped, survivors expressed feelings of loneliness, worthlessness, and depression. Two said that they heard voices in their heads telling them to jump. Another two said that they were still debating about whether to jump when bridge employees yelled and rushed toward them. If these men had approached them more calmly and spoken in a gentle manner, the survivors said, they might not have jumped.

Although jumpers fall 220 feet in four seconds, only one of the survivors Rosen talked to described this descent as rapid. The other five said that it seemed to take "hours" or "an eternity." This is consistent with the frequently reported phenomenon of people facing death for whom time seems to stand still—or to at least slow down a lot.

None of the survivors remembered life events or memories passing before their eyes during their jump. "One survivor," Rosen noted, "did experience the phenomenon of seeing the image of his father in an approaching bridge employee. It was his [the survivor's] opinion that what he experienced was the feeling that his deceased father was coming for him and trying to communicate with him."

Four of the six Golden Gate Bridge jump survivors blacked out before hitting the water or didn't remember hitting the water. All jumped feet first. One realized midway in his fall that he was heading toward a concrete piling. He was able to maneuver his body so that he narrowly missed it, and instead plunged into the water. Although he survived the fall, he almost drowned. The other survivor who was conscious throughout his jump said, "When I hit the water, I felt a vacuum feeling and a compression like my energy displaced the surface energy of the water. At first everything was black, then gray-brown, then light. It opened my mind—like waking up." When he surfaced, he was ecstatic. "I felt reborn. I was treading water and singing.... In that moment, I was refilled with a new hope and purpose in being alive. It's almost beyond most people's comprehension.... Everything is more meaningful when you come close to losing it. I experienced a feeling of unity with all things and a oneness with all people.... Surviving reconfirmed my belief and purpose in my life."

At the time that Rosen interviewed them, two of the six Golden Gate Bridge survivors were employed, two were planning to work, and two were receiving disability payments. All professed feelings of rebirth and spiritual transcendence immediately following their jumps, including one survivor who was a self-described agnostic before jumping and became a born-again Christian afterward. All six said that a barrier was needed to prevent others from jumping.

"It would discourage suicidal persons and it would enable people to think about it and possibly change their minds," one survivor said. Another stated, "It would make it [the bridge] less accessible. Even if it saved one person's life, it would be worth it."

The lone survivor of a San Francisco-Oakland Bay Bridge jump whom Rosen interviewed expressed many of the same sentiments. The thirty-year-old woman was upset because her children had been taken away from her recently. Feeling useless and depressed, the woman said that she drove to the Bay Bridge because it was the nearest bridge to her house. If the Golden Gate Bridge had been closer, she said, she would have gone there. She stopped her car mid-span, got out, and leaped with little or no hesitation. When she surfaced, she was angry and disappointed that she hadn't died. Her pelvis was fractured in the jump and she sent spent several months in bed. Six months after her attempt, she was treated for depression in a state hospital and released. Since then, Rosen said, she had not had a relapse and eventually she was reunited with her children. "I felt chosen because I didn't die," she told Rosen. "I was thankful." She recommended strongly that suicide barriers be erected on the Golden Gate Bridge and Bay Bridge to prevent future suicides.

Rosen concluded his study with the following:

> The fact that the Golden Gate Bridge leads the world as a location for suicides should be knowledge enough for us to begin to *deromanticize* suicide [his emphasis], specifically as it relates to the Golden Gate Bridge. In addition to *deromanticizing* suicide and death, especially as they relate to the Golden Gate Bridge, these findings point to a need to do something practical in order to prevent further suicides from that structure. I underscore and concur wholeheartedly with the survivors' unanimous recommendation that a suicide barrier should be constructed on the Golden Gate Bridge.

In the thirty-five years since Rosen's study, twenty-four people have survived suicide attempts from the Golden Gate Bridge. Paul Hudner, the son of wealthy parents in Marin County, jumped in 1986 at age nineteen, thirty-three years after his grandfather, a forty-one-year-old San Francisco socialite and auto dealer, jumped from the bridge. Hudner hurtled the rail at virtually the identical spot as his grandfather, landing near a fishing boat whose crew rescued him.

Michael Guss jumped in 1990 when he was twenty-six. He had been taking lithium and other drugs to combat manic-depression, but when his mood swings became unbearable, the Golden Gate Bridge beckoned. Five years after his jump, the former Wall Street options trader told his story to the media. From his apartment in San Francisco's Marina District, it was a short walk to the bridge. That was part of the bridge's attraction. The other part was what it represented. "The Bay Bridge wouldn't have interested me," he told a reporter. "It was more than just jumping off a bridge. It was jumping off the Golden Gate Bridge."

On the span, near the south tower, he paced anxiously for a few minutes. Then he put down his bottle of lithium, climbed over the railing, and with his back to the scenic wonders of San Francisco Bay all around him, he let go. Most people face out, toward the view, but Guss faced toward the bridge instead. He said later it was because he didn't want to watch.

Hurtling toward the moat surrounding the tower, he aimed for the water in the moat so that he wouldn't hit concrete. Still, when he landed in the water, it felt like concrete, he said. Despite multiple injuries, including a broken neck and collapsed lung, and despite not having his glasses on so that his vision was blurred, he was able to swim to the moat wall, pull himself up, and sit there until the Coast Guard arrived and rushed him to the hospital.

Following his jump, Guss moved to New Mexico. Still taking lithium, he told a reporter that anyone contemplating suicide should know that "there are people out there who want to help you. Once you have the bigger picture, it helps deal with the day-to-day pain you're going through."

Ken Baldwin knew what day-to-day pain was like; he had battled depression since adolescence. In 1985 he was twenty-eight years old, married, with a three-year-old daughter. He felt overwhelmed by the responsibilities of fatherhood; moreover, he was stuck in what he perceived to be a dead-end job as an office clerk. Two years earlier he had tried to kill himself by driving to a remote spot, sitting under a tree next to a stream, and ingesting a bottle of painkillers with a six-pack of beer. To his dismay, he woke up several hours later, groggy but still very much alive. He ended up driving home.

This time, he thought, "I needed to do something definitive. I had to do something that was going to work. I did not want to use a gun or hanging because of the fall out that my survivors would have to deal with. That's why I decided on the bridge. The statistics were pretty good that I would die and never be found." Another factor was that jumping from the bridge was something of a public statement. All his life Baldwin had gone unnoticed. He decided that he didn't want to be quiet about his death.

"Jumping from the bridge was going to force people to see me," he told a reporter later, "to see me hurting, to see that I was a person, too."

For days he agonized over when to do it. There was no question in his mind that killing himself was the best thing for everyone—that his family would be better off without him. When all you hear is an interior monologue about what a loser you are, he says, and it only gets worse because there's nothing to stop it, because it's a mental illness and you can't see it yet you're in the midst of it, you're not thinking straight. In your mind, you convince yourself that the people you love really will be better off if you're dead. They may be sad, but they'll get over it and ultimately their lives will be improved. Far from being selfish or self-centered, killing yourself is an act of supreme sacrifice. It releases those who love you from the burden of caring about you. This attitude doesn't make sense to individuals who think logically and rationally, but then the judgment of people who are suicidal is impaired.

Baldwin already had developed the capacity to make an attempt, as was demonstrated by his previous attempt. Now he just needed to choose a date. It turned out to be a morning in August. He woke up at 7 A.M. and told himself, "This is the day." He was relieved, almost euphoric. Many people don't understand that after a prolonged period of depression, suicidal individuals sometimes exhibit elevated mood swings shortly before killing themselves. The upbeat attitude is misinterpreted as a sign that the person is getting better, or that he or she is feeling more optimistic about life. In fact, suicidal people like Baldwin are upbeat because they've made a decision, they've taken control, and they believe that the end to their pain and suffering is near.

Baldwin told his wife, Ellen, that he was going to stay late at work to earn a little overtime pay. He hurried out of the house before she could ask any questions, got to work, sat fifteen minutes at his desk, then told his supervisor, "You'll never see me again," and left. In a little more than an hour, he drove from his home in Tracy to the Golden Gate Bridge. It was a beautiful day, not a cloud in the sky. After parking in a lot near the bridge, Baldwin started walking out on the span. Midway he stopped, looked over the railing, and counted to ten. He couldn't bring himself to jump, so he counted to ten again. This time he vaulted over the railing, afraid that his commitment might falter if he perched himself on the steel beam outside the railing.

As soon as he was airborne, he knew he had made a terrible mistake.

"Everything in my life that I thought was unfixable was totally fixable," he told *New Yorker* writer Tad Friend later, "except for having just jumped."

The last thing he saw leave the bridge was his hands. "It was at that time that I realized what a stupid thing I was doing," Baldwin says. "And there was nothing I could do but fall." The memory of his hands leaving the railing is still vivid in his mind twenty-five years later. He thought of his young family, and suddenly wanted to live.

Baldwin doesn't know if he blacked out when he hit the water or before. He remembers tucking his body into a cannonball position, then the water rushing toward him. The impact tore the back pockets off the blue jeans he was wearing and ripped off his wedding ring. When he came to, he was in the water hoping someone would save him.

He told Dr. Mel Blaustein later, "It was incredible how quickly I had decided that I wanted to live once I realized everything that I was going to lose, my wife, my daughter, the rest of my family."

He was plucked out of the water by the Coast Guard. On deck, a crewman leaned over him. "Do you know what you did?" the crewman asked. "Do you want to do it again?" Baldwin shook his head, amazed to still be alive. "No," he said. "No, once is enough."

He was taken to Letterman Hospital where doctors estimated that he had a fifty-fifty chance of surviving his injuries. Although his backside and feet took the brunt of the impact, causing major bruising, he didn't suffer any internal hemorrhaging or broken bones. He also didn't have any permanent injuries. When I asked him why he thinks he survived when so many others haven't, even though they, like him, probably regretted it the minute they went over the side, he says he has no clue. "I can never answer that question," he says. "Dumb luck." The fact that he had been a water polo player and diver in high school probably helped. Ironically, he had quit the school diving team because he was afraid of jumping off the highest platform.

In the hospital he learned that his jump had been witnessed, and that the Coast Guard had gotten to him in seven minutes. The quick response prevented both drowning and hypothermia since the northern waters of the Pacific Ocean are cold, about fifty degrees. He stayed in the hospital five days, then was released after promising to seek professional help. His wife, "who is a hero in my eyes," he says, went to therapy with him for five months, after which he was cleared, his depression gone. He was able to live a normal life for the first time in many years.

Nineteen-year-old Kevin Hines is another survivor. He jumped in September 2000. Hines started taking a medication called Tegretol at age ten after he had had an epileptic attack. It seemed to work, enabling him to participate on the Riordan High School (San Francisco) football and wrestling teams. When he was sixteen, he was taken off the medication because he hadn't had any further episodes. That same year, his mother and father, who had adopted him when he was nine months old, separated. The separation was traumatic for Hines, who was close to both parents. What no one knew at the time was that Hines was bipolar. In addition to treating epilepsy, Tegretol acts as a mood stabilizer. Without the medication, Hines experienced extreme manic-depressive swings. Overnight he changed from a sensitive youth who loved acting in school plays and was a tough athlete to being irritable and hard to control.

In January 2000 he had a big fight with his mother and moved in with his father, with whom he constantly butted heads. Then his drama teacher died by suicide and Hines's world was turned topsy-turvy. He was prescribed new medication and ended up, by his count, taking fourteen pills per day. He also had weekly therapy. Even so, his mood swings got worse.

He bought a knife and began cutting his wrist, intending to bleed to death. A last-minute change of heart led him to drop the knife, cover the wounds, and not tell anyone. Yet he continued to visit his dark place. On Friday, September 22, two days before he jumped, his girlfriend broke up with him. Over the weekend, he had hallucinations and heard voices. Sunday night, he wrote seven versions of a suicide note, trying to achieve a tone that didn't sound so angry—angry with himself, with his parents, with the world. The final version ended simply, "All. Please forgive me."

His father, Patrick Hines, a banker, sensed Kevin's torment. The night before he jumped, Pat was worried about Kevin and wanted to take him to the hospital. Kevin said no, he was okay— fully aware that he had just written a suicide note and was planning to kill himself the next day. The following morning Pat Hines told Kevin that he wanted to take him to work, that he was worried about him. Kevin said he had gotten a good night's sleep and was feeling better, and needed to go to school.

His father dropped him off at San Francisco City College, where Kevin was a freshman. Kevin kissed his father on the check, certain it'd be the last time he'd see him. He also gave his father a rare hug.

Kevin went to his first-period class, but left before the end. He took a bus to a Walgreens pharmacy to buy his last meal— Skittles and Starbursts candy. Then he caught another bus to the Golden Gate Bridge. Sitting in the rear, it dawned on him that he really was going to do it, he really was going to die. What happened next Hines has told hundreds of times, to reporters and audiences. It was 10 A.M. and the bridge was full of activity. There were walkers, joggers, bikers, and tourists. Red-eyed and distraught, Hines decided that if even one person asked him what was wrong, he wouldn't jump; he'd tell the person every-thing. Midway across the span he stopped and looked down more than two hundred feet to the water. His face was streaked with tears.

For thirty-five or forty minutes, he stood at the railing, sizing up the spot. It wasn't too close to a pillar. He'd hit the water and die. People passed by without saying a word, then a woman with a German accent approached. She asked Hines if he'd take her picture.

"I thought, 'What? Lady, I'm going to kill myself, are you crazy?'"

She was wearing sunglasses, he recalls, her hair was blowing in the wind, and she was probably a tourist. "All she could see," he says, "was this guy standing right where she wanted her pic-ture taken." He took several pictures of her, then gave her back her camera. As she walked away, Hines decided, "That's it. I'm going. Nobody cares." His backpack was on the bridge. He left a sign next to it that read, "The note is in here."

Like Baldwin, Hines didn't climb over the railing and pause on the chord. Instead, he took a few steps back, ran, and cata-pulted over the side. Instantly, he regretted it. As importantly, he knew that he had mere seconds to save himself. He threw his head back to hit the water feet first, at a slight angle. If he had hit even a fraction of an inch differently, doctors told him afterward, he would have severed his spinal cord and drowned. As it was, he shattered two vertebrae in his back and the pieces shot through some of his organs.

After falling the equivalent of twenty-five stories, he plunged deep underwater. It was dark and scary. At the same time, he marveled that he was still alive. He didn't know that that was possible. He couldn't move his legs so he used his arms to swim to the surface, toward the light. When his head broke through, he took a big gulp of air. He tried to call for help, but his words were lost in the current, which was sweeping him out to sea. The pain was overwhelming, and he felt himself sinking below the water. A large animal brushed against his legs, and Hines felt a new fear. Great white sharks have attacked people in San Francisco Bay. Even worse than drowning was the thought of being eaten alive. The animal kept circling around him, keeping him afloat. Hines believes now that it was a seal who was acting as a guardian angel.

Hines's jump was witnessed and the Coast Guard was able to get to him within minutes. He was taken to Marin General Hospital. His mother, Debbie, arrived first. Although Kevin was battered and highly sedated, he managed to mumble, "Hey, Ma. Hi." Pat Hines arrived a few minutes later. Kevin's first words upon seeing his father were to say that he was sorry. Pat, whom his son says isn't given to showing his emotions, broke down in tears. The moment served as an epiphany, causing Kevin to think that he had to fight his mental illness every day for the sake of his family, until he got better.

Kevin Hines was in Marin General for three weeks, during which time doctors inserted a metal plate in his back to replace the vertebrae he shattered. Pat Hines slept next to him, on a cot. After that, Kevin was transferred to a psychiatric unit at St. Francis Memorial Hospital, where he spent several months.

Since his jump, Kevin is most astounded when people ask him why he didn't shoot himself instead of leaping from the bridge. His response reinforces the fact that suicidal people often fixate on one means of death. "I'm like, 'What are you—nuts?'" he told a *Time* reporter in describing his reaction. "That scares the crap out of me. Pills were gross. I had already cut myself, it hurt like hell, and I hated seeing blood."

He had no money to get back on the bus that day and no bus pass. If he had had to pay even one dollar to walk on the bridge, he wouldn't have been able to jump. He also wouldn't have been able to get home after a thwarted attempt, a fact that he thinks about now.

"If there was a barrier," he said, "I would have had to go tell someone, or I would have been caught by the California Highway Patrol trying to climb over the thing. I would have been saved and put in a mental hospital, and then I'd be at home, dealing with my bipolar, hopefully doing it the right way."

Since their jumps, the lives of Ken Baldwin and Kevin Hines have changed dramatically. The first thing that changed was their attitude.

"Before, I didn't want to get better," Baldwin said. "I had become consumed by my depression." Afterward, he wanted to live. Despite feeling himself falling every time he closed his eyes, he never suffered flashbacks or nightmares. He was now willing to let others help him. Most importantly, his wife stood by him, determined to save his life. He shared his pain with her and she provided support. He also had therapy—only five sessions, but that seemed to be enough. His depression lifted and hasn't returned. There have been episodes of anxiety since, but nothing permanent.

Another change was that unlike his first suicide attempt, when he swallowed painkillers and beer next to a stream, his bridge jump was public. Everyone knew about it. The story had been reported by the press, and the circumstances leading to his attempt—the depression he lived with—no longer was hidden.

Five months after the jump, an architect who was sympathetic hired Baldwin as a draftsman. Seven years later, Baldwin was offered a position teaching drafting classes at Bret Harte Union High School in Angels Camp, California. Angels Camp is a small, one-time Gold Rush town in the foothills of the Sierra Nevada mountains. The miners left after the lode was exhausted, and today the biggest attractions are a handful of wineries and several caverns offering guided spelunking tours.

Baldwin has been at the high school for twenty years. Several weeks into each new school year, after his freshman students get to know him, he tells them about his suicide attempt. It's not something he's proud of, but it's also not something he tries to hide. Kids are smart and likely would find out anyway. The best thing, he believes, is to be up-front about it so that he can move on to other subjects. It happened before he started teaching, when he was severely depressed. He made a foolish mistake, and is fortunate to be alive.

I asked him whether incoming students expect to hear the story now, and how they react to it.

"The older kids are always asking, 'When are you telling the story?'" he said, "so most of my students do expect it, but some are surprised. The kids are awesome about the story. I have them listen to me tell the story of the day I jumped and then they can ask any question they want and I answer it truthfully. They are always very respectful when I tell it."

When I asked him whether he had any negative reactions from parents, he responded, "I have never had a discussion with a parent—ever. It could be they never hear about it [but] I doubt that.... Some parents may not know how to bring it up."

When he first arrived at the school, Baldwin was shown the classroom where he would be teaching. When he opened the drawer of his new desk, he found an old engineer's drawing. It was of the Golden Gate Bridge. The drawing had all of the measurements, like a blueprint. Baldwin decided that it must be a sign, and decided to display it. He still does, but says, "It's getting pretty ratty over the years."

I had read in one of his interviews that he divided his life in halves, the half before the jump and afterward, and asked him if it was still true. He said it is. Sometimes he and his wife will be talking and one of them will ask, "When was that?" Then they'll remember that it was before the jump or after the jump.

A high point of his life was being able to give his daughter her high school diploma. She graduated from the same high school where Baldwin teaches. She was too young—only three—to remember Baldwin's jump, but he has always talked openly about it with her. It helps that the outcome was positive and that she never saw him when he was depressed and wanting to disappear. Today she's in her fourth year of teaching primary school, and in 2010 she got married "to a wonderful young man," Baldwin says. He considers himself the luckiest guy in the world.

Kevin Hines's life is similarly divided, although he doesn't think of it that way. Before his jump he was despondent, convinced that he was worthless. After his jump he found a purpose—advocating for a barrier on the bridge and educating people about mental illness.

I was curious whether opposition to the barrier has surprised him. "Never once," he says. "We live in a culture that dubs certain public health issues, certainly mental health issues, and especially suicide attempts in general, as 'somebody else's problem.'"

Hines has become something of a celebrity, regularly interviewed by national publications and network television whenever there's a story on Golden Gate Bridge suicides. He's in demand as a public speaker, too, and he has an agent, although he'll appear for free if it's an audience—such as young people—that he wants to reach.

Unfortunately, from his point of view, reporters keep asking him to relive the moment when he hurtled over the railing. What went through his mind as he was falling? Did he black out before impact or was he conscious when his body slammed into the water? How did he feel when he plunged below the surface and realized he was still alive? What did he say to the people who rescued him? It's an experience that's hard to imagine, and the fact that he survived it when the vast majority of people don't gives him a unique perspective. At the same time, his life wasn't spared, he feels, just so he can tell people what it's like to jump from the Golden Gate Bridge. What's important to him is to stop others from jumping.

Several years ago, at a suicide prevention fundraising event, Hines was approached by a sixteen-year-old boy. The boy had just spent $300 of his own money to buy a large, color photograph of the Golden Gate Bridge in a silent auction. He told Hines that at one time he had considered jumping from the bridge, too, and asked Hines to sign his picture. These are the moments that

Hines lives for now. He wrote on the back, "Stay up. And never look down." Then he added his signature.

His parents have different opinions about his advocacy. His father believes it has been therapeutic. "Surviving, and having the ability to talk about it, gave Kevin a reason for life," Pat Hines told a *San Francisco Chronicle* reporter in 2005. "In many ways, this issue validates his existence."

His mother, a nurse, worries that Kevin is going to make a career out of it, that when he's fifty years old he's still going to be talking about a single, stupid moment in his life that happened thirty years earlier. She has been quoted as saying that it's time for him to move on. Moreover, she's not convinced that a suicide barrier is the best investment. Rather, Debbie Hines thinks that the money would be better spent treating mental illness, attacking the problem at its root.

On this issue, Kevin Hines prefers his father's voice. He has found his calling. It's to make the Golden Gate Bridge safe for others.

"If I could take it all back, I wouldn't," he told the *Chronicle*. "The places I've gone, the people I've helped, I'd have never met. I had heard that this was the easiest way to die, almost serene. It's not like that—you have a heart attack on the way down, or your limbs fall off and you drown."

Kevin is married now, and follows a strict schedule today in order to regulate his bipolar disorder. A combination of drugs and therapy enables him to control the manic highs and crushing lows of his illness. He also endures the physical consequences of his jump, the back pain that affects his everyday life and makes taking long car trips or riding in airplanes difficult.

For the first five years, on the anniversary of his leap, Kevin made a point of going to the bridge, walking to the same spot where he vaulted the railing, and dropping a flower into the water. "The first time," he says, "a sea lion popped up two feet next to the flower. I saw that as a sign—closure."

His sister carried on the tradition for a few years after that because Kevin was on the road a lot, then he told her to let it go. Today, he's in a far different place than he was when he jumped. His mental illness was diagnosed and is being treated, and he has the maturity of a thirty-year-old man rather than a twenty-year-old youth. The main thing that's changed, though, is his outlook.

"Life is beautiful," he says, "pain filled, but beautiful. Every day I awaken is a good day." It's a reminder both of how far he's come and how much is possible if given another chance.

To meet Janet Wilson, one wouldn't guess that many years ago she was poised to jump from the Golden Gate Bridge. Or that she suffers from a mental illness.[1] Wilson is a patients'

---

1. Nationally, more than ten million people have been diagnosed with a severe and persistent mental illness. This includes schizophrenia, bipolar disorder, and major depression. Schizophrenia is characterized by bizarre, grandiose, persecutory, or jealous delusions, auditory hallucinations (hearing voices), illogical thinking, blunted or inappropriate moods, and catatonia. Bipolar disorder is a mood disorder; a person experiences mood swings that are elevated, expansive, or irritable. Depression is a common emotional problem and a natural reaction to stress. Depression becomes more serious, however, when a person becomes immobilized and unable to function. It can be caused by chemical changes in the body, a situational life crisis and the way a person responds to it, or past events thought forgotten. If you're severely depressed, you don't feel like your usual self. You may assume that friends and family no longer "know" you and make it difficult for people to communicate with you.

There are dozens of additional mental illnesses. Among the more common are attention deficit disorder, conduct and anxiety disorders, attachment disorders, oppositional disorders, and eating disorders. Successful treatment usually requires medication and/or psychotherapy. Even many types of psychosis, where a person's distorted thinking and perceptions lead to a mistaken belief about what's real, respond rapidly to proper medication and professional counseling.

rights advocate with Mental Health Consumer Concerns, a nonprofit organization that represents mental health patients in administrative hearings in three northern California counties (Contra Costa, Napa, and Solano). She has been with the agency more than twenty-five years, since graduating from law school, and has held a number of positions, including executive director, a position she accepted only on an interim basis. Running an agency isn't nearly as fulfilling, she finds, as being in the trenches, working with and advocating for the rights of the mentally ill. This is because she knows how hard it is for people with a mental illness to ask for, much less receive, proper treatment. Wilson has suffered from bipolar disorder for years.

At age thirteen, she learned the truth about her father's death. Instead of being killed in a car accident when Janet was two years old, as her mother had told her, he shot himself in a car. "It was a defining moment in my life," Janet says, "and created a template for suicide."

Both of her siblings subsequently attempted suicide. At sixteen, Janet made the first of "eight or nine serious attempts," overdosing on pills that caused her to vomit.

In 1975, her sister jumped off an overpass in San Jose. She survived the fall, but ended up severely injured. Janet quit her job at Western Electric, changed her name, and knew—"sibling rivalry"—she says, "That I was going to try and do my sister one better," i.e. she was going to take her life by jumping from a taller, more dramatic structure.

The Golden Gate Bridge was the obvious choice. "There's something about it," she says, referring to its magnetic allure.

It was 1979. From her apartment in Oakland she drove her Ford Pinto across the Bay Bridge to San Francisco. She wasn't sure that she would jump, in part because she hadn't made provisions for her cat. Still, according to an inner voice the time seemed right. She didn't leave a note because she had no desire to write; there wasn't anyone she wanted to say good-bye to.

After parking on the Marin County side, she put her keys and wallet under the seat in her car and deliberately left it unlocked "in case it [jumping] didn't work." Then she walked out on the span. Like many days on the bridge, this one was overcast, windy, and cold. She used a hand-held calculus to determine the midspan so that she was sure to hit water. Like Kevin Hines, she didn't want to jump so close to a pylon that she'd land on concrete or rocks.

Two bridge patrol officers approached her and asked her what she was doing. She replied honestly, saying that she was looking for the best place to jump. She doesn't know why she was so straightforward, only that it didn't occur to her to lie. They drove her to a hospital in San Francisco, then she was transferred to Highland Hospital in Oakland. There she was placed in an unlocked ward, which stunned her. Although she considered herself a high suicide risk, she could have walked out if she wanted to; no one would have stopped her. She didn't have her car, house key, or any money, though. She also didn't have her glasses. A nurse took them when Janet was admitted, leaving Janet virtually blind.

Upon discharge, her mother drove an hour from Cupertino to pick her up, then helped her retrieve her car. After that, Janet self-referred herself to a day-treatment program in Oakland where she learned a problem-solving technique that she still uses.

"If I'm really suicidal and I do the problem-solving technique," she says, "everything changes dramatically."

The technique involves taking a sheet of paper and dividing it in half. On one side she lists all of the things she needs to do. On the other side she lists things that she can look forward to. She refers to the latter as STLFTs—Somethings To Look Forward To. The latter need to balance out the former, she says, and can't be as simple as saying on the to-do side that she needs to clean the house and on the other side that she looks forward to having a clean house.

She went to the day-treatment program three times a week for several months, then ended up volunteering there. In 1982, she started an unpaid internship at Mental Health Consumer Concerns, and she has been with the agency ever since.

Going to the bridge was the last time she thought seriously about suicide. At the same time, it's always on her mind. It's always an option even today, more than thirty years later. It's not the first option, however.

In honor of her father, she went to law school because he had been a lawyer. She had no interest in practicing law or even taking the bar, though. She wanted to follow his footsteps as far as law school, but no farther. After she graduated, she put it behind her.

June 12 is the anniversary of her father's death. She usually calls into work sick that day. In 2010, on June 12, she and a friend drove to the Golden Gate Bridge and walked across the span. It was the first time she had walked on it since 1979. The experience brought lots of memories, but that was all. She had no desire to jump, no immediate desire to die.

At the end of our interview, she hands me a ceramic tile, made to be hung, with the Golden Gate Bridge painted on it. "For you," she says. "Good luck with your book. I hope a lot of people read it, and that it helps end suicides from the bridge."

A small number of barrier opponents believe that lives are saved precisely because the bridge doesn't have a barrier. They maintain that when people are stopped from jumping off the bridge, they're directed to others who provide counseling and support. Suicide attempters may have never reached out to anyone before, and after they're stopped they're able to talk with someone about their problems. This enables them to get the help they desperately need. In a few cases, like Wilson's, the argument has validity. More often than not, though, it's specious. Many jumpers have received counseling and been prescribed antidepressants prior to their deaths. Some are so bent on suicide and fixate on the bridge so strongly that once they're stopped, treated, and released, they return and try to jump again. Equally important, while bridge police and California Highway Patrol officers intervene successfully in 65 to 70 percent of attempted suicides, they fail to save everyone else. How is it possible to justify leaving things the way they are when it means that people continue to die every month? Then there are the instances I've mentioned previously where a young child was thrown off the bridge. The correlation between their deaths and the low railing is undeniable. It's worth noting, too, that bridge personnel aren't resource specialists. They are not equipped to assess a person's needs—particularly a person who is mentally ill—and refer them to appropriate services. Their sole goal is to get someone who is suicidal off the bridge safely and as quickly as possible, then see that he or she is transported to a hospital. Lastly, not everyone stopped by bridge police or the California Highway Patrol is hospitalized. Some attempters are released on the spot if police feel that they don't present an immediate risk.

Richard Heckler is a therapist and the author of a book about suicide attempt survivors titled *Waking Up, Alive*. He talked with a reporter about the effect of surviving an attempt. "It is possible not only to recover from being suicidal, but it is possible to lead a rich, fulfilled life afterward," Heckler said. "When people come out of this experience, they don't say, 'I want to bulk up my 401(k)' or 'I want to build a second house in Mexico.' They've been touched very deeply."

That's the case with Janet Wilson, and it's also the case with Kevin Hines and Ken Baldwin. What they experienced changed them. Each chose to give back—Wilson through her patients' rights work, Hines through his advocacy for mental health programs and a bridge barrier, Baldwin through his teaching.

In 2007, the National Suicide Prevention Lifeline convened a group of eight suicide attempt survivors, including Kevin Hines. Participants described their experiences and noted key "turning points" in which their desire to live outweighed their desire to die. Feelings of self-worth and the ability to connect with others were common themes that assisted each person's recovery.

"I recognized my value to other people," one person said.

"I found I could do something for someone else. I could do something useful with my life," said another.

"When you are isolated from others," said a third person, "you can't see support around you. Once I really saw someone, it made a difference."

Surprisingly, perhaps, to people who aren't familiar with mental illness, the group agreed that a person's pain may not go away. Sometimes it does, but other times it returns. Even when it returns, though, it may return less frequently. Antidepressants help. So does talking. "Talking doesn't change the event," one participant said, "but can change how I feel about it and can make me feel less alone."

The Lifeline convened the group in an effort to better understand the thought processes of a suicidal person and to identify effective ways for phone counselors to support them. Even though their thinking was impaired at the time they tried to kill themselves, suicide attempt survivors are the only people who can speak about the subject from first-hand experience.

Similarly, when it comes to suicide on the Golden Gate Bridge, the only group of true experts are the handful of individuals who have jumped from the bridge and lived. They're the only ones who know the real mindset of people who jump, what leads them to the edge, why the bridge was their chosen means, and what would have happened if they were prevented from jumping. All eight survivors whom David Rosen interviewed in 1975 said they were in favor of a barrier. "If there had been a barrier," one said, "I would have gone home and forgotten about it." "The only solution is a barrier," another said. "That's it."

Most recent survivors—especially Kevin Hines—agree. Even Ken Baldwin, the high school teacher in Angel's Camp who told me he was in so much pain that even if the bridge had a barrier he would have found another way to die, acknowledges that a barrier will stop individuals from jumping off. You can't stop people from killing themselves, he believes, but you can stop them from using the Golden Gate Bridge to do it.

That's a good start. No one is naïve enough to think that once the Golden Gate Bridge has a suicide deterrent, the problem of suicide will be solved. Any kind of deterrent will save lives, though—and it doesn't end there. That's because one life represents more than one life. When you save someone, you save everyone who loves him or her from a lifetime of heartache. The pain of a loved one's suicide is deep and felt by all who knew the person. You also save generations of that person's family to follow. Future individuals have the opportunity to be born, grow up, marry, and have children because the lineage is continued. In addition, you save all of the professional skills that these future generations will acquire. As if that wasn't enough, you remove the dark cloud that hangs over one of the most beautiful man-made structures in the world. All this, and the only thing that's needed is a slightly taller railing or a net—something that, once it's up, will be taken for granted.

The few survivors of Golden Gate Bridge jumps know full well the value of making the bridge safe. They're living it. The only reason they're alive today is because of a confluence of factors bordering on the miraculous. First, they hit the water just right, neither too upright nor slightly askew, and were able to get back to the surface despite major injuries. Second, there were witnesses to the jump who reported it immediately. Third, there were either boaters nearby who rescued the person or Coast Guard crews who got there quickly. And finally, the person received prompt medical care for physical injuries and effective psychological treatment to deal with inner demons. Anything less at any point and the outcome would have been different. The person would have died—like so many others.

SIX

In Lieu of a Net

People choose to take their lives and it affects their families, but it also affects people like me who have to pick up what is left.

—Former U.S. Coast Guard crew member

Because the Golden Gate Bridge lacks a suicide barrier, the only safety net for jumpers is the one that's provided by the dogged efforts of mental health workers, the police, and the Coast Guard. These helpers and responders, on the front lines of crisis, often try valiantly to forestall tragedy. Their efforts save lives, but the need for a physical deterrent to make their work more efficacious is vital.

San Francisco has one of the oldest and busiest suicide hotlines in the country. Founded in 1962, the hotline receives 70,000 calls annually. Of these, 7,000 are actual suicide calls and 700 are deemed high risk, meaning that the caller has a plan, access to means, and probably has made a previous attempt. Frequently the plan involves jumping off the Golden Gate Bridge.

Eve Meyer has been executive director of San Francisco Suicide Prevention, which operates the hotline, since 1987. What strikes her isn't so much the nature of the work, it's that there's never any letup. "Count to 35 slowly," she says. "Before you finish, someone somewhere in the United States will attempt suicide. Every 17 minutes, an American dies by suicide. Suicide is the eighth leading cause of death in the U.S., and the second leading cause for college-age students."

She says that the reason why people call her agency is because they are in pain, but the pain comes and goes. Sometimes it seems unbearable, but then it subsides. People don't want to die, but when the pain is at its worst, they don't want to live with it, either. "The question is," Meyer says, "what do we do for people who are in so much pain that they want to kill themselves? Do we say that the problem doesn't exist? Or do we recognize it and say, 'This is bad. It can't continue.'"

Historically, according to Meyer, humans have chosen the former. "From the first to the tenth centuries," she says, "they buried you at the crossroads with a stake through your heart if you killed yourself. Your family lost its possessions. That stigma continues to the present. We are culturally programmed not to hear the word *suicide*."

At the same time, "asking about suicide opens up a door," Meyer says. "It offers a suicidal person an opportunity to think, to feel, to explain, perhaps to cry. It's a chance for someone to consider a dangerous decision one more time. Without asking, without taking that risk, nothing is prevented."

San Francisco's suicide hotline was founded under unusual circumstances. In 1961, an Episcopal priest named Bernard Mayes was working as a news anchor for the British Broadcasting Corporation (BBC). On assignment, he traveled to the United States to cover a story about suicide. America had a much higher suicide rate than England, and San Francisco's suicide rate was nearly three times the national average. In trying to find out why, Mayes learned something that stunned him: suicidal people in the United States had no one to talk to. While a network of community crisis lines manned by a federation of volunteers who called themselves "The Samaritans" crisscrossed Great Britain, providing easy access to people who were feeling hopeless and depressed, no such service existed in America.

Mayes cancelled his return ticket home and began training some of the people he had interviewed for the BBC story. Then he bought a red phone and installed it in a flophouse in San Francisco's low-rent Tenderloin district. Finally, he printed matchbooks with "Call Bruce" on the cover. Inside, the matchbook explained that "Bruce" was there to talk with people who were feeling down. Members of Mayes's group distributed the matchbooks to bars throughout the city. When someone called "Bruce," the red phone rang in the flophouse and one of the volunteers that Mayes trained answered it. That's how San Francisco Suicide Prevention was born.

Today, prospective phone counselors at the agency receive forty to sixty hours of specialized training before they handle their first call. This is the standard for all crisis centers that operate nationally certified suicide hotlines. By comparison, psychiatrists, psychologists, therapists, and other mental health professionals aren't required to take any training in suicide prevention to attain or retain professional licenses. Zero. Training in child abuse and domestic violence is mandatory, but training in suicide is optional despite the fact that most practicing clinicians have at least one suicidal patient in their caseload. For years, the American Psychological Association's massive *Diagnostic and Statistical Manual of Mental Disorders*, the bible of psychiatry in the

United States, has not provided any information to doctors on how to assess patients for suicide risk.[1] This may be one of the least understood facts about suicide prevention in our country. In many instances, volunteer caregivers are better trained and have more experience helping people who are suicidal than licensed professionals. Volunteers are there to listen, their time isn't rushed, and they have learned to suspend judgment. Most importantly, they're willing to ask about suicide because they're not afraid of the answer.

> "I get the feeling that you're thinking of killing yourself. Is that right?"
>
> "Do you have a plan for how you'd do it? Do you have a time frame?"
>
> "Have you put any part of your plan into action?"

Suicide rarely comes up in normal conversation. The stigma is so strong that most people—including physicians—miss vital signs because they haven't been trained to look for them. Studies show that nearly half the time, suicidal people see a physician within one month of killing themselves. Yet the doctor focuses on diagnosing the cause of a patient's physical pain, not mental anguish. Patients who speak of ailments that may seem imaginary from a physical point of view can be facing deeper, less visible hurt that's even harder to bear. If doctors don't do any probing, either because they don't know how or because they're afraid of what they'll find, the health and safety of their patients is jeopardized.

A case in point is Olivia Crowther, a twenty-three-year-old woman who jumped off the Golden Gate Bridge in June 2008.

---

1. The fifth edition, due out in 2013, will include a section on suicide assessment for the first time.

Prior to her jump she told doctors of "low moods" she experienced regularly and requested antidepressants, which were prescribed for her. Two months before she died she told her primary care physician that she wasn't sleeping well and questioned "the point in life." Her doctor didn't consider that she might be contemplating suicide. From outward appearances, she had everything to live for. She was pretty, well educated, and worked in the magazine industry. Only after her body was found in the water under the bridge, still wearing an iPod and shoulder bag, did her parents discover her intentions. While searching her computer they found that she had visited Web sites on ways to die by suicide.

According to *JAMA*, the Journal of the American Medical Association, training physicians to recognize and treat suicidal behavior is one of the two most effective ways to prevent suicide. The other way is to restrict access to lethal means.

Eve Meyer says that one doesn't have to be a mind reader to determine suicidal intent. Suicide is thought about much more often than people know. "Most people who are suicidal," she says, "leave a trail of clues that—tragically—become most obvious after it's too late. The clues are right there all the time, though; they can be read if you know what to look for." She ticks them off. "People who are thinking about suicide often allude to it indirectly. They may make statements that are not taken seriously, but should be, such as 'When I'm not around anymore' or 'I'll be going away for a long while' or 'I wish I could never wake up.'"

Another clue is putting one's affairs in order. "People who are planning suicide often wrap up their personal, business, and financial affairs quite openly," Meyer says. "Actions such as making or changing a will, closing bank and investment accounts, and assembling financial documents are often misinterpreted."

The person isn't showing new or renewed interest in his or her life; rather, loose ends are being tied up so that family members and friends don't have to deal with them.

Then there's the giving away of prized possessions. While people may be delighted with these gifts, says Meyer, "they miss the ominous underlying message: the giver won't be alive to use them anymore."

The clue that is most critical is when people acquire the means to kill themselves. This speaks to the issue of capacity, to the ability to overcome the human instinct for self-preservation. This clue is the easiest to miss, Meyer says, because unconsciously people deny it. Examples are buying a gun, stockpiling medication, or visiting bridges or other jump sites in person or via the Internet.

"Putting these clues together is a horrifying process," Meyer says. "What if you are wrong? What if you are right?" If you're wrong, the person may lose all trust in you. If you're right, you descend a dark hole and need to summon every ounce of training to see that both the caller and you get out.

At least hotline counselors have the advantage of knowing that callers are reaching out. Part of them wants to die, but another part wants to live. If there wasn't a part that wanted to live, they wouldn't have called. Phone counselors acknowledge the two parts, then talk to the part that wants to live.

I asked Meyer about what keeps her going, and how she has been able to stay in this field so long. "If you saw a child or an animal run into the street," she says, "and you got them to safety before a car would have hit them, you would feel wonderful. Saving someone from suicide feels the same way—if not even more so. Who wouldn't do this for as long as possible?"

I then asked her if there was any particular call that stood out in her mind. She thought for a minute.

One thing to know about her is that she has a dry sense of humor. On occasion she does stand-up comedy at San Francisco night clubs. She tells me about a person who came from out of town specifically to jump off the Golden Gate Bridge. The person was staying in an expensive hotel, not a Tenderloin flophouse, and called San Francisco Suicide Prevention's hotline. The crisis counselor contacted the police, then talked on the phone with the caller for two hours, only to learn that when the police arrived at the hotel, they didn't know which room the caller was in and didn't want to knock on every door so they ended up leaving. Meanwhile, the counselor convinced the person to go shopping since San Francisco has many famous stores. The caller verbally contracted with the counselor to do that, to shop rather than jump. That's how the call ended.

"We nearly lost them to the bridge," Meyer says. "Instead, we lost them to Macy's."

Over the years, Meyer has used logic as well as emotional arguments in an attempt to convince people of the need for a suicide barrier on the bridge. Because neither has brought about any kind of change, she now tries a different tact.

"If one or two golden retrievers jumped off the bridge," she says, "people would get serious about a safety railing. The public would demand it. Because it's lonely, troubled, depressed souls who are taking their lives, though, no one seems too concerned."

The reference to golden retrievers might sound whimsical, but among people who work for human service agencies it carries a lot of truth. There's a strong belief that the public, in general, is more sympathetic to the plight of animals than people—especially people who are afflicted by something so misunderstood as mental illness.

Meyer notes that recently there was an international outcry when a woman in Bosnia threw five puppies in a river. The country is war-torn, tens of thousands of people there are hungry and homeless, yet the international community focuses on the deaths of five dogs. That has to change, Meyer and others say. A dog may be loyal and obedient, a comforting companion, while someone who's clinically depressed may seem impossible to know in addition to being difficult to deal with, but behind the illness is a human being with feelings the same as anyone else. People who are mentally ill shouldn't be defined by their illness, just as someone in a wheelchair shouldn't be defined by an inability to walk. The illness or disability is part of who they are, but it's by no means all of who they are.

Another way to look at the issue, Meyer says, is to imagine that the Golden Gate Bridge doesn't exist. A pagan god comes to San Francisco and says, "I'll build you the most beautiful bridge imaginable. People will come from near and far to see it. It'll be one of the wonders of the world. In return, you have to sacrifice 30 people a year. Do you accept it?"

Once, on her way to a Bridge District hearing, Meyer was stopped in the parking lot by a barrier opponent. He said that instead of a suicide barrier, the district ought to put up a diving board on the bridge to make it even easier to jump. "Say that again," Meyer replied. "Say that they ought to put up a diving board on the bridge so that my son can jump."

When nameless, faceless people die, the lives of others continue uninterrupted with little or no thought of the deceased. When someone you know dies, especially when it's someone you love and the death could have been prevented, it's different.

Dr. Mel Blaustein is the medical director in the psychiatry department at St. Francis Memorial Hospital in San Francisco. Typically, he sees twenty-four patients each day, at least fifteen of whom express suicidal thoughts. When someone says that he or she plans to jump off the Golden Gate Bridge, Blaustein asks, "Why the bridge?" After all, there are lots of ways to kill oneself. Some of the responses, he says, include "It's classy," "It's quick," "It's fail-proof," "It's the way," and, "You're with all those people who jumped before."

People who are suicidal tend to be less connected to others. Jumping off the Golden Gate Bridge enables them to join for all eternity a large number of people who may be strangers, but with whom they have a common bond—a shared death. This point was made in a February 2010 editorial cartoon in the *Berkeley Daily Planet*. Viewed from underwater were mounds of human skulls, stretching as far as one could see. Above the water was the outline of the Golden Gate Bridge.

It's no surprise that the Golden Gate Bridge is the most photographed man-made structure in the world. It's one of the seven wonders of the modern world and is considered one of the top ten architectural achievements of the twentieth century. No other city has such a famous gateway. No other gateway has inspired more romance or poetry. It's not a stretch to say that life in the Golden State starts at the Golden Gate. When the sun sets over the horizon each night, the last and—some people believe—best views in the continental United States are from the Golden Gate Bridge.

There's an allure to the bridge, Blaustein says, that acts as a magnet to people who are in psychic pain. Add to this the pedestrian access, nearby parking lots, bus stops, and four-foot-high railing, and the pull is only stronger.

In addition to his work at the hospital, where he started in 1980, Blaustein is president of the Psychiatric Foundation of Northern California. It's a nonprofit organization of 1,200 psychiatrists and is affiliated with the American Psychiatric Association (APA). In recent years, the foundation's primary focus has been advocating for a suicide barrier on the Golden Gate Bridge. Blaustein has presented on the subject at every APA annual conference from 2006 to 2011. He also has published numerous opinion pieces and addressed many audiences, including members of San Francisco's prestigious Commonwealth Club. He tells people that although the Golden Gate Bridge and the Bay Bridge have three elements in common—they were completed in 1937, the roadway on each is more than two hundred feet high, and they connect at one end to San Francisco—the Bay Bridge doesn't have the mystique of its famous counterpart. According to "A Tale of Two Bridges," a 1982 study by U.C. Berkeley professor Richard Seiden, half the people who drove cars to the Golden Gate Bridge, then jumped, crossed the Bay Bridge to get there. No one went the other way, crossing the Golden Gate Bridge to jump from the Bay Bridge.

Because aesthetics are important, Blaustein talks about the fact that suicide barriers on the Eiffel Tower, Empire State Building, and Sydney Harbour Bridge haven't deterred people from continuing to enjoy these structures. The barriers have just prevented people from jumping.

When someone brings up the cost of a suicide barrier, Blaustein replies that money is a relative issue. "The Bay Bridge is costing $6 billion to be retrofitted," he says. "Andre Agassi sold his house [in nearby Tiburon] for $20 million. My wife is an alumna of the University of North Dakota where hockey is almost a religion. One of the alums donated $150 million for a hockey arena."

It's not money, Blaustein says, or aesthetics. "The real issue is the value we place on human life." For many years, Blaustein considered a suicide barrier on the bridge solely from a professional viewpoint. It was needed so that people he and others treated couldn't kill themselves as easily. His feelings changed, he told me, in 2005 after eighteen-year-old Jonathan Zablotny jumped. Blaustein's son and Jonathan were good friends. In addition, Dr. Ray Zablotny, Jonathan's father, was a close colleague. "After Jonathan's death," Blaustein says, "the barrier became a personal issue."

The barrier became a personal issue for Dr. Anne Fleming, too. Fleming is a professor of psychiatry at the University of California's medical school in San Francisco. She's also a consulting psychiatrist at San Francisco General Hospital, where most people who are stopped from jumping are taken for observation and treatment. The notation "BIBP from GGB" on a patient's chart is so common at the hospital that everyone knows what it means: "brought in by police from Golden Gate Bridge." Fleming has coauthored articles with Blaustein on the need for a suicide barrier. She also has co-presented with him at APA conferences. Her involvement grew after her friend and classmate in medical school, Dr. Phil Holsten, jumped in 2004.

I asked Blaustein why he thinks people in the Bay Area have opposed a barrier when residents of other cities with notable landmarks have come to accept them. After all, the same arguments pertaining to cost, aesthetics, and effectiveness apply. Why have people elsewhere been open to a barrier when local citizens haven't? Why is the attitude of people here different? Blaustein shrugs. "I don't know," he says. "Free will—this is California."

The foremost suicide prevention training program in the world is called ASIST (Applied Suicide Intervention Skills Training). It was created more than twenty years ago by a Canadian agency, Living Works, and is taught in dozens of countries, including the United States. It's the training program that's endorsed by the federal Substance Abuse and Mental Health Services Administration, U.S. Army, and National Suicide Prevention Lifeline. The training is intense, two full days. Almost without exception, people who complete the training say that they feel confident in being able to help a person who is suicidal.

An element in ASIST is a diagram that's referred to as the "River of Suicide." The river cuts through diverse landscapes—a city, suburb, farmland—ending in a waterfall. It represents the opportunities for suicide first aid. People enter the river from many different locations. If they don't get help, they can end up at the waterfall, which signifies a suicide attempt. The point of the diagram is that suicide prevention doesn't start at the waterfall; it happens all along the stream.

One of the people who knows this better than most is Dr. Jerome Motto, a long-time psychiatrist who worked with suicidal patients at the University of California San Francisco. Motto has studied suicide from every angle. He ran a suicide ward for more than three decades. He supervised psychiatric residents at San Francisco General Hospital. He published dozens of articles on suicide in medical journals which, at the time, generally ignored the subject. He also served as president of the American Association of Suicidology and has been on the boards of both San Francisco Suicide Prevention and the Psychiatric Foundation of Northern California.

One of the most often-told stories about Golden Gate Bridge suicides concerns a visit Motto made in the 1970s to the apartment of a recent bridge jumper. "The guy was in his 30s," Motto related, "lived alone. Pretty bare apartment. He'd written a note and left it on his bureau. It said, 'I'm going to walk to the bridge. If one person smiles at me on the way, I won't jump.'" Apparently no one did.

Motto doesn't understand why a suicide barrier on the bridge remains an issue. "If people started hanging themselves from the tree in my front yard," he told the *San Francisco Chronicle*, "I'd have a moral obligation to prevent that from happening. I'd take the limb off, put a fence around it. It's not about whether the suicide statistics would change, or the cost, or whether the tree would be as beautiful. If an instrument that's being used to bring about tragic deaths is under your control, you are morally compelled to prevent its misuse."

In 1964, when Motto first testified before the Golden Gate Bridge District directors in favor of a suicide barrier, he was forty-two years old. Three initiatives for a suicide barrier had been rejected previously; however, Motto assumed that once board members heard the testimony of mental health professionals like himself, that would change. He was wrong.

Over the ensuing decades, Motto and his colleagues have spoken before the board numerous times. Each time they thought would be the last time, that after hearing the facts, the Bridge District would take action. Each subsequent visit left them feeling stunned that the subject wasn't generating a greater sense of urgency. The Golden Gate Bridge was the most well-known public structure in the world that not only permitted but—by it's low railing and year-round pedestrian access—aided suicide. Didn't people care?

"It's like having a loaded gun on your kitchen table," Motto says. No matter how much one may try to ignore it, it's always there.

For the U.S. Coast Guard, at least the officers and enlisted personnel at Station Golden Gate, what's always there is the job of retrieving the bodies of Golden Gate Bridge jumpers—two to three per month. It's not something anyone signed up for. "No one came into the Coast Guard to do this mission [recover bridge jumper's bodies]," Leanne Lusk, sector San Francisco command center chief, told me. "We came in to save lives." "The eyes are the worst," one former Coast Guard crew member stated, referring to jumpers who are still alive but experiencing cardiac arrest. "It's just the eyes staring at you."

Based on the number of search and rescue cases, San Francisco Bay is the busiest place in the United States for Coast Guard personnel. Coast Guard Sector San Francisco, which is responsible for search and rescue operations in central and northern California, the Sacramento River Delta, and Lake Tahoe, and also encompasses Station Golden Gate in Marin County and Station San Francisco on Yerba Buena Island, had 1,557 cases in fiscal year 2010 (October 1 to September 30), and 1,664 cases in FY 2009, according to Lieutenant Commander Lusk. By comparison, the next closest Coast Guard sector in the United States had 979 search and rescue cases. One reason for San Francisco's high volume is because the bay is a top sailing spot. It draws a large number of boaters, windsurfers, kitesurfers, and other water enthusiasts. At the same time, the bay's strong currents, choppy water, and shifting shoals can fool even veteran sailors. In addition, there are multiple ports and waterways, plus ferry service in the bay, as well as boat fires and disabled vessels offshore. There's also the Golden Gate Bridge and, to a lesser extent, the Bay Bridge and Richmond-San Rafael Bridge (Station Golden Gate responds to all person-in-the-water calls near the Golden Gate Bridge while Station San Francisco responds to these calls for the other two bridges). All of this activity is why there are forty-five people at Station Golden Gate, forty of whom participate in search and rescue missions. It's one of the largest deployments of personnel in the Coast Guard.

There are four boats at Station Golden Gate. Two are forty-seven-foot motor life boats and two are twenty-five-foot response boats. The larger boats have four-person crews and the smaller boats have a minimum crew of three people. I asked Mark Allstott, commanding officer at Station Golden Gate, if the crews have a boat preference when doing person-in-the-water searches. He said that the larger boats are dispatched if they're available because they're more stable.

When Station Golden Gate receives word of a 10-31—police code for a jump—the crew on duty has four minutes to get dressed, run four hundred yards to the boat, and take off. They arrive within eight to fifteen minutes of the call, says Allstott. Even so, even with such a quick response, the jumper may be swept well beyond the Golden Gate Bridge, somewhere into the open sea. Smoke floats, dropped by police officers from the bridge near where the jumper was last seen, indicate the surface drift, assisting search and rescue teams in their efforts to find the body.

Given the inconvenience as well as the trauma of dealing with Golden Gate Bridge jumpers, some responders resent it. "It's a real thankless job," according to one former Coast Guard crewman. Another former crewman who worked at Station Golden Gate nearly ten years said that what bothered him the most were spectators. "It used to get me very upset," he said, "when people would come to where we were and try to get a glimpse of the people who jumped. Let them die in peace. Many died in my arms, and I did what I could to help them pass peacefully."

For officers on the Golden Gate Bridge Patrol who are constantly on the lookout for signs of potential jumpers, the job requires total concentration. Let your mind wander—even for a moment—and someone could die. The way it is, with ten million pedestrians and bicyclists using the Golden Gate Bridge every year—in addition to forty million vehicles—even being alert and acting quickly isn't always enough to save a life.

Furthermore, there's little formal training for the patrollers. It's more about staying focused and knowing what to look for. Jumpers usually are alone. Their body language hints that they're depressed. Instead of being in motion or stopping to look out at the view, they're inclined to linger in one spot and look down at the water.

According to information provided by Mary Currie, the Golden Gate Bridge District's public affairs director, 1,005 incident reports relative to suicide were filed between January 1, 2000, and November 22, 2010. Of this total, 274 were confirmed suicides, 59 were unconfirmed suicides, and 672 were people who were stopped by the Bridge Patrol or California Highway Patrol from making an attempt. In some cases the person was approached and talked to before he or she got a leg over the railing. Other times the person already was on the other side, standing on the chord and deliberating about whether to jump. In these instances, officers may spend hours trying to coax the person back to safety. When I talk with Captain Lisa Locati, who heads bridge security, she says that the longest intervention she remembers in her thirty-three years on the job lasted seven-and-a-half hours.

There's no particular model or method that officers use to talk to a potential jumper. Initially, the officer approaches, makes contact, and asks questions to confirm intent. After that, it's about helping the person find reasons to live—or at least choose not to die in the moment. Locati starts by saying, "Hi, my name is Lisa. I received a report of [or someone noticed] you acting like you might be preparing to jump. Is that true? Are you thinking about committing suicide?" After that, Locati says, "You lie, you do whatever you need to do to talk the person back [to safety]."

She says that the strategy has changed over the years. Early on, officers didn't mention suicide for fear that it would lead someone to jump. They didn't mention family, either, because that might be the reason why the person wanted to die. Today, officers know that asking about suicide is the best way to determine a person's intentions. It doesn't plant the seed in someone's mind because they're already at the bridge—they're already thinking about suicide. And questions are asked about the person's family ("Do you have a wife? Do you have kids?") because that may generate guilt. Again, anything that works.

Even so, every intervention doesn't end successfully. "If you have been doing this job any length of time," Locati says, "you've witnessed a jump and you've talked someone back down." She estimates that she has talked down more than two hundred potential jumpers over the years. Still, it's the jumps that occur after talking with a person that are haunting. "If you make contact and the person jumps, it's definitely harder," she says. "I was there when two people jumped at the same time. That will always be with me." She also remembers one person who jumped after seven hours of contact. The officers who were involved probably will remember that for a long time, she says.

If a bridge phone is used to report a jump or someone in the throes of jumping, the call goes to Bridge District's security command center. Sometimes a motorist tells a tollbooth worker, or someone in the control room notices the situation on one of the many monitors connected to bridge cameras. If a cell phone is used to call 911, it's answered by the California Highway Patrol. Oftentimes a call goes to both the CHP and Bridge Patrol. Then it becomes a matter of who gets there first.

There are more than fifty cameras on the bridge. Bridge District officials won't disclose the actual number of cameras for security reasons. The cameras are mounted on cables, bridge towers, struts, and elsewhere. Security police can change pictures in an instant to any section of the bridge, then zoom in. The images are live—looking down on traffic, following bicyclists and pedestrians, monitoring the toll plaza. The whole underside of the bridge, including the tower footings, also is monitored, and the control room is staffed twenty-four hours a day, seven days a week. The day I was there, one officer said that he had been on the job more than thirty years and the second officer more than twenty years. A smaller room next door has additional monitors and recording equipment. It's where Bridge Patrol officers go to rewind and review surveillance tapes.

Lights on the bridge make it possible to view camera images after nightfall. The bigger obstacle in terms of visibility is fog. From July to October—the worst months for misty conditions—two foghorns on the bridge sound continuously more than five hours per day. Small vessels that lack radar depend on the horns in order to enter and exit San Francisco Bay (each horn has a different pitch, and boats enter the bay between the two horns and exit between the mid-span horn and the north pier). When the fog is particularly dense, security personnel rely on sensors and alarm systems on the bridge that are activated by movement. Sightseers aren't out when visibility is low, so pedestrian traffic is minimal at those times.

Anytime bridge police have more than casual contact with someone, it's noted in a logbook. If the person isn't considered a serious risk, he or she is let go, but it's still noted in the logbook. The second logbook notation for an individual—or a more serious first-time attempt—results in a formal interview. The person is escorted off the bridge by security officers and taken into an interview room in the administration building parking lot. What happens next ultimately is left up to the California Highway Patrol, although Bridge Patrol personnel have a say. Persons who are thought to be probable jumpers are taken by the CHP to San Francisco General Hospital. At one time there were as many as fifteen hospitals that police transported people to for drop-in treatment or hospital hold, but many of them—like Letterman and Mt. Zion—are closed now. Once someone is off Bridge District property, responsibility is transferred to another entity.

In cases of actual interventions or suicides, Bridge Patrol officers file incident reports in addition to logbook notations. When an intervention is in progress, ironworkers on the bridge are alerted if they're on duty (they work 7 A.M. to 3 P.M. Monday to Friday). They're the only people authorized by the Bridge District to go over the rail and engage in what are referred to as "snatch and grab rescues" because they're wearing safety harnesses. The first officer on the scene is in charge and decides whether ironworkers will be involved. In worst-case situations where someone jumps during an intervention, debriefings are conducted and workers have access to an employee assistance program for posttraumatic stress disorder counseling.

Intervening in the lives of people who are suicidal can be dramatic, which is why Eve Meyer refers to suicide prevention as "opera without the music." It's filled with tragedy and personalities that start out small yet end up casting large shadows. She says,

> I could tell you dozens of stories, stories of people who are just like you, whoever you are. Male or female, young or old, rich or poor. Someone who is married with children, successful professionally, looked up to by others, or someone who is seemingly alone, without a supportive family or close friends, whose premature death nevertheless echoes throughout a community. The thing is, every suicide cuts short a life unnecessarily. As great as anyone's emotional pain may be, there are other options besides suicide. Call us and give us a chance to help you find them.

The common belief among the general public is that when someone picks up one of the thirteen specially-marked crisis phones on the Golden Gate Bridge, he or she is connected immediately to a suicide prevention counselor, most likely at San Francisco Suicide Prevention. Even some Bridge District officials believe this. In minutes from the district's January 27, 2005, meeting, board member Janet Reilly, a bridge barrier supporter, asked how many times the crisis telephones on the bridge are used. Kary Witt, the bridge's general manager, replied that four to five calls are made per year by suicidal individuals, and that the calls are routed to San Francisco Suicide Prevention. He was mistaken. In fact, Meyer says that her agency hasn't received a single bridge call since 1994. That's the year that calls started being answered by a police dispatcher—if they're answered at all. There are numerous photos on the Internet of "Out of Order" signs on Golden Gate Bridge phones. Salt air corrodes phone lines, and replacing them is costly and time consuming. People pose next to the phones for photographs, and sometimes pick up the receiver pretending to be suicidal, but they're seeking a memento, something to remember a walk on the world's deadliest span, rather than help.

Dr. Paul Linde is a psychiatrist in the emergency room at San Francisco General Hospital, where many potential Golden Gate Bridge jumpers are taken by police. He starts his book, *Danger to Self*, by saying, "I love my job when I'm not there." He explains that while the work is intellectually and emotionally demanding, when he's not there he has "a decent shot at separating out my job's trauma and drama from the rest of my life. But in my workplace, there's no place to hide." It's another way of saying that dealing with people who have persistent, severe, and complex mental illnesses—illnesses that often lead them to attempt suicide—is analogous to the intense theatrics of opera. The only thing that's missing is the music.

One important aspect to explore is the ambivalence that's behind every expression of suicidal intent. After all, it's unlikely that persons who are 100 percent committed to die will call a hotline or disclose much information to a psychiatrist. Often, they don't want to be talked out of it, nor do they want anyone to interfere. They just act.

Dr. David Jobes is a clinical psychologist who has treated hundreds of suicidal patients, written books on suicide prevention, and lectured around the country on the subject. One question he suggests that all mental health professionals ask of anyone who's suicidal is, "When you think of suicide, does it scare you or comfort you?" As hard as is it for most people to believe, the thought of suicide is comforting to individuals who are trapped in their own version of hell. It's a coping strategy to employ if their pain becomes too great. The suicidal person's perception of the world is so narrowed by his or her suffering that nothing else matters. It's analogous to getting your finger caught in a closing door. At that moment, your whole world narrows down to the finger and the door. You don't think about anything else. In the same way, people who are experiencing mental or emotional pain aren't likely to give up the thought of suicide. It's ever present in their mind. What counselors do is acknowledge that suicide is an option, which is important in building trust, then work to expand the person's perspective. They talk about loved ones who will be left behind, other options to deal with distress, the potential lessening of the person's pain over time, and the possibility that suicide would be a mistake. Clients and patients continue to maintain the freedom to make their own decisions, including the decision to take their life. The goal of helpers is to push suicide farther down the list of options, to convince someone that suicide isn't the only solution left.

In their article, "What Would You Say to the Person on the Roof?" psychologists Haim Omer and Avshalom C. Elitzur describe ways to put a suicidal person's pain in perspective: "In killing the nineteen-year-old Ron, you will also be killing the twenty-year-old Ron and the thirty-year-old Ron and the forty-year-old Ron. You will be killing also the Ron that will perhaps be a father and a grandfather. How can you choose for these other Rons, for a Ron that will be stronger and more mature? How can you choose for the Ron that you could become, but to whom you refuse to give a chance?"

In her memoir *An Unquiet Mind*, Kay Redfield Jamison describes what it's like to live with manic depression, a term she prefers to bipolar disorder. She has suffered from it since early adulthood.

When you're high, it's tremendous. The ideas and feelings are fast and frequent like shooting stars, and you follow them until you find better and brighter ones. Shyness goes, the right words and gestures are suddenly there, the power to captivate others a felt certainty. There are interests found in uninteresting people. Sensuality is pervasive and the desire to seduce and be seduced irresistible.... But, somewhere, this changes. The fast ideas are too fast, and there are far too many; overwhelming confusion replaces clarity. Memory goes. Humor and absorption on friends' faces are replaced by fear and concern. Everything moving with the grain is now against—you are irritable, angry, frightened, uncontrollable, and enmeshed totally in the blackest caves of the mind.

Jamison, a tenured professor of psychology who has written a number of books, including *Night Falls Fast: Understanding Suicide*, contemplated several methods of suicide before overdosing and surviving. She says that even factors that are considered buffers against suicide—love, success, friendship—aren't always enough. "Others imply that they know what it's like to be depressed because they have gone through a divorce, lost a job, or broken up with someone," she writes. "But these experiences carry with them feelings. Depression, instead, is flat, hollow, and unendurable.... You know and [others] know that you are tedious beyond belief: you are irritable and paranoid and humorless and lifeless and critical and demanding, and no reassurance is ever enough."

According to one attempt survivor,

In the midst of a dark period or deep depression, the process is so internal that the outside world fades and becomes less important and, in some respects, is not as real as what is going on inside a person's own head.... It is hard for someone else to understand how hard that can be and how dark some periods can be, or that untreated depression can be so deep. It also is hard for someone else to understand how peaceful it can feel to make a decision to end it and feel it is the right decision even though the world would scream that it is not the right decision.

The challenge for caregivers is that a moment of desperation can lead to a quick, impulsive, and fatal decision. "Once you've jumped over the four-foot railing of the Golden Gate Bridge and are hurtling downward," Paul Linde writes, "there's no turning back." In addition—and most importantly—suicide never ends the pain. It only transfers it to the people who love you. They carry it with them and now join the ranks of grief-stricken souls who are at high risk for suicide themselves.

"I know a hundred ways to die," wrote Edna St. Vincent Millay in a poem of the same name,

> I've often thought I'd try one;
> Lie down beneath a motor truck
> Some day when standing by one.
> Or throw myself from off a bridge—
> Except such things must be
> So hard upon the scavengers
> And men that clean the sea."

The Golden Gate Bridge facilitates suicides the same way that a blind curve facilitates auto accidents. While it might be hoped that everyone drives cautiously, as a society we recognize that some individuals are reckless. That a person may approach the curve too fast or slightly drunk doesn't excuse those in charge of the roads from telling people of the danger or fixing the problem. With the curve, flashing lights and warning signs are put up before the road opens, or at the latest after only one or two incidents, to signal drivers to slow down. In addition, guardrails are erected to keep cars from going off the road. No one complains that the signs or guardrails detract from the view because safety is considered more important. It's different with the Golden Gate Bridge. There's no hue and cry over the fatalities. No effort is made to stop the bloodshed. No one holds the people in charge accountable. Instead, the victims are blamed as if they're the ones who are solely responsible for their deaths.

There is someone else who is equally responsible, however. To be precise, there are multiple someones: the board of directors of the Golden Gate Bridge District. Their complicity and failure to implement reasonable safeguards over the past seven-plus decades has as much to do with bridge suicides as the mental and emotional state of the victims. Yet few members of the general public even know who the bridge directors are, much less their qualifications or how they operate. These are other elements of the story that have gone unnoticed. Like the tragedy itself, it's time to bring them out of the shadows.

SEVEN

Guardians of an Icon

I wanted to focus on whether we choose to see things
or not see things.
  —Eric Steel, producer of *The Bridge*

Although Golden Gate Bridge suicides aren't a secret, they have
received considerably less press than tragedies like this usually
generate. Historically, except for a brief flurry of articles whenever the Bridge District commissions a new barrier study, or
when the Marin County coroner issues a report, bridge suicides
haven't been covered by the media and the extent of the problem
has remained largely unknown. That's just the way Bridge District officials want it, and it has helped their cause that the California Highway Patrol and the U.S. Coast Guard follow policies
of silence as well.

This situation started changing in 2003 with the publication of
Tad Friend's article "Jumpers" in the *New Yorker*. In words that
were poetic, perceptive, and melancholy, Friend wrote about
people who leaped to their deaths from the Golden Gate Bridge.
Few national publications—and none with the stature of the *New
Yorker*—had covered bridge suicides before. The result was that
Friend's article opened many people's eyes to the problem for the

first time. Two years later, the *San Francisco Chronicle* published a seven-part series on Golden Gate Bridge suicides. The series, "Lethal Beauty," was featured every day for a week on the front page, with multiple interior pages devoted to it. The last day, the *Chronicle* included an editorial calling for a suicide barrier on the bridge.

Around the same time, a movie titled *The Joy of Life* premiered at the Sundance Film Festival. Produced by Jenni Olson, a local filmmaker, it was inspired by the death ten years earlier of Olson's close friend, Mark Finch. Finch, thirty-three, directed the San Francisco International Lesbian and Gay Film Festival, and his death haunted Olson. No one witnessed Finch's jump from the Golden Gate Bridge, in part because it was a rainy day. His briefcase was discovered mid-span, however, and six weeks later his body was found—twenty-five miles south of the bridge. "In the decade since Mark's death," Olson said, explaining her film, "I have alternately avoided the bridge and felt compelled to discover more about it. What I've learned is simple, true, and deeply melodramatic. If there had been a suicide barrier on the bridge, Mark would probably still be alive today."

Olson's movie added to the discussion of bridge suicides; however, it was overshadowed by another movie that came out right after it. It was a movie that brought the horror unapologetically and with disturbing force into theaters and people's living rooms, focusing a spotlight on the problem that people couldn't ignore or forget. This was because *The Bridge* by Eric Steel showed real people jumping to their deaths from San Francisco's world-famous span.

A New Yorker, Steel was in Manhattan on September 11, 2001. From his office window, he could see the twin towers of the World Trade Center engulfed in smoke from the terrorist attacks. He could see people on the top floors leap to their deaths rather than burn in the conflagration. Later, when he read Tad Friend's article, Steel thought back to 9/11. He thought about the deaths he had witnessed. He thought about what prompts people to kill themselves, the frame of mind a person must be in. Although jumping from a tall building to escape flames is different than jumping from a bridge to escape personal demons, there's a connection. It's a choice, in all likelihood the last choice a person will make.

Steel also thought about a painting by Peter Breughel, *Landscape with the Fall of Icarus*. Icarus was the figure in Greek mythology who tried to escape from Crete wearing wax wings made for him by his father. Icarus flew too close to the sun and his wings melted, dumping him into the Aegean Sea. The only evidence of Icarus in the painting is in the lower right corner. A pair of legs is disappearing into the water with so little splash that it goes unnoticed by other people in the painting. Even museum goers can miss it. Steel imagined that this must be what Golden Gate Bridge suicides are like, and he decided to make a movie about it.

A graduate of Yale, Steel started at Walt Disney Pictures, moved to Cinecom, a major film distributor, and was a producer of the movies *Angela's Ashes* and *Shaft*. He hadn't directed a movie before, but he was ready to. Moreover, he was familiar with tragedy. His brother died at age seventeen from cancer, and his sister was killed a year later by a drunk driver.

In thinking back to that time in his life, Steel told a British reporter, "I didn't feel suicidal, but I never felt it was all that far away. I knew there were people for whom the idea entered their heads and was there all the time. These were not people who felt foreign to me."

What did seem foreign to Steel, or at least different, was that most Golden Gate Bridge suicides took place in broad daylight, in front of others. While other suicides tend to occur in private settings—locked rooms, garages, closets, motel bathrooms—people who jump from the bridge don't mind being seen. Steel wondered why. He also wondered if it was possible to deduce their intent while they walked on the bridge. If so, what would that walk be like, from one end to the place where they decided to jump?

From the outset, he planned to combine observed footage of people on the bridge with their personal stories. The movie would include wide-angle views of pedestrians as well as close-ups of individuals jumping, plus interviews with surviving family members.

Steel imagined that Tad Friend's article didn't receive a lot of play on the West Coast, and was all but forgotten except by those who are in the business of suicide prevention. It's easy to forget something we read, but it's a lot harder to forget something we see, especially if the images are shocking and shown repeatedly. Who can forget the sight of commercial airliners flying into the World Trade Center? Because of their visual regularity, the images are burned into our consciousness. Steel hoped that his movie would do the same thing for Golden Gate Bridge suicides.

"I had a sense," he told a reporter, "that we would first show you the picture-perfect, postcard day at the bridge, with billowy white clouds, and people would say, 'That's beautiful.' Then ninety minutes later we could show you the same shot and you'd expect to see a splash. I wanted people to walk out of the theater and challenge the notion of the picture-perfect postcard."

The problem was that local officials would never allow it. They rarely even acknowledged that suicides occurred from the bridge; there was no way they would let camera crews set up and film people jumping. Moreover, if word got out that someone was shooting a movie about bridge suicides, it might increase the number of attempts. Given the media frenzy that took place years earlier, prior to the five hundredth and one thousandth deaths, the last thing anyone wanted, including Eric Steel, was to induce more suicides.

Steel flew to San Francisco, scouted locations, advertised for crew members, and applied for permits. Since disclosing his true intention was sure to result in rejection, he said that he was making a series of movies about national monuments, and the Golden Gate Bridge would be the first. According to the permit he filed with the Golden Gate National Recreation Area (GGNRA; his cameras would be placed on GGNRA land, not on the bridge), he aimed "to capture the powerful, spectacular intersection of monument and nature that takes place every day at the Golden Gate Bridge."

Steel's permit, costing $65, was approved. At the start of 2004, he placed two cameras at different vantage points and began shooting. One camera was in a fixed position and had a wide angle lens to capture the expanse of the bridge as well as the water below. All that the operator had to do was change tapes every hour, from sunup to sundown, and press the record button. The other camera had a powerful telephoto lens that captured individual people as they walked across the bridge. This camera was trickier to operate because millions of people walk, run, or bike across the Golden Gate Bridge every year, oftentimes obscured by heavy fog. The camera operator—more often than not Steel himself—had to choose which individuals to focus on, using whatever instincts he had.

From the outset, Steel established guidelines about when his camera operators should be observers and when they should intervene. It was important for everyone to remember that they were human beings first and filmmakers second, he said. Anytime an attempt seemed imminent, authorities were supposed to be contacted.

> We understood that if someone was walking alone, if he or she looked sad, lingered too long at one spot, or paced back and forth, this made them logical subjects to be filmed, but did not mean we should call the police to take them away. There were simply too many people who fit this description. We decided that if someone set down a bag or briefcase or removed shoes or a wallet—warning signs, we knew, from the article in the *New Yorker*, that the Bridge patrols paid attention to—or if someone made a real move to climb onto or over the rail, that trying to save a life was more important than getting footage. The bridge office was put on all of our cell phone speed dials.

The first two months of filming, Steel and his crew didn't observe anyone jump. They only knew that a suicide had occurred when smoke floats were dropped into the water and the Coast Guard responded. Later, in his office, Steel reviewed footage from the camera with the wide-angle lens and saw splashes in the water. He couldn't connect them, though, with any of the thousands of people captured on the telephoto lens. Then things changed.

> I [Steel] saw the first man actually climb onto the rail and jump. I am not sure to this day why I filmed him. He looked like he was enjoying a spring day. He was wearing a tracksuit and sneakers. He

walked briskly as if getting some exercise. He talked on his cell phone. He laughed heartily. And then he put down his phone as I called bridge police. He sat on the rail for a few seconds. He crossed himself. And then he jumped.

Over the ensuing months, Steel had a lot of time to think as he was sitting behind the camera, in all kinds of weather, looking at the bridge. "I thought if I stared at the Golden Gate Bridge long enough," he said, "I might crack its code, understand its fatal beauty. If is often undeniably stunning, awe-inspiring, but the bridge's most striking power is its ability to seemingly erase time. Within moments of death, it's like it never happened. Things return to normal, just like Breughel's painting."

There were twenty-four confirmed suicides from the bridge in 2004. Steel's cameras captured twenty-two of them (the two he missed occurred on the opposite side of the bridge, along the bike path, away from his cameras). Six are shown in the movie. Viewers see close up, through the telephoto lens, a person climb the railing and jump, with the wide-angle camera capturing the impact and splash. The only audio is the violent sound of the body hitting the water, sometimes in near darkness.

Steel said that he wanted to make a movie "about the human spirit in crisis, that showed but did not judge." He maintains that in six instances his crews saved lives by alerting Bridge Patrol officers in time to prevent a jump.

One of the most powerful images in the film is when Richard Waters, a visiting firefighter from Pittsburgh who was taking photos on the bridge, sees a woman who has climbed over the railing onto the chord. "She did it so casually," he told his home-town newspaper, "I was almost surprised." Seeing that she hesitated on the edge, he set down his camera, grabbed her by the jacket, and hauled her back to safety. In that moment, he said, "You don't even think about what to do. You just do whatever comes naturally."

She wasn't happy to be rescued, though, and started kicking him and screaming. He pinned her to the ground and called 911 while people—to his astonishment—passed by without asking what was going on. When the police came, he retrieved his camera and walked away, stunned by the experience. He estimated that he had been on the bridge no more than ten minutes before this incident occurred. Later, Steel informed Waters that the woman he saved was thirty years old and spoke seven languages.

The aim of Steel's interviews with the jumpers' family members was to make their loved ones real and their grief palpable, as well as to enlighten audiences about the challenges of mental illness. One family member says of schizophrenia, "It's like watching TV with 44 channels on at the same time."

Undoubtedly the most controversial segment in the movie concerns a thirty-four-year-old man named Gene Sprague. Tall, slender, with long, straight brown hair that continually whipped across his face, Sprague walked the full length of the bridge, starting at the south end. It was late morning, sunny, the air crisp. At different points Sprague, dressed in a leather jacket, stopped, looked out, and fingered the bridge's cables. When he got to the north end, he turned around and began retracing his steps, walking a little more quickly and making less of an effort to brush the hair out of his face. Steel's camera followed Sprague the whole time, for ninety-three minutes. Footage of him walking on the bridge is woven throughout, supplemented by interviews with those who knew him. When Sprague returned near his starting point, he hopped on the rail and sat on it, facing traffic, his back to the water. Moments later he stood on the rail, turned around, and in a position reminiscent of Christ being crucified, fell to his death. Not coincidentally since the movie starts and ends with Sprague, ninety-three minutes is the run time of *The Bridge*.

Steel never called the authorities about Sprague, a fact that some viewers find hard to accept. Given how long Steel's cameras focused on Sprague and what audiences learn about Sprague's life during interviews, he seems like an obvious candidate to jump. At the same time, the Bridge Patrol never identified Sprague as a risk, either. He was just another pedestrian on the bridge—one among hundreds that morning. He wasn't crying, and there were no outward signs that he was despondent. Steel acknowledges that Sprague's presence on the bridge made him anxious but, Steel says, "There was hardly a day when we didn't think we might be filming someone who was going to jump."

After filming was completed, and Steel's true motives were revealed, he was denounced by the Bridge District. Célia Kupersmith, the general manager at the time, and Mary Currie, the public affairs director, voiced outrage at Steel's deceit. They also said that the movie would make the problem worse by inciting copycat behavior. Even Tom Ammiano, the Bridge District board member who was the strongest supporter of a suicide barrier, called *The Bridge* "a snuff film." He and others said that the movie was exploitative, voyeuristic, and immoral because it showed real deaths. People picketed the San Francisco Film Festival when the movie had its West Coast premiere.

Even some suicide prevention advocates had misgivings. Dr. Mel Blaustein, president of the Psychiatric Foundation of Northern California, didn't like the fact that in all six cases where family members were interviewed, the jumpers had a diagnosed mental illness. Blaustein believes that this gives the impression that only people who are mentally ill attempt suicide. Another issue was that Sprague's death seemed both preventable and glorified. In addition, there was no number at the end of the movie that people could call for help (the toll-free number of the National Suicide Prevention Lifeline was added to the DVD version). Finally, the film made no reference to a suicide barrier.

Public opinion about the movie changed, Steel believes, only after victims' families—those in the film, and others—mobilized to say that the problem wasn't the movie, the problem was the bridge. As for his failure to reference a suicide barrier, Steel told me that he's strongly in favor of a barrier; however, he made a deliberate decision not to mention it in the movie. "What I was interested in," he says, "was starting conversations about suicide." He wanted to create a movie that caused people to think, feel, and care about suicides from the bridge in a way that they wouldn't forget easily. It's up to audiences, he believes, to supply the missing message, that a suicide barrier is needed.

Still, it baffles him that the movie didn't incite immediate action. "People didn't storm the bridge and say, 'What the hell is going on here?'" he said to me in a recent phone conversation. "That's the movie's failure, I think. It didn't ignite a response. It didn't hold people accountable." He paused for an instant, then added, "The Bridge District has a history of being incredibly disingenuous and calculating on this issue. Their strategy is delay, delay, delay. They're not haunted by the deaths, not driven to undertake changes to stop them."

Steel told ABC News, "If there was a two-mile stretch of road anywhere in this country, and two dozen people died at that stretch year after year after year after year, the people responsible for that stretch of road would feel compelled to take drastic action to stop 24 people from dying next year." It's a valid point. When something fails, whether it's the brakes on a car, the engine on an airplane, or the seal of a deepwater oil well, the person or entity that's responsible is blamed, sued, and forced to make changes. That doesn't seem to be the case with the Golden Gate Bridge, however. The few lawsuits that have been filed against the Bridge District have been dismissed without cause. The changes to the bridge that the district has approved have made the span safer for people with physical disabilities, but not mental disabilities. The stories about bridge suicides point out the issues of access—the low railing and year-round pedestrian access—but don't point a finger at the district that manages the span. Indeed, since the Golden Gate Bridge opened in 1937, the district has received a free pass where suicide is concerned.

In December 1997, a two-year-old girl named Gauri Govil was walking on the bridge with her four-year-old brother and their parents. Somehow she slipped through a nine-and-a-half-inch gap between the curb and the roadway, falling to her death. Carney Campion, general manager of the bridge then, called it "the fluke accident of all time." Even so, the Bridge District paid $1.46 million to the Govil family. In addition, funds were found to close the gap immediately, despite the fact that the likelihood of a tragedy like that ever happening again was remote. It was a matter of will and empathy.

The same will and empathy don't seem to exist when it comes to bridge suicides. If they did, a barrier or net would have been erected years ago, Steel believes. That, or people wouldn't be allowed to walk on the bridge, which is another option. It's not an option that the Bridge District has considered seriously, however, mainly because closing the bridge to pedestrians would be even less popular than a suicide deterrent. The bridge opened with people walking across it, and views from the bridge remain among the area's greatest offerings. The district briefly considered charging people to walk, run, or bike on the bridge, but dismissed the idea. Even a nominal fee would generate much-needed revenue, and in some instances it would be enough to deter a suicidal person. Kevin Hines, one of the few people to survive a bridge jump, spent the last of his money on a bus ride to the bridge. He didn't have money for return fare, and he couldn't have paid a toll to walk on the bridge if it had been in place.

"I suggested to the Bridge District that they charge people $1 to cross," says Patrick Hines, Kevin's father, who along with his son was interviewed in *The Bridge*. "They told me I was crazy. The Bike Coalition opposed it; they said it would be inconvenient for bicyclists." The response disgusts him. How inconvenient is it to pay a nominal fee to ride across the most famous bridge in the world? Resigned, Hines says,

> Fine. Don't charge them. Just charge people on the east side [the side with the pedestrian walkway]. Let people on the west side [the bicycle path] cross free. Almost all the deaths occur from the east side anyway. It would decrease the Bridge District's deficit and stop many of the deaths. My son had no money when he got to the bridge. If he had had to pay, he couldn't have gotten to a place to jump. But the Bridge District refuses to do it. They don't want to admit that one person jumps every ten days. They think it [suicides from the bridge] will just go away, and it might have except for Eric Steel's courage. What he showed on film is something that Golden Gate Bridge authorities have denied since day one.

The Golden Gate Bridge is the only bridge in California with its own board and staff. All other bridges come under the authority of Caltrans, the California Department of Transportation. In contrast, the Golden Gate Bridge District is an independent entity.

According to its Web site, the Bridge District's mission is "to provide safe and reliable operation, maintenance, and enhancement of the Golden Gate Bridge." One might think that such prominent reference to safety would include making the bridge safe for all, but that's not the case. For over seventy years, Bridge District board members have repeatedly voted against erecting any kind of suicide deterrent on the bridge.

There are nineteen board members, nine representing the city and county of San Francisco, four representing Marin County, three representing Sonoma County, and one each representing the counties of Napa, Mendocino, and Del Norte. Various entities, ranging from the mayor of San Francisco to county boards of supervisors, have the authority to elect or appoint individual Bridge District board members; however, the board as a whole is autonomous.

The current president of the board is Janet Reilly, who owns a restaurant with her husband (formerly she was a public relations manager and TV reporter). The first vice president, James Eddie, manages a family ranch. The second vice president, Dick Grosboll, is an attorney. The two most recent past presidents have been Al Boro, a retired phone company executive, and John Moylan, a retired union plasterer. Similarly, the occupations of the other fourteen board members have little if any connection to transportation, yet their opinions and decisions determine everything that happens on America's greatest bridge.

Board members are appointed to two-year terms, and aren't subjected to term limits. Four current members have been on the board fifteen years or more; one former board member served forty years. Collectively, they oversee the work of 825 employees, including two hundred who are devoted to the bridge itself. The latter include toll takers, tow truck operators, painters, ironworkers, electricians, engineers, communication technicians, and grounds crews, in addition to administrative employees.

Celia Kupersmith was the Bridge District's chief executive officer and general manager for ten years, starting in 1999 (she resigned from the $260,000 position in September 2010 to accept a job in Seattle). According to her, Eric Steel's movie missed the point. Rather than focusing on those who die, who "get ideas" (in Kupersmith's words) when Golden Gate Bridge suicides become public, Steel should have focused on the lives the Bridge District saves by having trained personnel keep a vigilant watch. In 2006, Kupersmith told ABC News,

> So far this year, we've talked back 65 percent of all of the suicide candidates that have arrived here at the bridge to do some sort of harm to themselves. We do that by training not only what you might consider your typical first responders, meaning your police officers, but we also train our ironworkers, our painters, our service operators—literally anyone whose job requires them to be out on the Golden Gate Bridge on a regular basis.

If one wanted to reduce illegal drug use, send the most virulent forms of cancer into remission, or rehabilitate hardened criminals, a 65 percent success rate would be laudable. It would be a sign of progress. But to say that two-thirds of all suicide attempts on the Golden Gate Bridge are thwarted doesn't seem like anything to brag about when it means that one-third of the people—twenty-five to thirty-five per year—are dying.

I asked Mary Currie, the Bridge District's public affairs director since 1992, if her opinion of *The Bridge* had changed in any way since it first aired five years. She had attended the opening and said, "I'm not critical of the film. We're not content cops." She said that the movie "did a good job showing the reaction of family members to someone who's suicidal." At the same time, "It was a shock and a surprise," and Steel was wrong to misrepresent his intentions in getting a permit. It undermined his credibility, she believes. I make the point that if he hadn't misled people, his permit wouldn't have been approved. This is said in the Bridge District's offices, in a meeting with Currie, Denis Mulligan (the former chief engineer who succeeded Celia Kupersmith as general manager), Bridge Manager Kary Witt, and Lisa Locati, the captain of bridge security. No one denies it.

I asked the other three if they'd seen the movie. Mulligan had, but Witt and Locati had not. Witt stated, "I haven't seen it, and I won't see it. To me, it's reprehensible and sick to see actual people dying." Locati agreed.

"Yet you watch real people jump from the bridge on videotape," I commented.

"That's our job," Witt said, "and we don't watch jumps very often—at least I don't. We don't do it for pleasure."

I was tempted to tell Witt that people who watch documentaries like *The Bridge* don't do it to be entertained; they do it to be informed. Being informed, however, hasn't been a high priority of Bridge District officials, at least where suicide is concerned.

As staff, Mulligan and, to a lesser extent, Witt and Currie report to the Bridge District board of directors. Board members set policies and provide general oversight while staff are responsible for day-to-day operations.

Depending on the source, the Golden Gate Bridge District tends to be depicted in two ways by the media and the public. On one hand it's portrayed as a regional powerhouse, beholden to no one, that manages a transit empire. In *Paying the Toll*, Louise Nelson Dyble chronicles decades of power brokering, secret deals, and mismanagement by district officials. Several local legislators, most notably Willie Brown when he was speaker of the California State Assembly, have introduced bills designed to dismantle the district and transfer responsibility for the bridge to Caltrans. So far, Bridge District officials have been able to fend off reforms.

On the other hand, the Bridge District is portrayed as something of a boutique agency with no equal to it in the state. The district manages one bridge, the buses that travel across it, and the ferryboats that traverse underneath it. Of the three functions, the bridge is far and away the top priority. It's the reason why people serve on the board; after all, there's no special distinction managing buses or ferries. There is status in being among a select group of people who manage a national monument—a group, incidentally, that's even smaller than the number of people who have survived a Golden Gate Bridge jump. The monetary rewards are minimal; board members attend twice-a-month meetings and are paid $50 per meeting day up to a maximum of $5,000, or $7,500 for the board president, who's an ex-officio member of all board committees. The prestige, however, is undeniable. After all, there's only one Golden Gate Bridge.

Current general manager Denis Mulligan equates the Bridge District to the Bay Area Rapid Transit system (BART), while board members tend to liken their role to guardians of an international treasure. They have sympathy for the families and friends of jumpers, but they believe there are larger interests to consider. First and foremost are the millions of tourists who come to San Francisco every year. Should their views and photographs be marred by a suicide barrier? Second are the thousands of commuters who cross the bridge every day. Their tolls help pay for the bridge's maintenance. Should what they see be affected by higher railings or a net? Third are all of the joggers and bicyclists who use the bridge. Marathons are run across it, and an estimated six thousand bikers peddle over it daily.[1] Fourth is everyone whose home or office looks out on the bridge. Each has paid dearly for the privilege. Should what they see be altered (albeit minimally) because a few people need psychiatric care? Last are other residents of the area for whom the Golden Gate Bridge isn't an everyday sight but, nevertheless, is a source of pride. Should they be reminded by the addition of a suicide barrier that there are people who want to kill themselves?

All are vocal about their likes and dislikes. This makes the issue of a suicide barrier on the Golden Gate Bridge a no-win situation according to Mary Currie, the public relations director. Whatever the district does or doesn't do, people will be upset.

Michael Martini was one of the board members who opposed a suicide barrier. He manages a winery in Sonoma County, fifty miles from the bridge. In a January 27, 2005, Bridge District meeting, the subject of bridge jumps came up and Martini asked whether there had been any suicides in the past few years. The question was notable for two reasons. First, it indicated that board members weren't receiving information on bridge suicides from staff. Second, Martini didn't seem to have a clue that there had been *any* suicides since December 2001 when Marissa Imrie—one

1. Bicyclists have twenty-four-hour access. Weekdays from 7 A.M. to 3 P.M., when work crews are on the bridge, the west side is closed because that's the only side that workers can mount the rolling platforms. During these hours bicyclists and pedestrians share the eastern promenade. After 6 P.M. during winter and 9 P.M. the rest of the year, when the pedestrian walkway is closed, bikers can press a buzzer next to the eastern gate at each end of the bridge. Security cameras zoom in, and if the person has a bike, whoever is monitoring the cameras can press a button, which allows the gate to open. At the other end, the same thing occurs in order for the bicyclist to get off the bridge.

of the few victims who lived in his district—jumped. More than seventy-five people had died in the interim and he didn't know it.

Martini and other Bridge District board members from the northern counties have been the strongest opponents of a barrier. In March 2006, when the board voted 14 to 2 in favor of proceeding with studies for a barrier, the two dissenting votes were from Sonoma County—Martini and Maureen Middlebrook. Martini called the issue a "distraction" from more pressing concerns while Middlebrook blamed barrier supporters for not having raised more money—as if it was the responsibility of others to make the bridge safe. In October 2008, when the board voted 14 to 1 to in favor of a safety net, the only "no" vote was cast by James Eddie, the family rancher representing Mendocino County. Martini and Middlebrook were no longer on the board, but Eddie said that the people in his district didn't think a barrier was needed. He may have been right, but only because the bridge is a good two hours' drive away—too far to have much relevance to his constituents. They don't see or use it regularly, and few of the victims live that far north.

At the same board meeting where Martini asked if there had been any suicides, he asked about the costs incurred by the Bridge District, Coast Guard, and local police dealing with bridge suicides. CEO Celia Kupersmith replied that the district had never tracked these costs and she didn't know if it was done by other agencies. No one on the board seemed to think it was an important point because there was no follow-up. The irony is that while several people on the board were quick to question the cost of erecting a suicide barrier of any kind, they didn't express any interest in knowing how much money it was costing the district or other entities *not* to have a barrier.

Calculating at least an estimate of the costs of suicide response and rescue at the bridge is likely possible, if the board really was interested. In response to my inquiry, the Coast Guard was able to provide some information. There's a "reimbursable standard rate," according to Lt. Commander Leanne Lusk, that is used to calculate costs. For the forty-seven-foot motor life boats used to retrieve the bodies of Golden Gate Bridge jumpers, it's $4,189 per hour. Even if a person's body is found immediately, by the time it's delivered to the coroner's office and the boat returns to the station, the cost is $4,000. If the search takes two to three hours, the cost can be more than $12,000. Multiply that by thirty searches and it totals $120,000 to $360,000 annually. And that's just for the Coast Guard.

The California Highway Patrol doesn't track its costs this way, or at least doesn't share the information publicly. Ken Holmes, the Marin County coroner, said that his office doesn't track the cost of conducting autopsies on Golden Gate Bridge jumpers, either, but probably could. When I ask Bridge District staff if a suicide deterrent will save the district money, Bridge Manager Kary Witt is quick to say that it won't because the same number of patrol officers and same amount of surveillance equipment will be needed to maintain bridge security anyway. His comment underscores the fact that Bridge District officials are far more interested in monitoring potential terrorist activities than worrying about people who end their lives on the bridge.

On average, more than 100,000 vehicles cross the Golden Gate Bridge every day. That's about 4,500 per hour or 350 every five minutes. If a section of the bridge collapsed suddenly, hundreds of people probably would be killed. Within seconds, blockades would be set up at both ends, and all traffic to the bridge would be diverted. Announcements would be issued across a variety of airwaves telling people to stay away. Large, can't-miss, Amber Alert-type warnings would be posted leading up to the bridge. Before the last body was pulled from the water, plans would be underway to replace the section with cost only a minor consideration. Meanwhile, the entity responsible for managing and maintaining the bridge would be attacked from all sides. Lawsuits would tie up local courts for years.

Despite more than fifteen hundred suicides from the bridge, there are no blockades, no announcements, no warning signs posted to stop them. There are only a few phones on the bridge that may or may not be working, which suicidal people tend to ignore anyway. Meanwhile, the entity that's solely responsible for managing and maintaining the bridge—the Golden Gate Bridge District—neither assumes nor is assigned by the courts, the media, or the public any responsibility for the deaths occurring on its structure.

In 2004, the Psychiatric Foundation of Northern California, comprised of 1,200 psychiatrists, established a Golden Gate Bridge suicide barrier task force to educate people about suicide and win support for a barrier. The organization, led by Dr. Mel Blaustein, launched a speakers' bureau, and members met individually with many Bridge District board members to make their case face-to-face. They also placed opinion pieces in northern California newspapers and brought together victims' families.

When Dave Hull learned of the Psychiatric Foundation in 2005, it was fifteen months after his daughter had jumped from the bridge. The timing also coincided with an event that raised his ire: the management of the Golden Gate National Recreation Area—part of the National Park Service (NPS) and Hull's longtime employer—criticized filmmaker Eric Steel for bringing unwanted attention to the bridge. Up to that point Hull had been silent about his daughter's death, believing that there was a "sacred circle of grief" around it that would have profaned her memory if mentioned to others. When GGNRA officials tried to cover up the problem, however, Hull decided that he couldn't be mute any longer. Not only was Kathy Hull dead because the bridge lacked a suicide barrier, he believed, but a year earlier a female park ranger had driven a GGNRA vehicle to the bridge and jumped.

Hull wrote letters to NPS officials relating his personal tragedy and expressing dismay over their tacit acceptance of bridge suicides. He said that the issue of a suicide barrier should be of primary interest to the NPS because the agency was responsible for the land on both sides of the bridge. "No one dies on the Golden Gate Bridge without crossing Park Service property," Hull stated. To their credit, NPS staff took Hull's letters to heart, and started having conversations with Bridge District board members and staff.

Meanwhile, Hull began attending meetings of survivors' families organized by the Psychiatric Foundation of Northern California. Half the people were mental health professionals and half were victims' families—"people in a lot of pain, driven to this table in hopes of finding something that could be done," according to Hull. The meetings were the first time that Hull talked publicly about his daughter's death. He couldn't maintain his composure doing it—he still chokes up today when the subject turns to her—but he forced himself to speak.

Hull found that the meetings weren't designed to support people in their grief, however, which was what he was most interested in. Instead, their purpose was to promote a suicide barrier on the bridge. To that end, Hull believed that educating people, particularly mental health professionals, wasn't enough. A broader approach was needed.

Two other Psychiatric Foundation supporters, Patrick Hines and Paul Muller, agreed. Hines was a corporate banker whose son, Kevin, was one of the few people to jump from the bridge and live. Muller, owner of a small San Francisco marketing firm, had been doing consulting work on the suicide barrier for the foundation, and he pushed to expand the task force's role. "If we don't broaden our constituency," Muller told Blaustein and other board members, "we'll repeat mistakes of the past." (Foundation leaders disagreed, and Muller was let go.)

For years, Jerry Motto and other psychiatrists had believed that they could convince Bridge District officials of the need for a suicide deterrent by the power of their arguments and their standing as physicians. Instead, their exhortations failed, largely because they constituted only one segment of the population. The majority of the public opposed a barrier, and until public opinion changed it didn't matter that the medical community was in favor. Collectively, it represented a single voice.

Muller, Hines, and Hull believed that the issue of a suicide deterrent on the bridge, like most issues, came down to politics and financing. They thought that success depended on wide-scale support, not intellectually reasoned arguments.

Through fortuitous circumstances, the three had a chance to pitch a San Francisco philanthropist who was interested in mental health issues. They explained the problem to her, as well as their general strategy, and she provided seed funding to launch a new nonprofit organization—the Bridge Rail Foundation. It had one mission: to see that the existing railing was raised or a net was installed so that suicides from the Golden Gate Bridge ended.

Marin County coroner Ken Holmes joined the all-volunteer organization, as did many survivor families. In district hearings and community forums, they told emotional, first-person stories of tragic deaths, all preventable if the bridge had had a barrier. They also created a poignant, traveling exhibit honoring everyone who jumped. In addition, the organization launched an active Web site, implemented a calendar of regular press activities to keep the issue alive and maintain pressure on the district, and met with federal legislators to identify potential funding sources. Most importantly, Bridge Rail Foundation members forged a partnership with Tom Ammiano, the Bridge District board member who was the strongest supporter of a barrier.

Ammiano had been on the Bridge District board for twelve years. He had read Tad Friend's article in the *New Yorker*, been moved by public comments of victims' families, and grown frustrated with what he calls all of the "sham studies" in which the results were "nitpicked to death." He told me that when he started on the board, "Opposition to the barrier was a class-level thing, an elitist thing. People on the board weren't educated about the issue and didn't want to be educated." Fortunately, things do change. "A lot of politics is fate," he said. "Some of the more resistant board members left. Once the complexion of the board changed, there was definite traction for the barrier."

In an interview with me, Denis Mulligan agreed that the Bridge District board "has evolved over time." Mulligan was hired as chief engineer in 2001 after working at Caltrans. He said that a combination of factors in 2005, all having to do with "changing societal values and changing perceptions of suicide," set in motion a series of events that culminated in the vote for a barrier three years later. There was $2 million to study the issue again, nearly all of it granted by the Metropolitan Transportation Commission at the request of Tom Ammiano. There was an agreement to revisit the criteria and the subsequent decision to accept a deterrent that couldn't promise to be 100 percent effective. There was the advocacy of the Psychiatric Foundation of Northern California, culminating in an event that featured bridge barrier designs of engineering students at U.C. Berkeley. There also was new and increasing press coverage.

"The *San Francisco Chronicle* ran a seven-part, page one, top-of-the-fold series on bridge suicides," Mulligan told me. "When has the *Chronicle* ever done that—for anything?" Indeed, the paper devoted more than 30,000 words to the subject, featuring bylines of eight reporters. It was a major commitment of time, space, and resources, and it ended with an editorial titled "Humanity over Vanity" that said, "It is time to confront the dark side of our glamorous attraction and build an effective suicide barrier."

I mentioned to him that I thought *The Bridge*, which also came out in 2005, put a face on Golden Gate Bridge suicides, a face that couldn't be ignored, and asked him how much impact he thought it had. "It didn't hurt," Mulligan said, adding that Jenni Olson's film was released around the same time. "A lot of things came together at once, including Tom Ammiano taking charge. You need champions for public service projects."

I asked Ammiano what he thinks of Eric Steel's movie now, reminding him that when it came out he called it a snuff film. He said, "I was ambivalent about it, but it did a lot of good. I was initially wary because something like this could be exploitative. In the end, though, the press coverage helped.... We broke the insular bubble of the Bridge District board."

In 2008, Ammiano was elected to the California Legislature, which meant that his tenure on the Bridge District board was ending. As one of his last acts, he moved that the district once again consider a suicide deterrent on the bridge. He sensed that the sympathies of the board had shifted, and knew that this would be his last chance to exert influence. Momentum was on his side, and board members who weren't fully committed to the idea nevertheless could see the writing on the wall.

On October 10, 2008, the board voted 14 to 1 to erect a suicide deterrent on the bridge. It was the first time in history that board members approved a physical deterrent. Specifically, they authorized the addition of a steel net underneath. Local suicide prevention advocates, predictably, were thrilled. Some of them, like Jerry Motto, Ron Tauber, Margaret Hallett, and Eve Meyer, had been lobbying for a barrier for decades. As early as 1960, ad hoc committees of mental health professionals, crisis center directors, interfaith leaders, and others met regularly to develop strategies to try and convince Bridge District board members that a suicide deterrent was needed.

Around the country, suicide prevention advocates applauded the Bridge District's decision as well, but had reservations about a net. No other major bridge has a net to prevent suicides; they all have taller railings. Because taller railings on bridges have proven to be effective while there's less evidence to support a net, and because whatever action is taken on the Golden Gate Bridge is likely to influence the decisions made on other bridges around the world, a net wasn't their first choice.

It wasn't Tom Ammiano's first choice, either. If it was up to him, he says, he would have opted for a higher railing. Nevertheless, the board approved something rather than nothing—at last.

According to Denis Mulligan, from an engineering standpoint there's little difference between a net and variations of a taller railing. "They all add extra weight and affect wind suspension," he said, noting that both the net and taller railing passed the wind tunnel study. That made both options viable. In terms of cost, he said, there's also little difference: "The bridge is 1.7 miles with sidewalks on both sides, so anything you do requires adding three-and-a-half miles of stuff. Whether it's a net on each side or a taller railing on each side, the cost per square foot is about the same."

Then he explained some of the details, starting with the fact that even a small change in a cross section can affect how long-span bridges like the Golden Gate Bridge perform. No one wants to see a repeat of the disaster that happened when the Tacoma Narrows Bridge in Puget Sound, Washington, collapsed. He also talked about installing attachments for the net. This will require removing the existing paint on the underside of the bridge—paint that's 67 percent lead-based and can't be released into the environment so it has to be contained. After that, the base steel has to be primed, and the attachments installed every twenty-five feet on both sides for the net to hang from. Because the new attachments will interfere with the couplings used now for the four rolling bridge painters' scaffolds, new scaffolds and couplings will have to be designed and fitted. Last but not least among the hundreds of things to consider is the cost of two Snooper trucks, used to retrieve anyone who jumps and lands in the net.

Bridge District directors chose a net for two reasons. First and foremost, it was the preference of people who voted for a suicide deterrent in the Bridge District's online opinion poll, as well as the option that was favored by the San Francisco Planning Department and the National Park Service. This made it more palatable politically. A net won't interfere with the views of people on the bridge; it'll only interfere with someone who wants to jump. The net will be stretched taut and angled so as to make climbing out of it difficult, though not impossible. Anyone who falls into the net will be likely to suffer broken bones and dissuaded from jumping again—or so the thinking goes.

If there is a jump, the person will be extricated with a special piece of equipment called a Snooper truck. The truck will have a hoist and bucket at the end like that used by utility workers to repair power lines and trim tree branches. A bridge worker, wearing a harness, will be lowered over the railing and into the net to rescue the jumper. The Snooper truck costs $250,000, takes ninety minutes to get to the site where the person jumped and ninety minutes to get back, and ties up one lane of traffic during that time. Bridge District officials aren't worried about the risk to bridge workers or the inconvenience of closing a lane of traffic for three hours, though. The purpose of the net isn't to save people after they've jumped; it's to deter them from jumping in the first place. A second Snooper truck, only smaller, will be used to retrieve garbage from the net.

The second reason why the net was chosen was cost. Whereas variations of a higher railing produce annual maintenance costs of $429,000 to $466,000 according to Denis Mulligan, maintenance costs of a net will be $78,000 per year. A major reason for the difference is because the net, made of marine grade stainless steel, doesn't need to be painted while a higher railing does (according to Bridge District officials, the net also will blend in more if it's unpainted). In addition, Bridge District officials don't want to inconvenience pedestrians or restrict access to bicyclists during construction. If taller railings were installed, the work would have to be done at night, resulting in overtime costs.

The evidence supporting a net comes from an unlikely source—a medieval castle in Switzerland. Prior to 1999, there were two to three suicides per year at Munster Terrace in Bern. After a net was installed there, suicides from the site ended.

Basing a decision on what happened at a castle in Switzerland might seem problematic. It doesn't necessarily equate with a bridge in San Francisco. Moreover, two to three suicides per year pales in comparison with the death toll at the Golden Gate Bridge. Nevertheless, a net is what has been approved, given the bridge's unique circumstances, and everyone is determined to make it work. Even the smallest deterrents—a stranger's smile, the inability to find a parking space, or a locked gate (which was enough to turn back Casey Brooks when she first went to the bridge)—can be effective, so there's every reason to believe that a net will do the job. One woman was prevented from jumping because her skirt was so tight that she couldn't swing her legs over the railing. She was too modest to take the skirt off, giving a patrol officer time to pull her back from the edge.

Now the big question is: When will the net be erected? Even though Bridge District board members approved it, they're adamant that future bridge tolls won't pay for it. The last of the construction bonds was retired forty years ago, and annual total revenues for the Bridge District exceed $85 million, yet the district is broke, according to the board and staff. Without sales tax or property tax revenues, the Bridge District has to rely primarily on bridge tolls and transit fares, which aren't sufficient to cover other costs, they claim, much less pay for a suicide deterrent. As a result, the last major hurdle is raising the money for construction. That's $45 million according to Mulligan—$30 million for the net system, $10 million for modifications to the bridge, $4 million for new, redesigned maintenance travelers (the four sets of rolling scaffolding for painters and other bridge workers), $500,000 for the two Snooper trucks, and $500,000 in miscellaneous costs. A $5 million grant from the Metropolitan Transportation Commission (again secured by Tom Ammiano) is paying for final plans, which are meant to be completed by spring 2012. After that, the project will be "shovel-ready," meaning that ground is ready to be broken or, in this case, that air is ready to be filled. If all of the funding is in place, work can start immediately thereafter since the final environmental impact report was approved in February 2010. If not, everything will be put on hold. Actual construction will take two years, according to Mulligan's estimates.

Because the Bridge District isn't willing to put up any money for the net, it's natural to wonder how committed officials are to ending suicides from the span. Some barrier supporters, such as Kevin Hines and his father, believe that board members voted for a net in 2008 in order to appear compassionate and take heat off of them, but really they have no interest in moving the project forward. If board members truly wanted to prevent suicides, critics believe, they would find the money, just as they did for the bike barrier. Instead, they're leaving it to others to secure the funding.

When I asked Mulligan how committed the district is to the net, he said unequivocally, "We welcome it and look forward to building it. It will save lives and will not mar the bridge."

As of this writing, however, no money has been identified to erect it. Bridge Rail Foundation volunteers have been pursuing a variety of legislative options, so far without success, and no one else is working on it. Unless there's a dramatic change— either the Bridge District decides to accept responsibility and budgets the amount needed, government funding is secured, or a wealthy donor steps forward—the deaths will continue.

I asked Eric Steel how he feels about the bridge today. He responds immediately, talking faster and with increasing passion until he stops himself mid-sentence and remarks that all of his feelings seem to have resurfaced after just a minute or two of conversation, even though it has been more than five years since his movie premiered. Once something changes, Steel believes, once you start to see it differently, you can't go back to seeing it the way it was. The Golden Gate Bridge is like that. Knowing all of the tragedies associated with the bridge changes one's perception of it. No longer can a person view the bridge simply as an architectural wonder and international icon. No longer can someone walk, bike, or drive across it blissfully. No longer is it possible to go sailing on the bay, turn on the radio to the Coast Guard frequency in order keep abreast of current weather and conditions, hear someone report, "Person in the water," and believe that it refers to something other than a suicide jump.

Still, there are people who continue to oppose any kind of barrier on the bridge. For some, the cost isn't worth it. For others, aesthetics trump everything—even human lives. By far the most commonly voiced argument, though, is that it won't be effective, that it will only cause suicidal people to choose another location or means. If they end up dying anyway, opponents believe, why worry about it? Why spend millions of dollars and change the look of the bridge if it will have no impact?

This is at the heart of the ongoing suicide barrier debate. It's not much of a debate, however, once one learns the facts. Intuitively, it makes sense to think that when one option is closed, a suicidal person will resort to another lethal means. If a gun jams, then swallow a bunch of pills. If your car doesn't start, then tie a noose. If a bridge has a barrier, then go to a train crossing instead. In reality, however, this isn't the case. As the next chapter shows, the evidence is overwhelming. Most people who are suicidal have a preferred means of death. If access to that means is restricted, they don't try to kill themselves another way. Instead, they resign themselves to living.

Casey Brooks, 17, jumped from the Golden Gate Bridge several months after this photo was taken by a friend. An excellent student, she had been accepted at Bennington College in Vermont—her first choice for college—where she planned to study environmental science and journalism.

SOURCE: *John Brooks*

In 2008, after their daughter died, John and Erika Brooks began
advocating for a suicide barrier on the bridge. It was too late for
Casey, but others could be saved.

SOURCE: *Marin Independent Journal*

Dave Hull's world stopped after his 26-year-old daughter jumped from the bridge. He didn't shave, get haircuts, or go to work for weeks.

SOURCE: *San Francisco Chronicle*

A young man contemplates jumping while Bridge Patrol and California Highway Patrol officers try to coax him back to safety. They were successful this time; however, several years later he returned to the bridge and jumped.

SOURCE: *San Francisco Chronicle*

Kevin Hines is one of the few people to survive a jump from the Golden Gate Bridge. Today, he travels around the country educating audiences about mental illness and advocating for a suicide barrier.

SOURCE: *San Francisco Chronicle*

Dr. Mel Blaustein pins an orange suicide barrier ribbon on Mary
Zablotny, who designed the ribbon after her 18-year-old son jumped
from the Golden Gate Bridge. Blaustein, a psychiatrist in San
Francisco, treats people who are stopped from jumping off the bridge.

SOURCE: *San Francisco Chronicle*

"Whose Shoes?" is an exhibit of footwear commemorating the more than 1,500 victims of Golden Gate Bridge suicides. It's topped by a pair of World War I boots in memory of the first known jumper, a WWI veteran.

SOURCE: *San Francisco Chronicle*

The body of a Golden Gate Bridge jumper is brought to shore by Coast Guard crew members. It's a thankless job, one they didn't sign up for.

SOURCE: *San Francisco Chronicle*

As the person responsible for conducting autopsies of Golden Gate Bridge jumpers, Ken Holmes knows the physical impact of falling from a great height and the emotional impact of suicide on loved ones. He's a strong advocate for a barrier on the bridge.

SOURCE: *Marin Independent Journal*

Dr. Sarah Cherny stands near the spot where her fiancée, also a physician, jumped in 2004. Afterward she learned that he had planned a surprise birthday party for her two weeks later.

SOURCE: *San Francisco Chronicle*

Renee Milligan visits the bench at a state park that was donated in memory of her daughter, Marissa Imrie. When she was 14, Marissa took a cab to the Golden Gate Bridge and jumped.

SOURCE: *San Francisco Chronicle*

In 2004, filmmaker Eric Steel set up cameras for a year and captured images of people jumping from the Golden Gate Bridge. He was criticized by Bridge District officials for misrepresenting his intentions, and praised by suicide barrier advocates for bringing the problem to light in a way that couldn't be ignored.

SOURCE: *San Francisco Chronicle*

Eric Hall (left), his two sons, and father were sailing on the bay in 2011
when a 15-year-old girl jumped from the Golden Gate Bridge. Hall
raced to the dive platform at the back of the boat and lay halfway in
the water to grab her, astonished to learn that she was still alive. He
kept her afloat until the Coast Guard arrived; she survived.

SOURCE: *Contra Costa Times*

EIGHT

The Barrier Debate

I'm an artist, and aesthetics are important to me. But
beauty that takes lives becomes ugliness.

—Mary Zablotny, whose son jumped in 2005

Knowing that the Golden Gate Bridge is the most popular suicide
site on earth, one is led to ask several obvious questions: Why
doesn't it have a suicide barrier? Why, among the world's great
architectural wonders, is America's most famous bridge the only
international landmark that people can jump off of so easily? Why
have the deaths been allowed to continue when, everywhere else,
preventative measures have been taken?

The answer to these questions is tied to the public's attitude
about suicide. For many people, suicide is morally reprehensible.
It's against their religion, or against their culture, or contrary to
their personal values.[1] Like other unpleasant subjects—incest,
disease, discrimination—it's avoided.

---

1. At one time Christianity, Judaism, and Islam took harsh positions when
it came to suicide. The Catholic Church considered suicide the work of the
devil and didn't permit memorial services or burial within the church for persons who killed themselves. Among Jews, suicide was a moral wrong, a rebel-
lion against God, and rabbis ruled that no mourning rites would be observed.

Some people believe that suicide is a choice, an individual's prerogative, and doesn't merit prevention or intervention. Further, persons who want to die should be allowed to do so; after all, it's their life. If they feel that it no longer has meaning, that they're worn out, or that they're a burden to others, they should be able to let go with society's blessing.

Overriding everything is the fact that suicide is so alien to most people—after all, the goal is to live longer, not shorter—that they believe it's impossible to dissuade someone who's intent on dying. This belief is a product of our Western culture, which emphasizes rational thought. We assume that all human behavior, including suicide, is rational when it's not. Some people are more likely to develop a mental illness than others, but all of

---

In Islam, Muhammad proclaimed that suicide victims were denied paradise and spent eternity in hell.

These attitudes have softened in recent years, partly because of greater understanding about why people die by suicide and partly because the public is more aware of the role played by mental illness. The result is a nuanced acceptance. For Christians, God can have mercy on people who kill themselves because they're not in their right minds, thus suicide isn't a sin. For Jews, people who can't cope with their problems and end up taking their lives now receive all rites of mourning because their actions are considered the result of temporary insanity caused by depression. For people of Islamic faith, the decision of whether a suicide victim goes to heaven or hell is in God's hands, as is everything else (in this regard, suicidal terrorists who believe that their acts will hasten entry to paradise are thought to interpret traditional Islamic teachings in a perverse and self-serving manner).

Culturally, some forms of suicide may be condoned, or all forms may be denounced. In India, the practice of *suttee,* where a wife throws herself on her husband's funeral pyre to prove her devotion to him, has been common for hundreds of years. The British government banned it in 1829; however, it continues in some areas today. In many Asian countries, the stigma of suicide is so strong that "mental illness" literally translates as "crazy illness." People readily seek treatment from doctors for physically injuries, but the closest they will come to admitting any kind of mental illness is to complain of headaches.

us—regardless of gender, age, race, culture, religion, sexual orientation, or socioeconomic status—have the potential to kill ourselves. This is what makes suicide so terrifying. Every person is a potential risk if his or her life spins out of control. As a society, we're afraid to acknowledge this, so instead we assume that suicidal people are different. We distance ourselves from them in order to protect us from a reality that we don't want to confront, much less accept.

Given this, it's understandable why suicide isn't talked about and why the usual compassion that people show others isn't evident. The prevailing sentiment seems to be: Why bother? Why invest time, energy, and resources in preventing people from doing something that seems unpreventable? In the United States today, with industry and technology all around us, with freeway overpasses, railroad crossings, and subway tracks everywhere on which to throw oneself, with an abundance of firearms that can be purchased on virtually any street corner, with over-the-counter drugs sold in bulk at thousands of places for quick and easy consumption, it's easier to take your life now than ever before. Why not just let people do it? It's legal, after all. Allow the rest of us time to turn our heads so that we don't have to look, and you can make a permanent exit.

The answer, quite simply, according to those who know, who have lost loved ones to suicide, is because if it was your son or daughter, sibling, parent, spouse, partner, or friend climbing over the railing, you'd want them to be saved. If you were there, and there was no physical reason for them to want to die, you'd be reaching for them frantically, trying to pull them back, working desperately to talk them out of it. If you knew that your loved one was headed to the bridge, or had a loaded gun, or had stockpiled medication, and planned to end his or her life, you'd do anything to stop the attempt. You'd stop it because you know something that your loved one doesn't—that suicide is a permanent response to what may be a temporary or manageable problem. Unfortunately, it takes time for someone to learn this. With suicide, time is the one commodity that's usually in short supply.

This brings us to the issue of a suicide barrier on the Golden Gate Bridge. There are three main arguments against a barrier. The first one is cost; a suicide barrier will be expensive. The second one is aesthetics; the Golden Gate Bridge is beautiful and a suicide barrier will mar it. The third reason has to do with effectiveness; if there's a barrier on the bridge, people will just kill themselves another way, so what does it matter?

In terms of cost, there's no question that a suicide barrier costs money. The actual amount is subject to debate—Bridge District officials estimate that each of the five options they considered, ranging from various forms of a taller railing to the option they chose, a net underneath, will cost $50 million. While it may be possible to construct a deterrent for less, the bottom line is that it won't be cheap. Then again, it also costs money to put airbags in cars, fences around swimming pools, child-proof caps on medications, and employ lifeguards at beaches, yet few people complain. These actions save lives.

As noted earlier, the original design for the Golden Gate Bridge included a railing that was five-and-a-half feet tall and angled in such a way as to make climbing over it difficult, but during construction the height was reduced to four feet. Lowering the railing at that point had little effect on the final cost of construction, and if the five-and-a-half-foot railing had been used as planned, the bridge still would have come in under budget.

Today, or course, it's a different story. Adding structural elements after the fact is a lot more expensive than incorporating them into the original design. Still, the district has a history of approving other types of additions to the bridge even when the cost is in the millions. For instance, in December 2003 a special barrier was erected on the Golden Gate Bridge to protect bicyclists from vehicle traffic. The barrier cost $5 million and was approved by the Bridge District despite the fact that no bicyclist had ever been killed on the bridge. What was the rationale? "Public safety" according to Denis Mulligan, chief engineer of the Golden Gate Bridge from 2001 to 2010 and currently CEO and general manager of the Bridge District.

The Bridge District also has approved a median on the bridge separating oncoming vehicle traffic. The cost estimates have ranged from $10 million to $20 million and held up construction, although Bridge District board members and staff are firmly committed to it for a simple reason: "Public safety," Mulligan says again. Since 1937, when the Golden Gate Bridge opened, fewer than forty people have died in traffic accidents on the bridge. That number pales in comparison to the more than fifteen hundred people who have leaped to their deaths. Thus, it's reasonable to wonder why a suicide barrier on the bridge isn't considered a public safety issue given the number of people who have died, and why it doesn't have the highest priority.

That said, money is still an issue. In today's economy, with the nation struggling to come out of a recession and the State of California plagued by huge deficits, funding for projects like this is hard to come by. It becomes a question of priorities.

Many people believe that addressing the root cause of Golden Gate Bridge suicides—mental illness—makes more sense than erecting a barrier. Instead of spending millions of dollars on a suicide deterrent, they say, use the money to treat people before they become so desperate that they want to kill themselves. Dave

Kahler used to be one of these people. In 2003, Kahler's thirty-two-year-old son jumped off the south end of the bridge, not venturing far enough out to land in water. Instead, he struck ground.

John Kahler had been diagnosed with bipolar disorder a decade earlier. He had a history of violence and needed to be institutionalized, but there were no long-term residential treatment options available to him. As a result, John lived at home with his widowed father, who tried to regulate his medications and behavior as best he could.

The day he died, John stood before Dave at 9:30 in the morning looking unusually well dressed, at least for him. There was a crease in his pants and he was wearing a green lumberjack shirt. Dave commented that he was "looking good" and asked John where he was going. John said he was visiting a friend in San Francisco. Dave challenged him on it because it was a Tuesday and he knew that the friend worked nine to five during the week. John mumbled something and hurried out the door.

Dave didn't give it much thought. John was an adult, with a car. Moreover, his attitude seemed more positive lately. "He was into a good space," Dave says, "taking meds that seemed to be working."

According to coroner's records, John's body was recovered at 11:20 A.M. so he probably didn't stop anywhere on the way to the bridge. Dave got a call at 3 P.M. from the San Francisco coroner's office asking if he knew a John Kahler. Dave replied that John was his son. The coroner asked Dave to describe the clothes that John was wearing, which he did. There was no need for Dave to physically identify the body; the clothing description matched. Because John landed on the ground, he still had his wallet, and his clothes weren't ruined by water.

The day before John's suicide, early in the afternoon, a woman was beaten to death along a popular walking trail. The trail was close to the Kahler's home and John Kahler was identified as a "person of interest" in the police investigation. Dave Kahler is adamant that this had nothing to do with this son's decision to jump. John died before the murder was public information; in fact, interest in John intensified only after police learned that he killed himself. Nevertheless, over the next few days Dave Kahler had little time to grieve. All of his energy was focused on clearing his son's name. Eventually, DNA tests exonerated John Kahler and implicated another man for the murder.

Ironically, John Kahler isn't considered a Golden Gate Bridge suicide. This surprised Dave Kahler when I told him. Since the autopsy was done by the San Francisco coroner, who doesn't attribute any fatalities specifically to the bridge, the cause of death is merely a fall from a great height. The fact that John's body was found below the bridge doesn't make any difference. Officially, it's the same as if it had been found in the courtyard of a hotel, the street below an apartment complex, or the foot of a high-rise office building.

Dave Kahler is convinced that his son's suicide was the result of a broken mental health system. Continuing cuts in funding have resulted in diminished services, overworked and overwhelmed staff, and only a small number of beds in treatment facilities for mentally ill people. The result is that family members have no choice but to become their children's own case workers. The answer, according to most mental health consumers and family members, is more money to pay for more resources. That's why Kahler originally was opposed to erecting a barrier on the Golden Gate Bridge. The cost wasn't worth it. He didn't oppose suicide deterrents, and in fact today supports a barrier. He just thought that $50 million could shore up some of the problems in the current mental health system, which ultimately would benefit more people.

The obvious point is that we should not have to make a choice, we should not have to choose between a bridge barrier and expanded mental health services. Practically speaking, however, there isn't enough money to do both, but that's only because the cost of fixing a broken mental health system far exceeds existing resources. The cost of a suicide deterrent on the Golden Gate Bridge, by comparison, is modest.

What's interesting is that there's evidence Californians—a majority of them anyway—really are interested in funding mental health services. The evidence comes in the form of Proposition 63, also known as the state's Mental Health Services Act. California voters passed it by more than a 2 to 1 margin in 2004, then reaffirmed it in a special election in 2009. The proposition added a 1 percent tax on individual incomes above $1 million with the money going to support local mental health programs. Admittedly, a major reason why it was approved was because most voters weren't personally affected. It did apply to 28,000 people in the state, though, with the resulting revenues—soon reaching $1 billion per year—representing the first new infusion of funding for mental health services in California in decades. A key provision in the act was that the money couldn't be used to supplant current mental health funding. Authors of the bill didn't want to repeat the mistake made years earlier when Californians approved a state lottery on the assumption that the revenues would provide new money for education, then saw state legislatures cut education funding and backfill it with lottery earnings. Prop 63 has opened the door for some new and innovative mental health programs; however, its passage also has coincided with major reductions in mental health services being made at the state level. The result is that new mental health programs are being funded and launched at the same that core mental health services are being defunded and dismantled. The hoped-for transformation of the system isn't occurring.

This as much as anything speaks to both the challenge and the benefit of funding a suicide deterrent on the Golden Gate Bridge. The challenge is reaching agreement on why money should be allocated when there are multiple, pressing needs. The benefit is that once a barrier is erected, the impact will be immediate and measurable, and no one will be able to take it away. Unlike proceeds from the state lottery or the Mental Health Services Act, which were implemented with grand intentions, there won't be negative consequences down the road. The barrier will be there as long as the bridge is standing, and suicides from the bridge will end.

In 2009, California Governor Arnold Schwarzenegger pushed for and got a rare, mid-year election. On the ballot were six propositions the governor said would help balance the state's budget. One proposition authorized the state to raid proceeds from the Mental Health Services Act for four years. California voters rejected it, as well as four of the five other proposals that Schwarzenegger championed. Even so, the election made clear that California leaders consider special pots of funding, designated by voters for specific purposes, to be at their disposal. Indeed, one of Jerry Brown's first acts after he succeeded Schwarzenegger as governor was to raid Mental Health Services Act funding.

A bridge barrier isn't like that. Once it's up, it's up. It's not subject to debate or money grabs.

It's hard to argue with the need to expand mental health programs and services. Yet there are no easy answers as to how this should be done or how it can be sustained. In contrast, the solution to the problem of suicides from the Golden Gate Bridge is clear and requires only a one-time expense. In the short term, it may not benefit as many people as using the money to patch holes in the current mental health system, but over time its impact could be greater, especially if one considers that at least six people—family members and close friends—mourn each suicide, and many others are affected.

Moreover, money for a suicide barrier on the bridge doesn't have to come out of mental health funding. In all likelihood, it probably won't. The Golden Gate Bridge is a key link in California's transportation system, and it's reasonable to think that transportation funds can be used to pay for a suicide deterrent the same way that they pay for other bridge improvements.

It's worth noting that in earlier days, when the economy was robust, there was considerable funding for public works projects and the Bridge District was operating with a surplus. The opportunity existed to deal with the problem for a fraction of the current cost—$200,000 if funded in 1953; $3 million if funded in 1993. Even as late as 2005, the Bridge District estimated that a barrier could be erected for $15 million. Doing nothing seems to drive up the cost almost exponentially, to say nothing of the emotional cost incurred by families of the deceased.

Bridge District CEO Denis Mulligan disagrees with the notion that delays result in high costs. He says that recent studies pertaining to a net indicate that the district has a clear picture of the costs, and the current budget numbers are real. Previous numbers weren't as flushed out, he says, or were provided by people who had a vested interest in selling a particular product. Furthermore, he believes that the current cost—$50 million, including $5 million already received from the Metropolitan Transportation Commission for final plans—is legitimate and will increase only nominally the longer it takes for the remaining funding to be raised. Time will tell if he is right.

The second reason why there isn't a suicide barrier on the bridge—and the argument that produces the strongest emotions among opponents—is because it will impact bridge aesthetics. The Golden Gate Bridge is beautiful; people come from all over the world to see it. The view from the bridge is equally breathtaking. Why ruin it with a suicide barrier?

After Casey Brooks jumped, John Brooks vowed that other parents would be spared the pain he and his wife were enduring. The only way to do that, he decided, was to join others who had lost loved ones to the bridge and advocate strongly for a suicide barrier. He knew it wouldn't be easy, however. In an opinion piece that was printed in the *San Francisco Chronicle,* Brooks wrote:

> We Americans hate to be inconvenienced, hate needless expenses imposed on us, and abhor any limitations on our personal freedoms. But this is not a popularity contest. We would probably not have helmet laws, seat belts, airbags, gun laws, controls on dangerous substances, to name a few—if they were put up for a public vote. We need a suicide barrier because we are supposedly a civilized and compassionate society that cares about the safety of our fellow citizens. This is a moral imperative.

Brooks acknowledges the passion behind the argument. It's not easily dismissed. Still, "by making 'the view' more important than saving lives," he wrote, "the message we're sending is that a few lives lost every month is but a small price to pay to preserve 'the view.' How do you defend that? Doesn't that make us look incredibly barbaric and at the very least shallow, selfish, and uncaring?"

Many people don't know that there actually is a barrier at the southern end of the Golden Gate Bridge. It's an eight-foot-high cyclone fence, 350 feet long, and has been there nearly thirty years. There's nothing pretty about it, but then it's not there for aesthetic purposes. It's there to protect people below, at Fort Baker, from being struck by debris tossed over the side. "We protect people from garbage," offered Eve Meyer, executive director of San Francisco Suicide Prevention, referring to this fence. "We just don't protect them from killing themselves."

Some of the designs proposed in the past for a suicide barrier on the Golden Gate Bridge would use flexible steel rods that are so thin they would be invisible from shore. You couldn't see them unless you were on the bridge, and if you were on the bridge they wouldn't block your view; they would just block someone from jumping.

A somewhat different design was used at the Prince Edward Viaduct in Toronto, Canada (also referred to as the Bloor Street Bridge because it connects Bloor Street with Danforth Avenue). Until 2003, this bridge was the second-deadliest suicide site in the world (after the Golden Gate Bridge), with nearly 500 fatal jumps. Then $4 million was spent on a "luminous veil" of stainless-steel rods constructed above the bridge's existing railing. Funds were allocated following the death of thirty-five-year-old Martin Kruze. Kruze jumped from the bridge after a man who was convicted of abusing him as a child received a lenient sentence in a well-publicized trial. Before he jumped, Kruze walked past toll-free phones that connected to the city's suicide hotline. The addition of a suicide barrier on the Bloor Street Bridge achieved the desired effect—the number of suicides dropped to zero and has stayed there. Of equal interest is the barrier's aesthetic beauty. Architect Dereck Revington envisioned that the 10,000 steel rods would create an open yet impenetrable wall and make the bridge look "strung like a Stradivarius." His barrier received the Canadian national engineering award for design elegance. Many people thought that aesthetics were enhanced because of it. Today, the barrier is referred to as "lifesaving art."

Lorrie Goldin is a clinician in the Bay Area. At one time she didn't have strong feelings one way or the other regarding a suicide barrier on the Golden Gate Bridge. What caused her to become a strong advocate for one was when a colleague told her about a fourteen-year-old boy who lived in Marin County and took a bus to school everyday in San Francisco. One day after school the boy got off the bus near the bridge, walked out on the span, and put his leg up over the railing, intending to jump. A variety of things were troubling him, and death would end his pain. At the last instant he changed his mind, took another bus home, and told his mother. She sought help for him immediately. That was in 2005.

"He's fine now," Goldin says, noting that in many instances "impulses pass, circumstances change, help is found, the balance toward affirming life over death shifts." Goldin's own daughter was fourteen at the time—one reason why the story resonated so strongly with her.

> Any lingering ambivalence I felt about the barrier evaporated. So much of the barriers to a barrier have to do with our failure to identify not only with the person who is suffering but with the hope that lies beyond the moment. A bridge barrier will not save every life, but it will buy precious moments that will save many lives.... Suicide

is not a freak accident, but a real and preventable risk. Imagine if it were you or someone you loved was about to swing a leg up over the rail. You might find the money and the ability to get used to a slightly different fabulous view."

The third and most-often cited reason against erecting a suicide barrier on the Golden Gate Bridge—and other bridges—is the mistaken belief that someone intent on suicide will go somewhere else to jump or, being thwarted, choose another lethal means. Opponents of a barrier use this argument as an alternative to appearing unsympathetic. They claim that if a barrier truly prevented suicides, they would be in favor of it. But if people really want to kill themselves, it's impossible to stop them, so why bother?

This belief in the inevitability of suicide is contradicted by the facts. For instance, it used to be that the most popular method of suicide in England was sticking one's head in the oven and turning on the gas. People died of asphyxiation in a matter of minutes. One psychologist referred to this as "the execution chamber in everyone's kitchen." Poet Sylvia Plath took her life this way in 1963. After oil and natural gas deposits were discovered in the North Sea, however, the majority of English homes converted from coal gas, which has a high carbon monoxide content, to natural gas, which is cheaper and much less toxic. With the conversion, the number of suicides by gas dropped from an annual high of 2,368 in the 1950s and 1960s to a low of 11 in recent years. Moreover, the country's overall suicide rate decreased by 26 percent. Since then, the suicide rate in England has remained at the lower level despite periodic high unemployment, which is directly linked to suicide. When it was no longer possible to die by breathing oven fumes, people didn't resort to another means.

Similarly, when the Australian government banned automatic and semiautomatic guns in 1996 after thirty-five people were killed in a shooting rampage, the number of firearm suicides dropped in half and has stayed there, while the number of suicides by other means has not increased. In 2006, the Israeli Defense Force stopped letting soldiers take their weapons home with them on weekend leaves. The suicide rate dropped 40 percent almost overnight with no increase in firearm suicides on weekdays.

In 1978 Richard Seiden, a psychology professor at the University of California in Berkeley, published a study titled "Where Are They Now?" The study was focused "towards answering the important question, 'Will a person who is prevented from suicide in one location inexorably tend to attempt and commit suicide elsewhere?'" To find out, Seiden and a team of graduate students tracked what had happened to 515 people who had attempted to jump off the Golden Gate Bridge and were stopped. Using a list provided by the California Highway Patrol, and crosschecking it against death certificate records, Seiden found that 94 percent either were still alive twenty-five years later or had died by means other than suicide. Only 6 percent subsequently ended up taking their own lives.

"At the risk of stating the obvious," Seiden told Scott Anderson, a *New York Times Magazine* reporter who wrote about Golden Gate Bridge suicides in 2008, "people who attempt suicide aren't thinking clearly. They might have a Plan A, but there's no Plan B. They get fixated. They don't say, 'Well I can't jump, so now I'm going to shoot myself.' And that fixation extends to whatever method they've chosen. They decide they're going to jump off a particular spot on a particular bridge, or maybe they decide that when they get there, but if they discover the bridge is closed for renovations or the railing is higher than they thought, most of them don't look around for another place to do it. They just retreat."

Seiden, now retired, told Anderson about a young man he interviewed who had decided to jump from a particular spot on one side of the Golden Gate Bridge. Somehow, by mistake, the man ended up on the other side of the bridge. Eventually he was nabbed by police because he couldn't bring himself to dart across six lanes of traffic—he was too afraid of being hit.

In 2006, three professors at the Harvard School of Public Health published a study regarding the public's belief in the inevitability of suicide. They surveyed nearly 3,000 adults across the country and asked them if they thought a suicide barrier on the Golden Gate Bridge would save lives. More than two-thirds of respondents said that most bridge jumpers would kill themselves another way, with 34 percent believing that *every single* jumper would have died by suicide regardless of whether the bridge had a barrier. The strongest predictor of this belief was owning a firearm. Forty-five percent of firearm owners believed that persons intent on dying would resort to any means available to kill themselves. The second strongest predictor was cigarette smoking; 43 percent of smokers believed that a person who wanted to die wouldn't be stopped by a barrier.

"These findings," wrote the authors, "suggest widespread and, at least among one-third of Americans, deeply held skepticism about the potential effectiveness of suicide prevention efforts, which rely on restricting access to highly lethal and commonly-used methods. It also may help explain why there has been little public demand to construct a suicide barrier on the Golden Gate Bridge."

Obviously, the people who were surveyed hadn't heard of Richard Seiden's study. In addition, they probably didn't know that only three of the thirty-two people known to have survived a jump from the Golden Gate Bridge have subsequently died by suicide. Most have chosen to live.

In 2008 the National Suicide Prevention Lifeline, a network of 150 independent crisis centers that collectively answer calls to America's two main suicide hotlines—800-273-TALK and 800-SUICIDE—issued a position paper in response to an increasing number of requests from transportation and bridge authorities who wanted to install bridge phones and signage with the Lifeline number rather than a safety barrier. Phones and signs are cheaper than barriers, and don't impact aesthetics. John Draper, a psychologist and the director of the Lifeline, drafted the paper. In addition to the "luminous veil" that was constructed at the Prince Edward Viaduct in Toronto, Draper noted a number of other instances where the addition of a suicide barrier on one bridge eliminated suicides from that location and didn't lead to increased suicides on neighboring bridges.

For example, from 1979 through 1985, twenty-four people died jumping off the Duke Ellington Bridge in Washington, DC. In 1986, an eight-foot-high anti-suicide fence was constructed. The fence was the result of three suicides in a ten-day period and the intense lobbying of Ben Read, former deputy secretary of state. Read's twenty-four-year-old daughter had died by jumping from the bridge. In addition, there were reports that one young woman had been thrown off the bridge while another had been held over the edge and told that she'd be dropped if she didn't submit to an attacker's sexual demands. Five years after a barrier was installed, only one person had jumped from the bridge. Furthermore, there was no increase in the number of suicides from the nearby Taft Bridge, which didn't have a barrier.

Another example is the Memorial Bridge located in Augusta, Maine. Between 1960 and 1983 there were fourteen suicides from the bridge; after a barrier was installed, the number of suicides dropped to zero. Two decades later, Dr. Andrew Pelletier, a researcher at the Centers for Disease Control and Prevention, reported that no other site in the area registered an increase in suicides after the barrier went up. Furthermore, there was an overall decrease in the number of suicides in the city. Pelletier concluded that the bridge barrier "was probably effective in lowering the overall suicide rate in Augusta."

Even so, in 2004 the Augusta city council debated whether the barrier was still needed. The bridge no longer was a magnet for suicides, and it was due to be renovated. City council members voted 7 to 1 to retain the barrier. "Some see that fence as something ugly," one council member told the local paper, "but I see it as something caring. The fence is a symbol that tells motorists and pedestrians that the capital city is concerned about the mentally ill who live here."

Draper cited examples from around the world. In Bristol, England, a partial barrier was erected on the Clifton Suspension Bridge. Over five years, the number of suicides from the bridge was cut in half, from eight to four. Researchers concluded that there would be even fewer suicides if a full barrier was in place. Moreover, they noted that there was no increase in jumps from other bridges. In Auckland, New Zealand, safety barriers were removed from the Grafton Bridge in 1996 after being in place sixty years. Over the six years following the removal there were fifteen bridge suicides. When the barriers were reinstalled in 2003, suicides from the bridge ended.

Closer to home, there were eighty suicides from the Arroyo Seco Bridge in Pasadena, California, from 1913 to 1936—so many that locals referred to it as the "Suicide Bridge." The bridge is 150 feet above a water-carved canyon, and was especially popular as a suicide site following the Great Depression. After a barrier was installed, there was only one suicide from the bridge in the next thirty-six years.

In 2006, England's National Institute of Mental Health studied a variety of "suicide hotspots," including bridges. The report concluded by saying, "The most effective form of prevention at jumping sites is a physical barrier, which literally restricts access to the drop." The Lifeline paper ends much the same way: "Decades of research clearly demonstrate that barriers are the most effective means of preventing [bridge] suicides."

In 2005, the Journal of the American Medical Association published the most complete review to date of suicide prevention strategies. Twenty-three physicians and scientists from the United States, Europe, and Asia authored the review after studying forty years of published scientific research. They concluded that the two most effective ways to prevent suicide are to restrict access to lethal means and to train health care professionals to recognize suicide warning signs and intervene when the risk is present. Treatment such as counseling and prescription medication provides long-term benefits, but in the moment, when a person feels that life is unbearable and suicide is the only way out, barring access to means—a gun, drugs, tall building, or bridge—makes all the difference.

The *JAMA* report noted that according to seventeen published studies, the rate of suicide deaths in gun-owning households is three to five times higher than in households without guns. At the same time, where guns are present, safety procedures such as using gunlocks and properly securing ammunition reduce the risk of suicide by two-thirds. The article also noted that in Australia, suicide from sedative overdose increased when medications were relatively easy to procure and decreased when access was restricted. A similar result occurred in England when legislation was passed in 1998 that limited the pack size of analgesics and prohibited pharmacies from selling more than thirty-two tablets per customer (non-pharmacies were restricted from selling more than sixteen tablets per customer). In 2004 the *British Medical Journal* reported that after the legislation was implemented there was a 22 percent reduction in suicides related to acetaminophen overdoses and a 30 percent reduction in liver transplants and hospital admissions to liver units (overdosing on acetaminophen severely damages the liver).

California's 2008 "Strategic Plan on Suicide Prevention," issued by the state Department of Mental Health, supports the *JAMA* findings. It notes, "Restricting access to lethal means can put time between the impulse to complete suicide and the act itself, allowing opportunities for the impulse to subside or warning signs to be recognized."

Despite this evidence, people hold onto the mistaken belief that someone who is suicidal will resort to any means available. Paul Muller of the Bridge Rail Foundation offers this response:

Much of what science tells us about the world we live in is counter-intuitive. Think about the relationship between the sun and earth. When I get up in the morning I see the sun rise in the east, then creep across the southern sky and set in the west. Everything about my experience says the sun revolves around the earth. And historically people believed this so fervently that it became a matter of religious faith. Yet now we know the earth revolves around the sun. So, too, with suicide. Common sense tells us that if a suicidal person cannot get a gun, he or she can just get a knife. If there are no knives, then pills will do. Yet the research tells us something very different. Restricting easy access to a single means of suicides reduces suicides. In every case studied where it was harder to get access to guns or poisons or carbon monoxide, the number of suicides went down. The same is true with bridges.

Scott Anderson, in his *New York Times Magazine* article, wrote, "If a man shoots his wife amid a heated argument, we recognize the crucial role played by the gun's availability. We don't automatically think, Well, if the gun hadn't been there, he surely would have strangled her. When it comes to suicide, however, most of us make no such allowance."

Thomas Joiner is a psychology professor at Florida State University and one of the preeminent suicide researchers in the country. In a recent book, *Myths about Suicide*, he dispels a number of false beliefs. One of them is the myth of means substitution; that is, if one method of suicide is unavailable, people will choose a replacement method. Imagine, he writes, if someone you know, a loved one, had a heart attack or stroke and was refused medical treatment because the prevailing public policy was that it didn't make sense to intervene, the person would just have another heart attack or stroke anyway. "It would be an outrage even if it were true," Joiner writes; that's no reason to deny care. Besides, it's not necessarily true that someone who has suffered from a heart attack or stroke will have another one. The odds may be greater; however, there's no certainty that it'll happen to any one individual. The same is true with suicide. Some people are at greater risk, especially if they've made an attempt before, but that doesn't mean they're sure to kill themselves. Far from it. No other public health problem is so stigmatized or misunderstood.

"It is unconscionable that a suicide barrier has not been erected on the Golden Gate Bridge," Joiner concludes. "The problem is not money and aesthetics, though if it were that would be appalling enough. The problem, rather, is ignorance and prejudice."

A different approach to countering the argument that people who are thwarted from one means of suicide will resort to another means is to apply that same thinking to a related project. Consider, for example, the planned multi-million-dollar meridian on the Golden Gate Bridge separating oncoming vehicle traffic. According to Paul Muller,

> If you think in terms of traffic safety, we build median barriers to prevent head-on collisions. Drunk or drowsy drivers cause many of these collisions, but who objects to building these barriers? Has anyone ever suggested that "the drunks will just go down the road, so don't bother with a barrier"? Likewise, no one believes that median barriers will solve drunk driving, but we recognize they are one necessary element in reducing the most extreme tragedies. Bridge barriers and nets do the same for suicides. They are not the solution, but one necessary means to reduce the most extreme tragedies.

Another argument against a barrier is that the number of people who jump off the Golden Gate Bridge is a small fraction of the total number of people who die by suicide in this country. Why focus only on them? Are their lives worth more? It's true that the number of suicides from the Golden Gate Bridge is negligible compared with more than 3,000 suicides per year in California, representing only 1 percent of the total. This doesn't mean that they're irrelevant, however. "Every suicide and accidental death is tragic," as John Brooks says.

> But if we have such an obvious, blatant, and shameful magnet for death in our community, how on earth can we be so blasé about it? If a few people a month jumped from a downtown high-rise—even if that accounted for a small percentage of the total—don't you think that access to that roof would be immediately barred? How about a particularly dangerous stretch of road notorious for deadly crashes? We don't ignore them because the fatalities are small relative to total fatalities. One life is not worth any more than another, but when this is so in-our-face, how can we ignore it?

It's interesting to note that if we were talking about reducing the homicide rate, even minimally, everyone would be in favor of it. Yet nearly twice as many people kill themselves every year in the United States as are murdered—35,000 suicides versus 18,000 homicides—and yet there are people who oppose taking action that would save lives.

In *November of the Soul: The Enigma of Suicide*, George Howe Colt wrote, "Clearly, we cannot and should not make the world 'suicide proof' nor our lives a twenty-four-hour suicide watch. Even if we could, suicides would of course still occur. But even if bridge barriers and gun control legislation were to have no effect on the suicide rate, there may be compelling reasons why such measures should nevertheless be taken. To put up or not put up a barrier says something about the way we feel about suicide and suicidal people." Colt recounts his conversation with a friend who believes that it's unfair to ruin the view for the sake of a few, and who asks, "If they want to die so much, why not let them?" Colt responded, "It troubles me that so many otherwise kindhearted people should object to preventative measures. For how far is it from this passive condoning to the voices one sometimes hears when a crowd has gathered at the base of a tall building to watch the weeping man on the ledge high above, shouting, 'Jump, jump, jump?'"

It turns out that it's not far at all. As Tad Friend reported in the *New Yorker*, an engineer named Roger Grimes walked back and forth on the Golden Gate Bridge for several years wearing a sandwich board with a heartfelt message: "Please Care. Support a Suicide Barrier."

"He gave up," Friend wrote, "stunned that in an area as famously liberal as San Francisco, where you can always find a constituency for the view that pets should be citizens or that poison oak has a right to exist, there was so little empathy for the depressed."

"People were very hostile," Grimes told Friend. "They would throw soda cans at me, or yell, 'Jump!'"

Heidi Benson was one of the *San Francisco Chronicle* reporters who contributed to the newspaper's 2005 seven-part series on Golden Gate Bridge suicides. She wrote, "The assumption that suicide is not preventable is an enabling one. It enables the public to remain passive."

It is this passivity more than anything else that fuels the suicide barrier debate. People who believe that a barrier won't make a difference see no reason to have one. Why spend money to ruin the view when the impact is negligible?

Mary Zablotney doesn't buy it. As the mother of an eighteen-year-old son who jumped from the bridge, she's incensed that people are so unconcerned. "What kind of monster would stand there before me and tell me that aesthetics are more important than my son's life?" she wrote in a blog. Several people responded that it wasn't the bridge's fault. Individuals who use the bridge as a place to kill themselves, they said, are to blame.

Their comments had the same tone as gun owners who maintain that firearms aren't responsible for the country's high homicide and suicide rates—that the people who use them inappropriately are.

What has been ignored is the fact that at least three children under age five have died because the Golden Gate Bridge didn't have a suicide barrier. Their fathers were able to throw them over the railing because it was so low. These children weren't trying to kill themselves; they were murdered. The Golden Gate Bridge was the weapon.

Also ignored is the fact that bridges are supposed to be safe. A net was installed during construction to protect the workers. A barrier was built to protect bicyclists. A meridian will be erected to protect motorists. If the bridge is going to be accessible to pedestrians, then people who walk on the bridge need to be protected, too, sometimes from themselves. A taller railing would do that. So would a net. To let the deaths continue and take no immediate action to stop them runs counter to the policy governing every other roadway in this country, as well as every other one-time suicide magnet in the world.

In 1979, a thirty-three-year-old woman in Berkeley, being treated for depression, used what little money she had to take a bus to San Francisco, then a cab to the Golden Gate Bridge. She scribbled a note of apology to her seven-year-old son, then walked out on the span. In her words, "I had been suffering from severe, immobilizing, tortuous depression for several months, and was simply obsessed with killing myself to end the agony that no medication seemed to touch." She took off her glasses ("I figured if I couldn't see the water too clearly, it would be easier to jump"), and climbed over the railing onto the thirty-two-inch-wide beam on the other side. She couldn't bring herself to jump, though, and climbed back onto the pedestrian path. Then she climbed over the railing again, trying to summon the will to fall. Once again her survival instinct was too strong, and police were able to intervene. A few weeks after that she was put on new medication and her depression lifted. "I was suddenly back to normal, no longer in torment," she said. Twenty-five years later, she has had no further thoughts of killing herself.

In one of his many letters to the editor following the death of his daughter, John Brooks wrote, "Before this tragedy, I had never had a close encounter with suicide, never gave a suicide barrier a second thought, and pretty much felt that a suicidal person could not be stopped. The Golden Gate Bridge was nothing more than the highlight of my daily commute from Marin [County] to San Francisco. Imagine how it feels now?"

Ever since her son jumped, Mary Zablotny has referred to the Golden Gate Bride as "that damn orange thing." It's impossible for her to see any beauty in it, she says.

Renee Milligan, the mother of fourteen-year-old bridge jumper Marissa Imrie, doesn't see any beauty in the bridge, either. "I just feel haunted by it," she said. "And living in the Bay Area, you can't get away from it."

Milligan's comments were made to a reporter shortly before she testified in 2005 to a Bridge District committee that, once again, was considering a suicide barrier. "I'm here for all the moms, all the dads, all the aunts and uncles and sisters and brothers who have lost someone on the Golden Gate Bridge," she told committee members. "Yes, my daughter must have been suffering from some type of mental illness and you might say, 'How did you miss it, Renee?' I was there, I would pick her up from school, I don't know how I missed it, but I did."

"We are given a rare opportunity to make a difference, to save lives, to decrease suffering," says psychiatrist Mel Blaustein. "As people of conscience, how can we allow these suicides that we can prevent to continue?"

How, indeed?

Epilogue

The way to end suicides at the Golden Gate Bridge and every other problem bridge in the world is simple and straightforward: erect a barrier. In every instance in which a barrier has been added to a bridge, tall building, freeway overpass, or train crossing, suicides from that site have been reduced dramatically or ended altogether. Moreover, once a barrier—either a tall railing or a net—has gone up, suicides haven't increased from neighboring sites, nor have most people who fixated on the bridge decided to kill themselves another way. Many members of the public choose to believe otherwise, but their belief is based on intuition rather than facts.

A national study of bridge suicides is the first step in addressing this public health issue. To date, there hasn't been such a study even though suicides have occurred from more than sixty bridges in the United States. In contrast, a study was commissioned quickly after a spate of suicides at railroad crossings on the San Francisco Peninsula, south of the city. The study, to be completed by the American Association of Suicidology and funded by the

Federal Railroad Administration, aims to answer why particular sites become hotspots for train suicides, and why people—especially young people—choose that means of death.[1] In addition, a rail safety campaign called Common Sense was launched to reduce pedestrian deaths from trains, and on the Peninsula security has been beefed up along fifty-two miles of tracks. According to Caltrain spokespersons, the agency spent more than $17 million in 2009 for signs, fencing, and pedestrian gates at street crossings to try and prevent train-pedestrian fatalities. Still, there were eleven Caltrain suicides in 2010, and nine through the first half of 2011.

In California, sixty people per year, on average, are killed by trains. Many of these aren't suicides—joggers, transients, and others are struck unintentionally. It leads one to ask, though, why bridge suicides which occur just as frequently receive less attention. One reason may be because of plans for future high-speed rail service between northern and southern California. Suicides along existing tracks engender negative publicity that could deter development.

No such consideration comes into play with bridge suicides. In fact, one has to go back to the 1950s and 1960s to find anything remotely analogous. That's when it was proposed that the Bay Area Rapid Transit (BART) system be expanded into Marin County by adding train tracks on the underside of the Golden Gate Bridge. A New York engineering firm, hired by the Bridge

---

1. In 2009 there were fifteen train suicides on the Peninsula, and eight train suicides through the first nine months of 2010. The majority of victims have been teenagers, including four students in the span of six months from Gunn High School in Palo Alto. The crossing where each of them was killed is 1.7 miles from the school. Another crossing is closer. Meanwhile, several other high schools in the area are situated right next to the tracks yet have had no train suicides.

District, reported that the bridge could support two trains on it at the same time if the trains didn't go faster than thirty miles per hour. A subsequent report by Clifford Paine, one of the bridge's original engineers, said that the added weight of the trains, tracks, and passengers would cause the roadway to sag up to eight feet, potentially jeopardizing the entire structure. Ultimately, the Bridge District board vetoed the idea before any thought was given to the aesthetic impact of tracks and trains on the bridge.

In many cities, concerns for safety are prompting action. Suicide barriers have been added in recent years to bridges in Pasadena and San Pedro, California, as well as bridges in Maine, Ohio, Massachusetts, and Washington, DC. Outside the United States, barriers have been installed on bridges in Auckland, New Zealand; Sydney and Melbourne, Australia; in Montreal and Toronto, Canada; and in Bristol, England.

Currently, a Milwaukee sheriff is advocating for a suicide barrier on the Hoan Bridge, the site of sixteen suicides in the past ten years. Barriers also have been approved or are being considered for the Cold Spring Bridge in Santa Barbara, CA, the Coronado Bridge in San Diego, CA, the Sunshine Skyway Bridge in Tampa, FL, the Rio Grande Gorge Bridge in Taos, NM, and the Tappan Zee Bridge in Nyack, NY. Predictably, opponents in each of these communities are citing reasons that are identical to arguments against a suicide deterrent on the Golden Gate Bridge: (1) suicidal people will kill themselves another way so it doesn't make a difference; (2) the number of people who jump represents a small portion of local suicides; and (3) the barrier will negatively impact bridge aesthetics.

The Aurora Bridge in Seattle, WA, formally referred to as the George Washington Memorial Bridge, has been the number two suicide site in the country after the Golden Gate Bridge. Since the bridge opened in February 1932, about 250 people have died jumping from it, including the first suicide, by a thirty-two-year-old shoe salesman, a month before the bridge was even completed. Through the first eleven months of 2010 there were three suicides from the bridge. The Aurora Bridge is similar to the Golden Gate Bridge in several ways. It's an historic landmark, included in the National Register of Historic Places. Also, it's tall, although at 180 feet the roadway isn't as high as the roadway on the Golden Gate. In addition, there are walkways on both sides of the bridge, which offer easy access for pedestrians. Finally, the bridge's owner and operator, the Washington State Department of Transportation, installed six emergency phones and signage on the bridge in an attempt to reduce suicides, with no effect.

After years of debate regarding the need for a deterrent, work started in August 2010 to end suicides from the Aurora Bridge. A barrier nearly nine feet high, originally estimated to cost $8.1 million but reduced to $4.6 million because steel costs were down and local construction companies bid competitively for the job, was approved by Seattle's landmark preservation board and the state legislature. Completed in February 2011, the barrier consists of steel rods spaced close together on each side of the bridge. In addition to saving lives, the barrier frees emergency workers from having to respond to bridge jumps, according to city officials, as well as spares people who live and work in the area below the bridge—an area that has become increasingly developed—from witnessing a frequent tragedy.

Tim Durkan is one of many people to breathe a sigh of relief. He's the Lake Union District coordinator for the City of Seattle, where the Aurora Bridge is situated, and his office is directly underneath the bridge. In a blog and subsequently in an e-mail conversation with me, he talked about what that has been like.

> It gives me shivers and saddens my heart even thinking about it.... One of the last successful attempts was during a discussion with my nineteen-year-old college intern (on her first day) about what to do in case a jump occurred. The words hadn't left my lips when we heard the man's scream and the horrible impact fifteen feet from our front door. Words could never describe.... The tourists walking by, the driver heading to lunch, and the crumpled body of a dying man outside our office on N. 34th—all frozen in a horrible moment. Despite the efforts of myself and two medics who happened to be training across the street by coincidence, there wasn't anything to be done except place a blanket over the body.... I think about him a lot—his scream, the horrible impact, and watching him pass as I knelt over him."

Unlike the Golden Gate Bridge District, the Washington State transportation department opted for a taller railing after considering a net. Officials felt that a net would obstruct bridge inspections, ensnare birds, collect trash, and present risks to emergency personnel who responded to bridge jumps. Thus, raising the railing made more sense.

Tourists don't flock to the Aurora Bridge for the view, though, the way they do to San Francisco's famous span. Moreover, the Golden Gate Bridge is longer and more heavily trafficked than most other bridges, which adds to the cost of making it safe.

Until things change, the Golden Gate Bridge will remain an anomaly, an icon of beauty and death. Millions of people will continue to come from all over the world to see it, while twenty-five to thirty-five people per year will continue to jump from it. Since the bridge opened, it has simultaneously inspired more dreams and ended more lives than any other structure on the planet.[2]

The installation of a net on the Golden Gate Bridge is moving quickly or slowly, depending on whom one talks to. Denis Mulligan, general manager of the Bridge District, says it took "only two-and-a-half years" for the environmental impact report to be completed. "That's one of the fastest EIRs in California," he told me, "faster than it took San Francisco to complete an EIR for the city's bike plan, which is a much less complicated project." Mulligan says that Caltrans didn't do as thorough a job in preparing for the Cold Spring Bridge suicide barrier. As a result, it opened the door for a lawsuit that's delaying the process more.

Some barrier proponents aren't so sure that the district is truly committed to ending suicides on the bridge. A 14-to-1 Bridge District board vote in favor of a net seems convincing. It seems to indicate a strong desire to stop bridge suicides. It seems to indicate a willingness to make the bridge safe for the first time. It seems to recognize the pain and suffering that loved ones of bridge jumpers have endured, while demonstrating a sincere commitment to spare others from the same fate. Yet since October 2008, when the net was approved, progress has consisted of an environmental impact study and $5 million in funding from the Metropolitan Transportation Commission to finalize architectural and engineering plans—funding that the Bridge District didn't solicit

2. One bridge that eventually may eclipse the Golden Gate Bridge in terms of suicides is the Nanjing Yangtze River Bridge in China. Nanjing has a population of six million people, many of whom cross the four-mile bridge every day. At least one suicide occurs per week from the bridge, which is 130 feet above the Yangtze River. The Chinese government has used guards, signage, and even butter (butter is smeared on bridge railings so that they might be too slippery to climb) to try and discourage suicide attempts. To date, nothing has worked.

(state assemblyman and former board member Tom Ammiano requested it). District officials have taken no action to try and raise any of the remaining $45 million needed for construction. They say that that they'll cooperate in every way with efforts to secure federal funding, but suicide prevention advocates have to lead the charge.

At the same time, the district is moving ahead with plans to upgrade the visitor information area in anticipation of events commemorating the bridge's seventy-fifth anniversary in 2012. And that's just the beginning. The long-term goal is to raise enough money from donations and sales of bridge memorabilia to build a museum and visitor center near the toll plaza that showcase stories of the bridge's history. While board members and staff can't find money for the net, they don't mind actively fundraising for the museum. Once again, a project aimed for tourists is taking priority over improvements that will save lives.

Members of the Bridge Rail Foundation are working to secure funding for the net. In November 2010, Bridge Rail convened a meeting of supporters and family members to map out a strategy intended to "make the net real." First up was to reintroduce in Congress an amendment to the National Transportation Act that allows local authorities to apply for federal transportation funds for construction of suicide deterrents on bridges. It's not forbidden now, but it's not expressly permitted. After that, the strategy was to advocate for the addition of $200 million to the Federal Highway Administration's $41 billion budget in order to pay for a net on the Golden Gate Bridge and deterrents on other bridges that have become suicide sites. Unfortunately, when the new Congress was seated in 2011 the chair of the committee that oversees transportation issues, as well as most of the committee members, many of whom had been contacted by Bridge Rail volunteers, were no longer in office or no longer on the committee. Now the education process and the building of support have to start all over.

While supporters are frustrated, they're also encouraged by the fact that the Golden Gate Bridge is closer to having a barrier than ever before. A deterrent has been approved. A net has been chosen. An environmental impact report has been completed. Final plans have been funded and are being drafted.

Advocates are well aware, however, of the urgency in accomplishing their mission. Every month that there isn't a suicide deterrent on the Golden Gate Bridge, two to three more people die. Five to seven more people attempt to jump and are stopped. Countless others continue to think about jumping, and possibly formulate plans.

Of equal importance, social movements depend on momentum. Past efforts on behalf of a suicide barrier have petered out, and advocates are determined not to let that happen again. The Bridge Rail Foundation's traveling "Who's Shoes?" exhibit in which the footwear of many Golden Gate Bridge jumpers is displayed at strategic locations, is designed to keep pushing the issue. Ongoing meetings with key lawmakers, as well as continuing efforts to inform the general public through print and electronic means, are having an impact, too.

"This is what keeps me going," John Brooks says of the fight for a suicide barrier. It's too late for his daughter, Casey, but it's not too late for the daughters, sons, spouses, siblings, parents, and friends of other potential victims.

Brooks and thousands of others who have lost loved ones to the Golden Gate Bridge have made the ultimate sacrifice. When the deaths end and the bridge has a barrier, these sacrifices won't be known to future generations who have been spared a similar tragedy. Families and friends won't know that their loved one is alive because the world's number one suicide magnet no longer exerts a deadly pull. They won't know—except in a general way—of the losses that others have suffered, largely in anonymity, or even that their loved one would have been at risk because jumping from the bridge was so easy. There won't be any thought given to the fact that the bridge is now safe from suicide, much less any thanks to the people responsible for it.

Brooks was laid off from his job at Wells Fargo Bank several months after Casey's death. He and his wife also moved. Recently, he completed a 425-page memoir that he's trying to get published about being a father and losing his only child to suicide from the Golden Gate Bridge. "The basic arc of the story," he says, "is how I wanted so much to be a dad in life, struggled to become a dad, then a good parent, and then lost it all. The resolution comes out of how I reconcile that and find some way to reclaim at least something of what I lost."

One concern for bridge barrier proponents is what's going to happen to the primary source of information about Golden Gate Bridge suicides, the Marin County coroner's office. Effective January 1, 2011, it was merged with the sheriff's department and coroner Ken Holmes retired, as did Gary Tindal, the longtime assistant coroner. A sergeant has taken over, and one of the three investigators in the coroner's office has been laid off. The question is whether the new coroner, coming from the law enforcement side, will be as proactive in analyzing and publicizing Golden Gate Bridge suicide data as Holmes. If not, then that's another reason to move quickly on the barrier front, before the extent of the problem ceases to be reported. (In August 2011, just before this book went to press, I tried to get updated information from the current coroner; he didn't return my calls.)

Of final concern, work is nearing completion on the $6.3 billion project to replace a section of the nearby Bay Bridge. This bridge has two sections, one running from Oakland to Yerba Buena Island and the other from the island to San Francisco. It's the second section, from Yerba Buena Island to San Francisco, that's being rebuilt. In at least three ways, the new section is being modeled after the Golden Gate Bridge. First, at its highest point the roadway will be 220 feet above the water, the same height as the Golden Gate. Second, there will be a fifteen-foot-wide pedestrian path (to this point, pedestrians haven't been allowed on the Bay Bridge). Third, in order to provide sweeping views, the railing will be only four feet, seven inches high—just tall enough to comply with the current fifty-four-inch minimum height requirement of railings on bridges, but not tall enough to keep someone from jumping. Although mental health professionals have advocated for a taller railing, and members of the Coast Guard, among others, worry that pedestrian access is going to lead to more suicides, construction is proceeding according to the original design.

More public mobilization is needed. The toll exacted month in and month out is lost to everyone except those who are directly affected—loved ones, witnesses, police officers, and Coast Guard personnel.

In the fall of 2010, a sixteen-year-old girl jumped from the Golden Gate Bridge after she had been stopped three times previously by the Bridge Patrol. The fourth time, police officers were too late. According to her bereaved parents, the lure of the bridge was too strong. At about the same time, one of my board members at the Contra Costa Crisis Center told me the story of a friend of hers who said that she didn't know anyone who had died by suicide. Then, just a few days later, a person the friend knew well, a man whom she swam with regularly in a community pool, jumped off the Golden Gate Bridge. The woman was so shaken that it was months before she was able to return to the water. No longer does she have the luxury of being unaffected.

In March 2011, a high school student from Windsor, CA, jumped off the bridge while on a field trip with forty-five class-mates and two teachers. He became the thirty-first person to survive the fall when he was rescued by a surfer, taken to shore, and transported to San Francisco General Hospital. He told the surfer that he jumped "for kicks." The incident raises a whole new specter of alarm. Will others be foolish enough to try and test their luck and survival skills this way?

While the jumper was being treated for broken bones, many of his classmates were in shock and needing mental health services. Undoubtedly, it will be a long time before they're able to forget the horror they witnessed—if they're ever able to forget it. In all likelihood, from this point forward they'll associate the bridge with their classmate's leap. So, one imagines, will school admin-istrators, who probably won't plan future field trips to the bridge. And what of the jumper himself? Will he be idolized or ostracized? Encouraged to get help or motivated to test fate again?

A month later, in April 2011, another teenager jumped. She, too, survived, in large part due to an extraordinary series of events.

Four or five times a year, Eric Hall, his two teenage sons, and his father rent a boat for the weekend and go sailing in and around San Francisco Bay. Usually they rent a vessel that's built for rough seas given that the bay is characterized by strong tides, major swells, and heavy winds. This particular weekend, how-ever, none of the boats they normally rent was available. To their

dismay, they ended up with a Beneteau 373, which has a high pro-
file in the water, high sides, a small rudder, and isn't designed for
inclement weather. Instead, it's designed for staying in one place,
and has a dive platform off the rear.

Normally the Halls drop anchor Saturday night in Paradise
Cove, on the eastern side of the Tiburon peninsula. They sleep on
the boat, have a leisurely breakfast Sunday morning, then sail
across the bay to San Francisco where they follow the waterfront
under the Golden Gate Bridge and out into the open sea. This
time, for reasons Hall can't explain, they dropped anchor in Rich-
ardson Bay, on the western side of the peninsula, got up early
Sunday morning, and sailed from Sausalito across the shipping
lanes. This put them in closer proximity to the Golden Gate
Bridge for a longer period of time.

Around 10:30 A.M. on Sunday, near the bridge, Eric Hall noticed
a smoke flare in the water. He also noticed an ambulance on shore
racing to Fort Point, on the San Francisco side of the bay. In addition, there were people on the bridge pointing down to something. Hall's boat was the only boat in the area, and his youngest
son thought people were pointing to a whale. As their boat drew
close, however, the Halls could see, through heavy fog, that it was
a partially submerged body. The person's face was covered with
blood, which was wiped away as ocean water swept over it. Eric
Hall assumed that whoever it was was dead. Then he heard a faint
moan and saw the person vomit saltwater. That's when he became
excited. It meant the person was still alive.

Hall did a quick stall, dropping the sails, putting the boat's
motor in neutral, and heading into the wind. He tossed several
devices into the water—a rescue horseshoe and a life sling—but
the person was unconscious and couldn't take them. He then

jumped from the helm to the back of the boat, lay down on the dive platform, snagged the body with a boat hook, and held onto it by the scruff of the neck, his own body half in the water. He didn't want to lift the person onto the boat because he or she might have broken bones so he just held on, trying to keep water from washing over the person's face. He told his younger son to be the spotter, to keep his eye on the person in case Eric lost his grip. Meanwhile, his older son took the helm while Hall's father radioed the Coast Guard.

Fortunately, the Coast Guard had been alerted and already was en route. After several minutes—time that "seemed like an eternity," Hall says, "like forever"—a boat pulled up alongside the Hall's boat. Two Coast Guard crew members, near the waterline, snatched the body with boat hooks and hauled it on board. It was only at that time that Hall realized the person he saved was a girl, Asian, with short black hair. He didn't know her age—sixteen—until it was reported in newspapers the following day. It also was reported later that the girl, from southern California, had been vacationing on the bridge with her family when she handed her diary to sister, then jumped. The diary contained a suicide note.

The girl was taken to Marin General Hospital. At last report, she was the thirty-second person known to survive a fall from the Golden Gate Bridge.

"It was a very odd day for all of us," Hall tells me. "So many unique things came together. We were in a boat we didn't like, but it turned out to be perfect for grabbing someone in the water. We spent the night in a place we don't normally go to, left earlier in the morning than usual, took a different route than usual, happened to be in the exact spot to find someone—in heavy fog—whose body was mostly submerged, and we were capable of dealing with it. Also, the Coast Guard was already in the area, and she was alive. It all happened exactly perfect."

He adds that they also had exactly the right number of people on board—four. Any fewer and an important task would have gone undone, while any more and they would have run into each other.

Hall, who grew up in the Bay Area, says that although he has sailed in and out of San Francisco Bay many times, he never gave the Golden Gate Bridge much thought before this.

"It used to be," he says, "that we'd sail under bridge and one of us—usually one of my sons—would say, 'I hope no one jumps on the boat.' After this experience, we won't say anything like that again. After this experience, I'll never be able to think of it [the bridge] the same way."

While one might hope that this is the last time such heroic action is needed on behalf of a bridge jumper because preventative measures have been taken, the reality is that it won't be. Indeed, only a few weeks later, in May 2011, a fifteen-year-old girl from Danville, CA searched for directions to the Golden Gate Bridge on her computer. Then she rode her white and purple mountain bike to a BART station nine miles away, boarded a train to San Francisco, got off at the Embarcadero Station, pedaled across the city to the bridge, and jumped.

Her body wasn't found after a two-day search, and it is apparent that she died.

"We have evidence that shows she walked onto the bridge around 10 A.M., but never walked off," Bridge Patrol captain Lisa Locati told the press. Locati didn't say what the evidence was, but in all likelihood it was a review of surveillance tapes for that day. Shortly thereafter, one thousand people attended a candlelight vigil in the girl's memory.

It is time—past time—for action. Only through a concerted effort of study, public mobilization, and construction of a safety net can we end the sad litany—more than fifteen hundred and growing—of Golden Gate Bridge suicides.

May that day come soon.

APPENDIX A

EXPLAINING SUICIDE

About one million people around the world die by suicide annually. It's impossible to obtain precise statistics because many countries don't maintain—or at least don't make public—data about it. High rates of suicide reflect poorly on those in charge. Moreover, suicide is underreported, mainly because of stigma. As a result, one million is considered by many to be a conservative estimate. Still, it's equal to the number of people who are killed in wars around the globe every year.

In the United States, more than 35,000 people die by suicide annually. To put that number in perspective, it's equivalent to 9/11 occurring almost every month. It's also the equivalent of a fully-loaded commercial airliner crashing every two days. By comparison, there are about 18,000 homicides in the United States every year. A person wouldn't know it from reading or watching the news, where each day brings fresh stories of violence, but almost twice as many Americans die by suicide as are murdered.

If this fact seems surprising, one reason why is because of media coverage or, in the case of suicide, the lack of it. The social taboo that keeps individuals from talking about suicide—unless a celebrity is involved—also keeps media outlets from covering it. Another reason is television. It's estimated that by the time a person reaches age eighteen in this country, he or she has seen 40,000 murders portrayed on TV. Every day of the week, on network and cable stations, people are shot, stabbed, strangled, poisoned, dropped, drowned, burned, or blown up in various dramas. There are suicides, too, of course, but they're not proportionate—the same viewer will see roughly 800 suicides during that time. Audiences know at some level that what they're seeing isn't real. With the advent of so-called "reality" shows, however, the distinction becomes blurred. Thus, the mistaken belief exists that murder is common while suicide occurs less frequently. In fact, it's the reverse. Suicide is much more prevalent than most people— particularly most Americans—realize.

Whenever someone dies by suicide, loved ones and friends invariably ask the same question: Why? Why did he or she do it? There's no satisfactory answer because it's almost impossible for anyone who hasn't seriously contemplated suicide to assume the frame of mind of someone who dies that way. At the simplest and most basic level, there's the explanation of Nick Adams's father in Ernest Hemingway's short story, "Indian Camp." The elder Adams is a doctor who delivers a woman's baby at the same time that her husband, who's also in the room, slashes his throat. Nick witnesses the horror and asks his father why the Indian killed himself. "I don't know, Nick," the father replies. "He couldn't stand things, I guess."

It's reasonable to think that a suicide note provides telltale clues; however, this is rarely the case. First off, only 20 percent of suicide victims leave any kind of note. Most don't. Few members of the general public have ever seen a suicide note. Second, there aren't any rules about what one should include in the note or even who it should be addressed to. Does one ask for forgiveness from loved ones, cite reasons of rejection and isolation in order to hurt others, or provide general instructions about money and insurance or the disposal of the deceased's remains? Third, among the relatively small number of people who do leave a note, the contents tend to be so meager that they lack the passion and desperation usually associated with suicide. In many instances, the note appears to be an afterthought.

This is the case with notes left by Golden Gate Bridge jumpers. In 1969, a doctoral student at the University of California at Berkeley, Ronald Tauber, working with Dr. Richard Seiden, compared authentic notes left by ninety-seven jumpers from three Bay Area bridges, the majority from the Golden Gate, with notes that were hoaxes (i.e., made to appear real but in fact weren't connected with a real jump). The biggest difference he found was that the fabricated notes contained more content and feeling than the authentic notes. Indeed, of the authentic notes Tauber said, "It is as if some of the suicides were, in a psychological sense, dead when they penned the note." Here are a few samples:

"My darling, I cannot ask for forgiveness but I can say that I've loved you with all my heart. Please try and make a new life which you so richly deserve."

"Dear Mother, everything I have done has been a lie. Everything Dad did was a lie. I am going to do away with myself before I do further harm to people."

"Honey, I know that anything I have done or do is all on myself. Something was and is wrong with my makeup and there is not anything that anyone can do about it. I love you. Goodbye."

"Spent all day yesterday walking around San Francisco deciding what to do. This is the only thing I could do with all the trouble I have caused. Please remember I loved you very much. Take the insurance money and settle the bills."

Because there are rarely clear answers to the question of why someone decides to die by suicide—after all, suicidal behavior is complex, and usually precipitated by multiple causes—it's often left to researchers to explain. The challenge is that while suicide is a universal phenomenon, affecting all ages starting as young as ten, all ethnicities, all cultures, and all socioeconomic groups, the incidence of suicide varies considerably between nationalities, races, religions, and professions, as well as between men and women. Suicide rates around the world are highest for the elderly, for example, and in every country except China elderly men are at greatest risk. In China, elderly women have the highest suicide rate. In the United States, elderly white men have the highest rate, especially those living in western states. Seniors of other races, as well as those living in the East, have lower rates. Among youths, Native Americans are most at risk, gay and lesbian teens have elevated rates, and girls attempt suicide three times more often than boys, although more boys die by suicide than girls. How does one explain the differences?

Physicians and prostitutes have high rates of suicide, but why? Suicides increase during times of economic crisis and decrease during times of national crisis, but why? It's a fact that far fewer people died by suicide in the United States on February 22, 1980—the date of the Olympic hockey team's "Miracle on Ice" victory—than on any February 22 in the preceding 20 years or the following 20 years, but why?

How is it possible to understand mass suicides in cults? Why is suicide associated more frequently with anorexia than with bulimia? Why is self-injury by cutting or piercing a gateway to suicide even though it's rarely intended as a suicidal act?

It's like trying to put together a puzzle when some of the pieces missing. One may think that he or she knows what the puzzle is supposed to look like, but with empty spaces it's hard to know for sure.

In 1897, a French sociologist named Emile Durkheim published the first empirical study of suicide. Citing a variety of statistics, Durkheim concluded that: (1) suicide is more common among men than women, although women make more suicide attempts, (2) the elderly are more likely to die by suicide than younger adults or youths, (3) individuals who are divorced have higher rates of suicide than those who are married, and (4) adults who are childless kill themselves more often than adults who are parents.

Durkheim discounted the influence of mental disorders and psychological distress in explaining suicide. Instead, he believed that suicide rates were related to social factors, in particular to social integration. Simply put, when people feel part of a larger group they're less likely to attempt suicide, and when people lack social bonds the likelihood of suicide increases. Working people are more integrated than those who are jobless, Durkheim reasoned, which explains why suicide rates are lower during boom times when unemployment is low and higher during recessions when unemployment is high. Married people, as a rule, are more socially connected than those who are single, divorced, or widowed, Durkheim said; therefore, they're more protected against suicide. Parents with children are even more protected because they tend to be more integrated. Durkheim cautioned, however, that married people living in societies where divorce is common are less protected than those living in societies where divorce is rare.

Geographic mobility is a factor, too. Durkheim observed that starting in the latter half of the nineteenth century people were moving farther away from home in order to pursue educational opportunities, employment, and a better way of life. Once on the go, they continued to move, resulting in the disruption of social networks and kin support, which are especially needed during times of crisis. In 2001, the national Centers for Disease Control and Prevention reported that frequent moves are one of the more significant predictors of suicide.

From the vantage point of current research, there's a lot to critique in Durkheim's work. For one thing, Durkheim considered suicide to be predictable and regular when it's neither. Suicides do occur with predictable regularity, and some populations are at greater risk; however, even in instances where a group such as elderly white men has a high rate, the vast majority of people in the group never attempt suicide. Moreover, we know now that individuals who have seriously considered killing themselves and even may have made an attempt don't think about suicide every waking moment of the day. The desire to die, to be free of suffering, comes and goes. In addition, suicidal feelings vary in intensity depending on a variety of factors—they're not static. Thus, it's difficult to predict when or if an attempt will occur.

Attributing suicide entirely or even primarily to social factors also is flawed. While some external circumstances such as divorce, job loss, death of a loved one, or failure in school can precipitate a suicide attempt, they're considered triggers rather than causes. Instead, mental disorders—in particular severe depression that's untreated—play a major role, especially when combined with alcoholism. According to the National Institute of Mental Health, up to 90 percent of the people who die by suicide suffer from major depression, schizophrenia, or bipolar disorder. Not everyone who's mentally ill is a suicide risk, however. The majority of people with mental disorders don't kill themselves. At the same time, mental illness substantially increases the risk.

Durkheim's definition of *suicide*—when a person consciously does something or avoids doing something that leads to his or her death—also is debatable. It includes heroic sacrifice, for instance, and excludes madmen when today it's the reverse; heroic sacrifice usually isn't viewed as suicide and the death of a madman—a lone gunman or suicide bomber—is. In addition, Durkheim failed to acknowledge the moral reasons and material interests (such as life insurance benefits) that lead suicide to be underreported. Also, in explaining the disparity between suicide rates by age, Durkheim didn't note that questionable deaths of youths are less likely to be declared suicides because youth suicide carries the greatest shame, while seniors not only have fewer people left to care about them but they also may have no one around to hide the cause of death.

That said, Durkheim's work still represents a milestone. It demonstrated the value of statistics and methodology, laying the groundwork for future research. Indeed, the June 2008 issue of *Suicide and Life-Threatening Behavior,* a publication of the American Association of Suicidology and the principal journal in the United States for suicide studies, noted that Durkheim's book, published iii years earlier, was cited forty-four times in academic articles from 1997 to 2001, ranking it eighteenth among 8,004 reference sources.

In 1918, a year after Emile Durkheim died in Paris, Edwin Shneidman was born in Pennsylvania. The juxtaposition of

Durkheim's death and Shneidman's birth wasn't exactly a passing of the torch. Shneidman, a psychologist who was educated in southern California, was more interested in individual behaviors than social behavior. He made the study of death—thanatology—and in particular suicide the focus of his professional life when, early in his career, he was asked to write condolence letters to the widows of two veterans who had died by suicide. In researching their cases, he discovered a vault at the Los Angeles County Coroner's office that contained all of the suicide notes that the office had collected over the years. There was so much data, unmined at that point, that Shneidman felt as if he had struck gold.

In the next fifty-plus years, Shneidman published twenty books and hundreds of articles on suicide. He wrote the entry for *suicide* in the *Encyclopedia Britannica*, a book he read in its entirety in high school. He founded the Suicide Prevention Center in Los Angeles, which in 1958 launched the country's first suicide hotline. Six years later he founded the American Association of Suicidology, which today is the preeminent suicide research institute in the United States. During a three-year stint as the head of suicide prevention studies at the National Institute for Mental Health, he traveled to forty states sharing his views as a clinician and researcher of the unbearable psychological pain that leads people to contemplate suicide. This pain, for which he coined the word "psychache," is the key to understanding suicidal behavior, Shneidman maintained. Social statistics and physiological factors have a place, but suicide is the desperate action of individuals in extreme emotional duress who can't see other options for relief. Backed into a corner psychologically, they resort to the one option that's available to them and offers a guaranteed end to their pain.

Shneidman said that the only way to explain suicide is to delve into people's private history, to learn their personal stories and glimpse the emotional circumstances behind their desire to die. When one does this, conducting what Shneidman called a "psychological autopsy" to determine a person's intentions, the most perplexing of all human behaviors starts to make sense.

He had little regard for research that studies physiological factors. "You don't understand psychopathic murder by slicing [Jeffrey] Dahmer's brain," Shneidman said in a *Los Angeles Times* interview in 2004, "and you won't get $E = MC^2$ by slicing Einstein's brain. Unfortunately, it's in the mind. And the mind is not a structure. It is an ephemeral concept."

There's growing evidence, however, that decreased levels of serotonin in the brain contribute to feelings of depression and, thus, influence suicidal behavior. Serotonin is a neurotransmitter and sometimes is referred to as one of the "feel-good" hormones. Decreased amounts have been found in patients who are depressed and have a history of suicide attempts, as well as in the postmortem brains of suicide victims (drugs such as Prozac, Paxil, and Zoloft often are prescribed to reduce depression because they increase serotonin levels). Additionally, researchers at Johns Hopkins and elsewhere are beginning to study potential links between chromosomal genes and suicidal behavior, indicating that some people may be genetically predisposed to suicide.

In treating individuals, Shneidman was emphatic in his support for people whose loved ones died by suicide, recognizing that they were at heightened risk.

"The person who commits suicide," he said, "puts his psychological skeletons in the survivor's emotional closet."

Shneidman died in 2009 at age 91, after battling a variety of ailments. To the end, he maintained that in dealing with suicidal people the only two questions any helper needs answers to are "Where do you hurt?" and "How may I help you?" He also continued to write, publishing his last book, *A Commonsense Book of Death*, at age 90. In it he wrote:

> Death is not your ordinary garden-variety topic. There is a whiff of sulfur about it. Death has a Brueghel-like and Hobein-like quality.... It is associated with dread and tears. It has a scary, taboo aura. We don't like to think about it or talk about it. But death—the dying patient, the suicidal person, the grieving survivor—has been my life's topic. Being a professor of thanatology, I could rather be objective about it, until recently. Now, at 90, widowed and existentially alone, death has a definite personal bite to it.

Aaron T. Beck, a psychiatrist, sees the problem of suicide somewhat differently. In the 1980s he created the Beck Hopelessness Scale and Beck Depression Inventory to rate degrees of hopelessness and depression in psychiatric patients as a predictor of suicide. In these models, the more one perceives life events as overwhelming, the more despairing he or she becomes. When events such as the ending of a relationship, death of a loved one, legal problems from being arrested, job loss, financial crises, or medical illness exceed a person's coping abilities and capacity for tolerance, suicidal thoughts and behaviors can develop.

Obviously, people deal with stress in different ways. Moreover, what's unbearable for one person isn't necessarily unbearable for another. Nevertheless, Beck believes, the extent to which a person has developed effective skills to deal with adversity can mitigate feelings of hopelessness. He studied 207 hospital patients who had been admitted five to ten years earlier because of suicide ideation, not for a recent attempt. Before learning what happened to them, he used his hopelessness scale to correctly identify 91 percent of those who ended up dying by suicide. A subsequent study of 2,000 outpatients yielded similar results, with Beck correctly identifying 94 percent of the patients who eventually killed themselves.

Today, experts agree that psychological pain and extreme hopelessness are important pieces of the puzzle, as is social connectedness. At the same time, a key question that virtually no one addressed until fairly recently was this: How do people acquire the ability to kill themselves? Wanting to die is one thing, but acting on it is altogether different. After all, self-preservation is the strongest of all human urges. Voltaire called it "the most powerful instinct of nature." How, one asks, is it possible for some people to voluntarily end their existence before—sometimes way before—age or illness do it for them? Is this a sign of weakness, wanting to escape life, or an indication of fearlessness, being unafraid to die? It's not unusual for anyone who looks down from a great height to imagine what it would be like to fall. Common sense and good judgment stop most of us from doing anything more than imagining it, though, and if there isn't a solid guardrail, we're careful not to get too close to the edge. In the same way, many individuals who want to die can't bring themselves to jump from the precipice, pull the trigger, swallow poison, cut themselves, or otherwise inflict self harm. Yet a smaller number of people have this capacity and, moreover, follow through on it. What makes them different?

Thomas Joiner is the author of numerous books and studies on suicide. Suicide is both a professional interest of his and a personal one because when Joiner was in graduate school, his father drove to an office park a mile from home and killed himself in the back of a van.

Joiner believes that capacity combined with desire is the key to understanding suicide. People not only have to want to die, they have to overcome the natural instinct for self-preservation. How? Through practice and repeated exposure to pain and death. He uses rock star Kurt Cobain's suicide as an example.

As a young man, Cobain was afraid of needles and heights. Eventually, though, by continually challenging himself to surmount these fears, he became a self-injecting drug user and someone who scaled thirty-foot platforms during concerts. Cobain also abhorred guns, and when a friend invited him to go shooting, Cobain wouldn't get out of the car. On later excursions Cobain got out of the car, but wouldn't touch a gun. Still later, he let his friend teach him how to aim and fire. Cobain died in 1994 of a self-inflicted gunshot wound at age twenty-seven. Through continued exposure, he conquered his fear of needles, heights, and guns. In so doing, Cobain "worked up" to the act of suicide, Joiner says, by becoming accustomed to pain and danger.

In much the same way, nonlethal self injury such as cutting yourself with a razor blade, knife, or piece of glass, as well as self-induced starvation (anorexia), is a gateway to suicide, Joiner believes. Though the intent rarely is lethal, cumulative and escalating experiences prepare a person to be less afraid of dying. Similarly, body piercings, tattoos, and cosmetic surgery can increase someone's pain threshold the more he or she has them, progressing to the point where even extreme acts, such as dousing yourself with gasoline and setting your body on fire, no longer seem terrifying.

Past suicide attempts also lead to increased capacity, of course, even if an attempt didn't seem serious to others at the time. Individuals who are, in essence, "trying out" suicide, working it through in their minds in order to decide on a means and perhaps a location, may make some sort of "test run" such as consuming a large but nonlethal dose of medication or visiting a jump site like the Golden Gate Bridge multiple times. This can place them at much greater risk the next time they test because the danger is less threatening to them. While family members and friends may consider these acts as calls for attention rather than genuine attempts, they contribute to a person's ability to overcome the natural instinct for self preservation.

"Some people think that those who commit suicide are weak," Joiner says. "It's actually about fearlessness. You cannot do it unless you are fearless, and this is behavior that is learned."

A person doesn't have to experience pain and injury personally, however, in order to develop the capacity to kill oneself. Joiner believes that repeated witnessing of pain, violence, or injury is sufficient. This explains why physicians and prostitutes have high suicide rates. Every day, through their work, they're exposed to pain and suffering and gradually they become inured to it. The same is true for police officers and servicemen, with an added risk. While physicians and prostitutes have access to drugs that can be lethal depending on how much is consumed, cops and soldiers have even easier access to firearms, which are far more deadly. Oftentimes this access continues long after they've retired because people in these professions tend to keep guns around them.

In this light, it's not surprising that veterans account for 20 percent of all U.S. suicides. While considerable attention has been paid in recent years to the number of suicides among active personnel serving one or more tours of duty, as well as those recently discharged, what's overlooked are the number of suicides by veterans. More than 150,000 Vietnam veterans have died by suicide—three times the number of soldiers whose names are engraved on the Vietnam Memorial. Veterans are twice as likely to die by suicide as non-vets, giving new meaning to the phrase "collateral damage." Once used to refer to civilian deaths that occurred during war, it's being used more frequently now to refer to a high rate of military suicides, both on the battlefield and at home. It's not coincidental that the first confirmed suicide from the Golden Gate Bridge was a veteran.

The capacity to kill yourself isn't enough, however. One must also have the desire, which Joiner says derives either from a perception that a person is a burden to others or to a feeling that he or she doesn't belong. Joiner trained a group of people to evaluate real suicide notes according to the concept of perceived burdensomeness, as well for hopelessness and general emotional pain. What the raters didn't know was that half the notes were written by people who had killed themselves and half were written by people who survived their suicide attempt. The result was that perceived burdensomeness was more prevalent in the notes of those who died than those who survived. The former made more lethal attempts because their desire to die and leave others better off was stronger. There was no statistical difference when the notes were evaluated for hopelessness or emotional pain. These findings support an earlier study in which people who survived a serious suicide attempt characterized their desire to die as a way to relieve others of the burden of caring for them, while people who engaged in self-injurious behavior that wasn't suicidal (primarily cutting) characterized their behavior as an expression of anger or a desire to punish themselves.

Lack of social connectedness—what Joiner calls thwarted belongingness—parallels Durkheim's theory of suicide. In a Norwegian study, one million women were tracked over fifteen years. Those with six or more children had suicide rates five times lower than other women. A Danish study in 2003 compared 18,000 people who died by suicide with 370,000 others who were randomly selected. It concluded that having children—especially young children—is a buffer against suicide. Another study the same year found that twins have lower rates of suicide regardless of their gender, even though there's evidence that suggests twins may be slightly more likely to develop mental disorders than non-twins, which in other circumstances would increase their risk of suicide.

"One of the more interesting facets of the possible association between thwarted belongingness and suicide," Joiner says, "is the 'pulling together' effect at times of national tragedy." When it seems as if people should be most depressed because a calamity has befallen the country, in fact they experience the greatest sense of social connectedness. The shared experience of a crisis increases an individual's feelings of belonging. For instance, suicide rates in the United States declined during World War I and World War II, then increased immediately afterward. They also declined following the assassination of President John F. Kennedy; in fact, a study of twenty-nine U.S. cities found that there wasn't a single reported suicide for eight days after Kennedy's death, from November 22 to November 30, 1963, even though there had been suicides between November 22 and November 30 in the years before and after. Similar data emerged following the 1986 explosion of the Challenger space craft and the 9/11 terrorist attacks. Even people who were physically isolated during these events felt socially connected, as if they weren't alone because people all around them were experiencing the same sense of loss. The country was united in its grief, and individual feelings of depression and despair were counterbalanced by the thought that this was normal, what everyone else was feeling.

For the same reason, suicides rarely occur in concentration camps even though a person's desire to live would seem to be at its lowest point. Despite starvation, cold, torture, and separation from or loss of loved ones, people don't kill themselves (if they survive the death camps, though, they may die by suicide later as noted Italian writer Primo Levi did).

Joiner was able to combine his professional study of suicide with his personal love of sports to demonstrate that the camaraderie and sense of pulling together that result from being a fan provide another form of connectedness. When a city's football, baseball, basketball, or hockey teams—professional or collegiate—win a national championship, there's a temporary decline in the suicide rate. Conversely, after a loss the rate goes up. People literally live and die with the success and failure of their team. The U.S. Olympic hockey team's 1980 victory over the Soviet Union—the so-called Miracle on Ice—came at a time when the Iran hostage crisis had gone on 111 days and Russia's invasion of Afghanistan was a month old. Millions of people in America had never seen a hockey game, didn't know the rules or the names of any of the players, yet were glued to their TV sets and radios rooting the home team to victory. It's not surprising, Joiner says, that the suicide rate in the United States was unusually low that day, February 22, 1980, compared with February 22 twenty years before and twenty years after. (It may have been unusually high in Russia, although there's no data available to verify this.)

Joiner's theory that people die by suicide because they've developed the capacity to kill themselves and have the desire to do so can be applied to mass suicides as well, he maintains. In 1978, in the jungles of Guyana, Jim Jones induced 914 of his Peoples Temple followers to drink grape-flavored Kool-Aid laced with cyanide. In 1997, in Los Angeles, Marshall Applewhite coerced thirty-nine of his Heaven's Gate brethren to ingest a lethal mixture of Phenobarbital and vodka. In both instances, prior to the fateful day there were discussions and explicit rehearsals for suicide, designed to overcome people's fear of dying. On multiple occasions, Jones tested the loyalty of his followers by giving them a drink that he said contained poison (it didn't) and telling them to swallow it. In Jonestown, people worked long hours in oppressive heat farming and constructing buildings, receiving little food— another way that they became accustomed to suffering. In Heaven's Gate, eight of the eighteen men who died had undergone voluntary castrations.

It's possible to argue that a sense of belongingness exists in cults. After all, people work side by side, eat together, worship together, cohabitate, sometimes share sex partners, and often engage in communal child rearing. Outsiders are demonized, adding to the cult's solidarity, and dissidents are expelled. In fact, though, the connection of followers to one another is minimal. Crises are invented to keep the focus on the leader, and close relationships are disrupted so that alternative forms of authority don't develop. As a result, followers don't belong to a group—they belong to the leader, who's not interested in developing community bonds. His interest (cult leaders almost always are male) is exerting and maintaining power.

Understanding why people die by suicide is critical in preventing it. At the same time, no two individuals—even identical twins—are exactly alike. While circumstances may push one person to the brink, causing him or her to consider suicide, the same circumstances can result in different choices for others. It doesn't help that the only person potentially capable of explaining his or her suicidal intentions may not be alive to do so; nevertheless, even people who attempt suicide and survive can't always articulate their motives. If one's judgment is impaired because of a mental disorder, alcohol, drugs, or intense psychological pain, being able to describe accurately what he or she was thinking or feeling at the moment of an attempt isn't necessarily possible. Moreover, it assumes that a person *was* thinking when, in fact, some suicide attempts—especially by adolescents—appear to be impulsive.

In 2001, researchers at the University of Houston studied 153 people who made a nonlethal suicide attempt. What they found was that the vast majority—87 percent—thought about suicide for fewer than eight hours before acting. In fact, for 70 percent their attempt occurred within one hour of making the decision. Most astonishing of all, 24 percent said that they attempted within *five minutes* of deciding to kill themselves. In other words, the interval between thought and action for most of the group was only an hour, and for one out of four people almost no time elapsed between the impulse to kill themselves and the attempt. Clearly, suicide was something that most people in the study gave little thought to despite its enormous consequences.

Examining how people die by suicide can be as important in preventing it as understanding why people resort to suicide. It may lack the weight of existential study—Albert Camus referred to suicide as "the only serious philosophical problem" while Shakespeare's Hamlet poses the question that's at the heart of suicide: "To be or not to be"—at the same time, a study of methods used in suicides has the benefit of being concrete. We may never know for sure why a person takes his or her life, but we can determine with near 100 percent certainty the method used. Gunshot, poison, hanging, jumping, drowning, stabbing, cutting—each is unmistakable.

Worldwide, the leading method of suicide is hanging. People don't always have access to a gun, medication, motor vehicle, cliff, tall building, or bridge, but they can fashion a noose out of just about anything. In China, where pesticides are readily available for agricultural purposes, poison is the top choice. In Norway, which is surrounded by water, a disproportionate number of people kill themselves by drowning. For many years, the most popular method of suicide in Sri Lanka was jumping into a well. Then indoor plumbing was introduced and wells became obsolete. Today, the leading method in the country is pesticide poisoning.

In the United States, where the number of firearms exceeds the number of people, guns are used in 60 percent of all suicides. States with the highest suicide rates—Nevada, Alaska, Idaho, Arizona, and New Mexico—are those with a high percentage of males and liberal gun laws. The reason why more males die by suicide than females even though females make more attempts is because males tend to use a firearm, which almost always is fatal, while females historically have overdosed, which is less lethal and offers more opportunities for intervention.

The choice of method rarely is random. Usually it's related to the means that's most available to a person. Police officers shoot themselves because they have ready access to a firearm. Physicians overdose because they can obtain lethal quantities of drugs easily. Prisoners hang themselves because the only means available to them are bed sheets, shirts, and shoelaces. In *November of the Soul: The Enigma of Suicide*, George Howe Colt noted three unusual deaths: one man killed himself by jumping into a vat of beer, a second man locked himself into a high-altitude test chamber, and a third man lay in front of a steamroller. The means they resorted to were explicable, however, once one learned that the first man was a brewer, the second was an Air Force technician, and the third was a construction worker.

"It takes a tremendous amount of energy to figure out how you're going to kill yourself," one woman told Colt. She considered various options, dismissing them either because death wasn't certain or she didn't want loved ones to find her body. Had she lived near San Francisco, her choice would have been simple— the Golden Gate Bridge. Easy access, no mess, and death a near-certainty. As it was, she parked her car away from home and tried to inhale carbon monoxide. She was found alive, though unconscious, and revived at a hospital. Afterward, she said, "I kept thinking about what would be easiest for everyone else. Of course, the easiest thing would have been if I lived."

Well-known poet Anne Sexton also resorted to carbon monoxide, killing herself in 1974 at age forty-five. Several years before her death she wrote a poem titled "Wanting to Die." It contains these lines: "Suicides have a special language. Like carpenters they want to know which tools. They never ask why build."

The tools, in the case of the Golden Gate Bridge, are simple. No firearms, no pills, no motor vehicles, not even rope or a razor blade. Just hoist yourself over the short railing and in the blink of an eye you're gone. That's what Lois Anne Houston did. Even though she was seventy-five years old and overweight, she was able to surmount the railing without difficulty.

The challenge for those who study suicide, as well as for caregivers and survivors, is to understand as much as possible about what drives someone to the edge—and beyond. The more we learn, the less taboo the subject becomes and the more our misperceptions disappear. This isn't easy when funding for suicide studies is relatively paltry. In 2010, the National Institutes of Health spent $3.1 billion for AIDS research and 1.3 percent of that—$40 million—for suicide research, even though twice as many people in the United States die by suicide as from AIDS.

Thomas Joiner concludes his book *Myths about Suicide* this way: "We need to get it in our heads that suicide is not easy, painless, cowardly, selfish, vengeful, self-masterful, or rash…that it is partly genetic and influenced by mental disorders, themselves often agonizing; and that it is preventable (e.g. through means restriction like bridge barriers) and treatable.…Once we get all that in our heads at last, we need to let it lead our hearts."

APPENDIX B

HELP AND RESOURCES

Anyone who is feeling suicidal or worried about a loved one who might be suicidal can call the National Suicide Prevention Lifeline. The Lifeline consists of 150 independent crisis centers across the United States, and calls are routed automatically to the center nearest the caller. Licensed professionals and highly trained volunteers answer the calls 24 hours per day, 365 days per year, providing confidential counseling and emotional support. The Lifeline also has an extensive Web site.

National Suicide Prevention Lifeline
800-273-TALK (8255)
800-SUICIDE (784-2433)
888-628-9454 (Spanish)
800-799-4TTY (4889; Hearing Impaired)
www.suicidepreventionlifeline.org

The following organizations promote research, education, and training programs to understand and prevent suicide. In addition, the American Association of Suicidology certifies crisis centers across the country while the American Foundation for Suicide

Prevention has a public policy and advocacy division that was enhanced when the Suicide Prevention Action Network (SPAN) was merged into it. All three organizations publish a variety of information as well as maintain comprehensive Web sites.

American Association of Suicidology
5221 Wisconsin Avenue, NW
Washington, DC 20015
202-237-2280
www.suicidology.org

American Foundation for Suicide Prevention
120 Wall Street, 22nd Floor
New York, NY 10005
212-363-3500
www.afsp.org

Suicide Prevention Resource Center
55 Chapel Street
Newton, MA 02458
877-438-7772
www.sprc.org

APPENDIX C

GOLDEN GATE BRIDGE
SUICIDES

Confirmed Golden Gate Bridge Suicides by Year

1937	4	1950	17	1960	11	1970	37	1980	30	1990	11	2000	16
1938	6	1951	12	1961	18	1971	35	1981	29	1991	18	2001	17
1939	5	1952	14	1962	21	1972	40	1982	23	1992	17	2002	27
1940	11	1953	21	1963	18	1973	31	1983	16	1993	23	2003	24
1941	4*	1954	12	1964	28	1974	23	1984	23	1994	39	2004	24
1942	2*	1955	15	1965	14	1975	24	1985	22	1995	45	2005	23
1943	3*	1956	12	1966	18	1976	32	1986	26	1996	23	2006	31
1944	5*	1957	8	1967	28	1977	42	1987	23	1997	33	2007	39
1945	12	1958	16	1968	29	1978	36	1988	13	1998	25	2008	34
1946	7	1959	10	1969	17	1979	32	1989	17	1999	22	2009	31
1947	13											2010	32
1948	24											2011	24*
1949	8											Total	1,575

SOURCES: Golden Gate Bridge District, news articles, Marin County coroner's office
(1991 on)

* Data incomplete

The following is a list of 1,200 people known to have killed themselves by jumping from the Golden Gate Bridge through 2010. The list is comprehensive, but by no means complete. Individuals whose deaths were confirmed but whose bodies weren't identified are excluded. Also excluded are people suspected of jumping but whose jumps weren't witnessed and whose bodies haven't ever been found. The latter includes Leonard Branzuela, Casey Brooks, and Matthew Whitmer, who are discussed in this book, as well as hundreds of others (the Marin County coroner included these suicides in the above table starting in 2006, which accounts for the increase in the past five years). In addition, this list omits the names of the three children under the age of five who were murdered when their parents threw them over the short railing, then followed them to their deaths.

The list was compiled by Dayna Whitmer, Matthew Whitmer's mother. She created it from newspaper articles, archives of Malcolm Glover (a longtime newspaper reporter in San Francisco, now deceased), and names released by the Marin County coroner's office. Because the San Francisco coroner's office doesn't separate Golden Gate Bridge jumps from other falls, no information is available on jumpers whose bodies were autopsied in San Francisco.

I consulted with colleagues and did a lot of soul searching before deciding to include the list in this book. Although death records are public information, victims' families haven't consented to their loved ones being identified. In the end, I decided that the list puts a face on bridge suicides in a way that no statistic can. It's like reading the names of soldiers on the Vietnam Memorial. Also, excluding it would perpetuate the stigma of suicide as something not to acknowledge or talk about.

This list is a memorial to those lost. Publishing it may help people understand the extent of the tragedy, a tragedy that continues uninterrupted today.

Date	Name	Age	Sex
8/7/1937	Harold B. Wobber	47	M
10/2/1937	Louis Levin	60	M
10/5/1937	Rafaello di Regolo		M
11/26/1937	Frank Clevenger	62	M
1/19/1938	John W. Prohoroff	35	M
3/9/1938	Agnes Harrington		F
8/24/1938	Harold M. Juda		M
10/1/1938	Edwin D. Pierson		M
11/15/1938	Albert Ransauer		M
12/30/1938	Ruth Steiner	25	F
2/13/1939	J. M. Silvey		M
4/3/1939	Joseph Tricaso	42	M
4/4/1939	Paul J. Umland	25	M
6/24/1939	George Verhaghen		M
5/14/1940	Matthew Wuerstle	52	M
6/10/1940	Arthur John Fisher	26	M
6/10/1940	Ruth Tumelty	36	F
8/19/1940	Drederick Bisordi	17	M
10/17/1940	Mathias Anderson		M
10/21/1940	Andrew O. Glover	74	M
10/28/1940	Henry J. Flexenshar		M
11/2/1940	Lloyd Edward James	26	M
11/4/1940	Mildred Gibbs	38	F
11/20/1940	Kathleen L. Johnson	45	F
11/21/1940	Warren H. Dickinson		M
1/30/1941	Paul S. Johnson	56	M
2/24/1941	Matthew Gleason	~70	M
3/1/1941	David H. Zimet		M
10/20/1941	Julia B. Hunter	41	F
4/14/1942	Guiseppe Quaresima	52	M
5/26/1942	Julian S. Haswell	60	M
3/22/1943	Charles Lee Brewer	45	M

Date	Name	Age	Sex
10/8/1943	John Mariani	68	M
12/29/1943	Eugene Joseph Fagothey	54	M
2/1/1944	Carl Irvin Oscarson	17	M
3/6/1944	Arline H. Kellner	39	F
4/2/1944	Charles George Baltzer	65	M
6/28/1944	Eveleen Ward	39	F
7/18/1944	Frank C. Reed		M
4/3/1945	Neva Wilson	46	F
July 1995	Edward F. Carnahan	49	M
7/23/1945	Marilyn DeMont	5	F
7/23/1945	August DeMont	37	M
8/28/1945	Annie Hunt	59	F
9/19/1945	Helen Nissen Goree	47	F
9/20/1945	Charles A. Stephens	78	M
9/25/1945	Edward Albert Beurman	58	M
10/31/1945	Carl Ludwig Breitling	37	M
11/1/1945	Justin Dimick French	46	M
11/2/1945	Leola Myers	42	F
11/19/1945	James McCowan	65	M
5/31/1946	Rudolph O. Luders	75	M
7/24/1946	Charlotte Lunn Winton	47	F
8/8/1946	Marie C. Percy	53	F
10/10/1946	Derinda Barber McFarland	46	F
1/20/1947	Marie Borrello	49	F
3/20/1947	Ernest K. Loeres	68	M
4/2/1947	Richard Ernest Ott	46	M
4/19/1947	Carl Hansel	44	M
4/21/1947	Benjamin Harrison Henry	56	M
5/5/1947	Warren Pfander	62	M
5/15/1947	Thomas P. Hughes	28	M
6/26/1947	Margaret Ann Murphy	24	F
8/22/1947	Mark G. Rajkovich	47	M
11/17/1947	Lugo Henry Winfield	52	M
11/19/1947	Meyer Brazer	56	M
11/19/1947	William K. Powell	60	M
1/4/1948	Edna A. Steinmann	48	F

Date	Name	Age	Sex
1/23/1948	Patrick James Warren	59	M
2/6/1948	Alfred "Dusty" Rhodes	32	M
2/27/1948	Jacqueline Felzer	21	M
3/4/1948	Eulis K. Williams	50	M
3/11/1948	Philip Sheridan III	31	M
3/30/1948	Ralph Walter Martin	60	M
3/31/1948	Leona Strauss	55	F
5/21/1948	George Benninghoff	36	M
5/29/1948	Jay Darwin Bacon	56	M
6/13/1948	George E. Studebaker	56	M
6/16/1948	Neal Hammond	66	M
6/28/1948	Fortunato Ornelas Anguiano	50	M
8/5/1948	Miner Waddinton Smith	36	M
8/20/1948	Roy P. Knickerbocker		M
9/23/1948	Gaspar T. Pelletier	39	M
9/30/1948	Noble T. Biddle	44	M
10/5/1948	Andrew Lewis Pomerville	72	M
11/5/1948	Edward Hugo Herr	58	M
11/29/1948	George H. Derr	51	M
12/14/1948	Edward H. Doherty	53	M
12/21/1948	Albet C. Hartford	44	M
1/3/1949	Earl Craw		M
4/7/1949	Philip Capra	40	M
5/23/1949	Marion Paul Hughes	35	M
7/18/1949	Trygve Arnesen	45	M
8/3/1949	Glenn R. Eubank (Burbank)	38	M
8/11/1949	Joseph Edward Kossick	38	M
11/28/1949	August Karl Rauhut	77	M
1/5/1950	Andrew Pearson	63	M
4/7/1950	Quong Lee Jew	70	M
4/13/1950	Henry Feldman	42	M
4/17/1950	George A. Wadham	20	M
5/3/1950	Eleanor Lillian Whelan	71	F
5/12/1950	Alga V. Jones	67	M
6/24/1950	Ernesto C. Guetierrez		M
6/27/1950	John Nestor Soderman	66	M

Date	Name	Age	Sex
7/20/1950	Joseph Jelick	58	M
7/28/1950	John Kiernan		M
8/9/1950	Benjamin Franklin Eastin	64	M
9/17/1950	George F. McNair	59	M
11/7/1950	Anna Shane	44	F
11/16/1950	Joseph Andrew Egenberger	54	M
11/25/1950	George H. Chance	33	M
12/10/1950	Frank Mederios	55	M
12/20/1950	Effie Mae Witt	67	F
3/15/1951	Laura Brower	49	F
3/21/1951	Maude Jessie Cohen	45	M
3/22/1951	Eugene Paton	37	M
4/7/1951	Nora Lee Rohr	50	F
4/18/1951	Edmund Samuel Ciprico	49	M
5/21/1951	Harry Francis Purt	44	M
6/17/1951	Alex W. Partington	44	M
6/30/1951	Margaret J. Easterlin	42	F
7/15/1951	Richard D. Holman	28	M
8/13/1951	Pierre Oron	50	M
2/17/1952	Mae Carroll	46	F
3/6/1952	Carter James Buck	43	M
4/19/1952	Iva Hagemann	46	F
4/21/1952	Gerald W. Whismand	26	M
4/22/1952	Margaret Holmes Durant	61	F
4/25/1952	Martin F. McDonough	39	M
5/1/1952	Eugene Cronin	32	M
6/17/1952	Hollister Benjamin Smith	44	M
7/31/1952	Stephen Noel Podesta	34	M
8/29/1952	Elmer Lee Clark Jr.	22	M
9/8/1952	Gabrielle J. Leibbens	43	F
9/9/1952	Kent M. Barnes		M
12/12/1952	Thomas Davis	54	M
2/13/1953	Bruce McCollum	49	M
3/10/1953	Stanley D. Kasper	26	M
3/10/1953	Ella Christinalar Rohde	58	F
3/18/1953	Ezra David Bourland	37	M

Date	Name	Age	Sex
4/1/1953	Robert Hughes	69	M
Unknown	George E. Ruff Jr.	41	M
6/9/1953	Helen Benjamin	41	F
6/12/1953	Muriel Whelan		F
6/21/1953	Charles H. Raven	41	M
7/1/1953	Ernest Oliver Ames	38	M
8/1/1953	Morris Hirsch	49	M
8/14/1953	Gene Lee White	21	M
8/24/1953	Virginia Crosby Bancroft	49	F
8/23/1953	Arthur J. Cohen, Jr.	39	M
12/1/1953	Marie L. McCormick	24	F
12/7/1953	Everett Lawrence Hubbard	48	M
12/11/1953	Arthur Raymond Burt	61	M
12/18/1953	Gustave F. Aguilar	65	M
4/19/1954	William M. Coulter Jr.	28	M
7/23/1954	Barney William Johnson	66	M
7/30/1954	Mavis Marie Boesch	33	F
9/24/1954	Kay Hagop Balekian	46	M
9/27/1954	Charles S. Gallagher Sr.	45	M
10/1/1954	Charles S. Gallagher Jr.	24	M
10/21/1954	William Allen Roach	58	M
11/19/1954	Bruce Roscoe Burch	63	M
11/21/1954	John Thomas Doyle	46	M
11/30/1954	Vera Faye Emerson	32	F
12/16/1954	Bruno Herman	67	M
2/21/1955	William John Llewellyn	70	M
2/28/1955	Clarence F. Wight Jr.		M
3/16/1955	Cecil V. Williams	50	M
5/11/1955	Victor Hesselberg	35	M
5/11/1955	Gertrude Tufts	56	F
5/23/1955	Ben Risvall	62	M
7/30/1955	Antonio Rocco Buletti	53	M
7/29/1955	Joseph Rieger Eppler	58	M
7/20/1955	Weldon Kees		M
8/4/1955	Earl Harold Burlingame	64	M
8/25/1955	Frank Charles Leone	50	M

Date	Name	Age	Sex
10/4/1955	William Joseph Crosby	50	M
10/26/1955	Matthew Ferdinand Wuerstle	27	M
10/31/1955	Walter John Felix	52	M
12/14/1955	Albert Bender	51	M
2/6/1956	Genevieve Major		F
3/4/1956	Victor Hesselberg	35	M
3/16/1956	William Patrick Keane	49	M
4/2/1956	Doris Marie Dickinson	60	F
5/10/1956	Fam Kong Poon		M
6/4/1956	George Clark McConnell	23	M
6/6/1956	Francis Patrick Boylan	23	M
8/6/1956	Joseph Ignatius Gallagher	54	M
8/10/1956	Lucille Wagner	51	F
9/4/1956	Charles Lee Waters	23	M
9/14/1956	Eddie Fromme	67	M
9/16/1956	Michael Wyatt	27	M
1/29/1957	James Ross	54	M
3/15/1957	Caroline Ann Page	36	F
6/9/1957	Lewis Bruce Bagby	60	M
8/4/1957	Donna June Tracy	30	F
9/14/1957	Hazel A. House Clark	59	F
10/15/1957	William Berger	63	M
12/30/1957	Joyce Marvelle Scheuer	32	F
4/4/1958	Gareld G. Mills		M
4/29/1958	Imigi Pockar	54	M
7/5/1958	Julian A. Bates	30	M
7/18/1958	Manuchr G. Howakey		M
12/3/1958	Joyce M. Scheuer	33	F
1/8/1958	Dave D. Lala	33	M
1/13/1958	John H. Pearson	25	M
8/10/1958	Howard S. Cook Jr.	37	M
8/12/1958	Eilert Johnson	70	M
10/5/1958	Gladys W. Johnson	32	F
10/4/1958	Fred T. Bernstein	32	M
10/22/1958	Barbara Mae Wasemiller	33	F
11/22/1958	John Losky		M

Date	Name	Age	Sex
11/25/1958	Albert L. Morris	42	M
12/4/1958	Cesare Bardini		M
2/3/1959	Arthur Frederick Gunn	73	M
2/11/1959	Carl Rosvall	35	M
3/31/1959	Fritz August Meyer	64	M
9/28/1959	Alan E. Moran	48	M
10/6/1959	Sheldon K. Goldfus	24	M
10/11/1959	Madeline Pera	41	F
10/11/1959	Theodore W. Vanderhoof	31	M
11/25/1959	Clarence True	59	M
12/30/1959	Thomas C. Elliott	41	M
1/30/1960	Jack H. Cleaveland	33	M
4/26/1960	Jeanne E. Hamilton	42	F
7/22/1960	Carl J. Fisher	80	M
5/5/1960	Albert L. Keehn	21	M
6/17/1960	Pyung Chung	31	M
6/22/1960	Jay Bruce Storm	27	M
6/29/1960	Adolph Roy Uribe	29	M
9/12/1960	Epitacia D. Santos	43	M
9/16/1960	George E. Mulcahy	65	M
10/1/1960	George A. Clarke Jr.		M
12/30/1960	Iva L. Mazurek	39	F
1/4/1961	Betty Anne Brown	38	F
1/30/1961	Arthur Irwin	51	M
2/5/1961	Richard Dixon		M
2/14/1961	Raymond C. Lewis	57	M
3/15/1961	Herbert Gifford		M
3/31/1961	Frances J. Cantu	41	M
4/4/1961	John Clarence Walker	61	M
4/10/1961	Clifford A. Cullis	48	M
4/14/1961	Joseph L. Fong	39	M
4/22/1961	Ernest O. Gross	61	M
Unknown	Charles Martina	59	M
9/28/1961	Arthur Karge	62	M
10/10/1961	Charles L. Epidendio	48	M
11/4/1961	Frances C. Hurliman	23	M

Date	Name	Age	Sex
11/8/1961	Makiko Hata	24	M
12/13/1961	Frances Patrick Kennedy	20	M
1/15/1962	Harold S. Hartley	62	M
1/23/1962	Cynthia Flannery	33	F
1/26/1962	Herb L. Livesey	39	M
1/28/1962	Walter Morse	62	M
2/5/1962	Oliver J. Gustafson	30	M
2/11/1962	Norman Nordling	26	M
2/27/1962	Sharon L. Grijalva	19	F
5/20/1962	Dorothy Drummond	50	F
5/26/1962	Louis G. Scurini	26	M
6/3/1962	Beverly J. Landry	28	F
6/11/1962	Seymour Webb	33	M
6/14/1962	Ronald C. Milligan	23	M
7/11/1962	Cecil P. Herrman	33	M
8/12/1962	James T. Foss	39	M
9/8/1962	Vladimir Valanykin	62	M
9/13/1962	Guy R. Crone	73	M
9/13/1962	James McNeill	70	M
9/13/1962	Patricia S. Rathbun	35	F
9/20/1962	Stephen O. Mason	73	M
9/22/1962	Glenn W. McCurdy	36	M
11/5/1962	Barbara J. Woodard	40	F
2/16/1963	Steve L. Bossi/Bassi	39	M
2/17/1963	Marilyn J. Moss	30	F
2/21/1963	Brenton D. Caldwell	60	M
3/4/1963	Ephime V. Tzvetnitsky	73	M
3/22/1963	Warden John Smith	70	M
4/27/1963	Clara K. Levine	36	F
7/5/1963	Alice A. Bivins	23	F
7/8/1963	William B. Anderson	45	M
7/13/1963	Patricia R. Williams	38	F
7/14/1963	Donald A. Laquet	31	M
7/16/1963	Margaret D. White	47	F
7/29/1963	Louise A. Jennings	45	F
8/17/1963	Joseph K. Lee	33	M

Date	Name	Age	Sex
8/28/1963	John M. Fulle	19	M
9/10/1963	Hickman Price III	20	M
9/13/1963	Roland C. Frost	73	M
11/1/1963	Arnold M. Kaplan	37	M
12/13/1963	Marshal N. Israel	34	M
1/4/1964	Richard R. Gray	42	M
1/7/1964	John L. Hunting	37	M
1/26/1964	Thomas A. Dean		M
3/5/1964	Gary G. Girton	20	M
3/15/1964	Frederic G. Ferree	40	M
4/14/1964	Thomas Dillon		M
4/24/1964	Cecil H. Boyd	55	M
5/5/1964	Alfred L. Bosse Sr.	77	M
5/25/1964	Mary E. Keegan	45	F
6/5/1964	Joseph J. Kakez	50	M
7/5/1964	Elsie M. Larsen	72	F
7/5/1964	William H. Romine	67	M
7/23/1964	Leonard M. Jenkins	45	M
7/22/1964	Drake E. Rogers	19	M
7/26/1964	Richard H. Gillespie Jr.	23	M
7/29/1964	Emma Barsi	58	F
7/28/1964	Edward R. Mitchell	67	M
8/2/1964	Carl B. Anderson	51	M
8/6/1964	Merrell Augustus Sisson	55	M
8/20/1964	Betty Lou Storm Hunsucker	30	F
8/22/1964	Morris McClellan	48	M
8/25/1964	Marion D. Elder	50	M
10/8/1964	Robert C. Jennings	21	M
11/7/1964	Edward K. Smith, Jr.	31	M
12/7/1964	Harold J. Larson	64	M
12/12/1964	Warren C. Gustafson	33	M
1/12/1965	Murry R. Baird		M
2/24/1965	Stanley R. Klopstock	54	M
2/25/1965	Blossom Marie Grim	38	F
2/26/1965	Harry Greenblat		M
3/24/1965	Yoshio P. Furukawa	41	F

Date	Name	Age	Sex
6/5/1965	Shiras White	46	M
6/14/1965	Jill E. Thompson	29	F
8/7/1965	Clyde M. Korman	41	M
8/11/1965	Clyde F. Casey	42	M
8/20/1965	Juanita R. Daneri	42	F
9/9/1965	F. P. Johnson		M
11/10/1965	Karen A. Silverstein	31	F
11/22/1965	Perry Charlton	39	M
1/3/1966	George F. Pendleton	36	M
1/7/1966	Edward C. Hawkins		M
1/11/1966	Waverly F. McGehee	46	M
1/17/1966	Adrienne L. Haxton	21	F
2/18/1966	Otto Herman Weidanz	80	M
2/27/1966	Berta Spoerri	56	F
3/2/1966	Gee S. Poon	33	M
3/12/1966	Fred H. Marciel		M
3/24/1966	Barbara Y. Hayslip	26	F
4/11/1966	John Michael DeTata	20	M
4/24/1966	Faye G. Hoffman		F
5/6/1966	Ferdinand Pechin, Jr.	26	M
6/29/1966	Walter Elwood Liston		M
7/13/1966	Russell F. King	58	M
7/20/1966	David Lee Prescott, Jr.	28	M
7/22/1966	William C. Thomas		M
8/30/1966	Rudolph H. Van Bilderbeck		M
10/24/1966	Robert E. Hanson		M
1/13/1967	Edward Walsh	38	M
2/13/1967	Sam Cantu		M
3/9/1967	Irving Estes		M
3/16/1967	John R. Wilson		M
3/20/1967	Shirley Ann Overmiller	34	F
4/11/1967	Walter G. Weeks	33	M
4/16/1967	Robert E. Eddington		M
4/19/1967	Paul Mezei	44	M
5/7/1967	Irving Levenson		M
5/13/1967	Lucinda Cheney	25	F

Date	Name	Age	Sex
5/17/1967	Maria Caldera	76	F
7/6/1967	Mildred J. Carberry		F
7/16/1967	Sylvia Hensler		F
7/21/1967	William C. Hannigan		M
9/14/1967	Helen Somoff	41	F
9/17/1967	Ruth Lee Reed		F
10/22/1967	Louis Roben		M
10/24/1967	Gardner A. Dailey		M
10/24/1967	John M. Harte		M
10/25/1967	William G. Lyon		M
10/26/1967	Dorothy DeCleene Jochim		F
11/6/1967	Kimberly Lehan		F
11/7/1967	James Wono		M
12/8/1967	Ann B. Mayer		F
12/28/1967	Harry Candy		M
1/27/1968	Virginia Ann Hunt		F
2/16/1968	Thomas K. Liatas		M
3/25/1968	Betty Lee Carson		F
4/3/1968	Joel R. Roscoe		M
4/8/1968	Hildegard Heim		F
4/10/1968	Thomas J. Cairns		M
4/21/1968	Lewis E. Salter		M
4/22/1968	Dianne Strei		F
4/22/1968	J. Doetts		F
5/1/1968	Iris Arther		F
5/15/1968	Frank Hess		M
5/17/1968	Robert Mark Bacjman		M
5/21/1968	Ernest V. La Lone		M
5/26/1968	James Thul		M
6/4/1968	Robert C. McCloskey		M
6/18/1968	Janet Grumwald		F
6/24/1968	Richard Todhuner		M
6/28/1968	Ruth A. Snyder		F
7/14/1968	Collin Huuter		M
7/17/1968	Helen Freedman		F
8/28/1968	Bonita F. Batts		F

Date	Name	Age	Sex
8/30/1968	Irene G. Hofstad		F
9/4/1968	Kathryn W. Layton		F
11/2/1968	Diane Porter		F
12/7/1968	Daniel A. Monje		M
12/16/1968	Edwin Mann		M
12/20/1968	Martha Y. Kamecka		F
2/8/1969	Sam Rosenberg	50	M
3/13/1969	Cleo Cora Nelson	35	F
4/17/1969	Michael J. Dalton	22	M
4/25/1969	Kelvin S. Dunnigan		M
6/15/1969	Daniel J. Lenihan	34	M
8/20/1969	Lynn Marie Bottarini		F
10/16/1969	Peter V. Davis		M
10/23/1969	George L. Hagemann		M
10/24/1969	Karl E. Bybee	48	M
11/6/1969	Charles H. Stebbins, Jr.	22	M
12/28/1969	Molly DeMartini		F
1/27/1970	Michael R. Beavers		M
2/17/1970	Raymond Joseph Tanguay	59	M
2/19/1970	Dennis John Marinos	26	M
2/24/1970	Evan L. Thomas	19	M
3/26/1970	Jeffrey Gneri		M
5/3/1970	Pamela F. Hall		F
5/12/1970	Ed M. Hickman		M
5/13/1970	Charles Carroll		M
5/19/1970	Linda Oberhansley		F
7/8/1970	Ronald Miller		M
7/14/1970	Arthur Greenberg		M
7/20/1970	LeRay S. Solano		M
7/24/1970	Ronald A. Sorenson		M
8/5/1970	Forrest G. Rye		M
8/14/1970	Douglas P. Verduzco		M
8/27/1970	David S. Whitcher		M
9/8/1970	Mary Lou Vroman		F
9/9/1970	Gregory Hasler		M
9/10/1970	Margaret Ann Allen		F

Date	Name	Age	Sex
10/2/1970	Marina Joan Brush		F
10/12/1970	Evelyn Menda		F
10/17/1970	Martha Harrington		F
10/22/1970	Joyce B. Treadway		F
10/26/1970	James Norman Lest	26	M
11/20/1970	Paul L. Sorenson		M
12/1/1970	Robert Bourgerie		M
12/24/1970	Paul Derimoan	24	M
12/28/1970	Giah L. Sae-ow		
2/12/1971	Edith M. Eldridge	24	F
2/13/1971	Glenn L. Gillespy	34	M
2/27/1971	Patricia M. Clark		F
4/27/1971	Nancy Rehm	20	F
4/30/1971	Lola M. Reich		F
5/8/1971	Kevin V. McCarthy	22	M
5/11/1971	Marian A. Clark	59	F
5/15/1971	Albert B. Fierstine		M
6/16/1971	David E. Brigham		M
6/17/1971	Michael P. Lamm		M
6/17/1971	David El Rae	31	M
6/22/1971	Alice Mayer		F
7/7/1971	James L. Decleur	20	M
7/18/1971	Mary E. McKeown	22	F
8/9/1971	Christiana A. Luna	23	F
8/9/1971	William A. McClanahan	44	M
8/12/1971	Patricia S. Cox	29	F
8/30/1971	Darcy Jill Van de Reit	18	F
9/12/1971	Maxine I. Pennington	42	F
9/19/1971	Susan Nahinu	21	F
10/2/1971	David A. Jeffrey	56	M
10/6/1971	Rhey Lee Bartlett	32	M
10/16/1971	Dolores G. West		F
10/23/1971	David Cleveland		M
10/26/1971	Vina Hamann		F
11/29/1971	Juliet Ravlin	19	F
12/4/1971	Lee S. Hagar	57	M

Date	Name	Age	Sex
12/4/1971	Delores Bolstad		F
12/30/1971	James A. Black		M
1/7/1972	Louis P. Kovacevich	35	M
1/8/1972	Tajima Yoshiaki	39	M
1/18/1972	Wah Han Ng	61	M
1/18/1972	James A. Caggiano	70	M
1/26/1972	Bruce McBain Austin	25	M
1/26/1972	Frank A. Basile	34	M
2/20/1972	Tullia S. Teasauro	35	F
2/21/1972	James Wilson	19	M
2/22/1972	Michael Courter	21	M
2/27/1972	Richard J. Grimm	21	M
3/4/1972	Enid E. Weiss	24	F
3/22/1972	Edwin K. Moellman	24	M
4/14/1972	James F. Gough	36	M
5/1/1972	Daniel Tudkovic	31	M
5/8/1972	Marcella Aragon	19	F
5/11/1972	Cynthia Daneri		F
5/12/1972	Earle M. Brown, Jr.	47	M
5/24/1972	William Blesingame		M
5/30/1972	Kathleen Clancy	32	F
6/8/1972	Douglas R. Martin	21	M
6/26/1972	Akiko Barchard		F
8/16/1972	Pauline Brummer	44	F
8/22/1972	Robert B. Mackowsky	22	M
8/22/1972	Chris Welles	27	M
9/21/1972	Robert M. Koshland	50	M
10/11/1972	Peter Weldon	23	M
10/15/1972	Ed Shalhawski	36	M
10/18/1972	Richard Thule		M
11/2/1972	Jane Killebrew	21	F
11/29/1972	James G. Roy	22	M
12/28/1972	Jeffrey Nesbitt	21	M
2/13/1973	Arthur W. Loder Jr.		M
4/12/1973	Armando E. Estrada	~50	M
4/21/1973	Bobette Boyer	32	F

Date	Name	Age	Sex
5/25/1973	Phyllis Garland	25	F
6/23/1973	Jeanette Durr	37	F
6/23/1973	Ellen Shift		F
6/28/1973	James S. Dodge	28	M
7/24/1973	Byron Wiederkeber	58	M
8/18/1973	Pierre Beal Lee	27	M
8/17/1973	Kenneth W. Gilvert	40	M
8/29/1973	Janice L. Eskildsen	44	F
9/5/1973	Candy Polycove	24	F
9/9/1973	Ephram C. Oliva	20	M
9/12/1973	Nancy Chisholm	56	F
10/11/1973	Stephen Hoag	26	M
10/10/1973	Lila K. Haynes	48	F
11/6/1973	David E. Gunder		M
12/1/1973	Salvador Arredondo		M
12/11/1973	Joe B. Jentick	19	M
12/30/1973	Heather Forsythe	25	F
1/29/1974	Donald DeVola	24	M
2/5/1974	Richard T. Sanchez	24	M
2/7/1974	Eutiquio Trevino		M
2/20/1974	Hermann Fielder	60s	M
4/16/1974	Adrienne L. Brown	21	F
Unknown	Maria P. Malkerson	39	F
4/23/1974	Stanley E. Jacobson	58	M
5/24/1974	Oroville Conrad		M
6/19/1974	Atley B. Carlough	37	M
6/22/1974	Robert W. Jopes	55	M
6/24/1974	Winifred Love	52	F
7/30/1974	Dorothy Mae Lamerdin	54	F
10/9/1974	Marjorie M. Horton	36	F
10/12/1974	Barbara M. Baker	49	F
10/17/1974	Nancy Donna MacKenzie	38	F
11/11/1974	Keiko Sakamoto	26	F
12/8/1974	Kenneth R. Lampkin	29	M
Unknown	Patricia Ann Bourdon	45	F
12/22/1974	Mark Zimmerman		M

Date	Name	Age	Sex
2/7/1975	Regina Webster	49	F
2/13/1975	Auguste L. Goupil	30	M
4/14/1975	Fletcher L. Harrison	21	M
4/15/975	Robin G. Ray	31	F
5/5/1975	Leland Fong Soon	24	M
5/6/1975	Ingebord Rathe		F
5/19/1975	Billy Bob Strickland	29	M
6/5/1975	Robert Allen Buys	~30	M
6/11/1975	Alan Jay Meinhofer	31	M
6/23/1975	Robert Russell Kennedy	29	M
8/27/1975	Allen M. Culver	22	M
9/2/1975	Robert E. Keane		M
9/25/1975	Ronald Stetzel		M
11/16/1975	Dennis Reid Kneeland	32	M
12/10/1975	David Lyle Robbie		M
12/26/1975	Patricia Rae		F
1/3/1976	Steven T. Hemeter	27	M
1/11/1976	Susan Heitmeyer	26	F
1/23/1976	Raymond Earl Hagerman	56	M
1/24/1976	Pauline Allerton	34	F
2/2/1976	Harry Olsen Jr.		M
2/16/1976	Sally Jane Hanson		F
2/28/1976	Margaret Ann Puckett	28	F
3/9/1976	William B. McCreery	55	M
3/27/1976	Phyllis Maschiaverna	48	F
4/5/1976	Terence L. Monroe	29	M
4/13/1976	Jain Ellen Porth		F
4/16/1976	Douglas R. Ranieri	29	M
4/22/1976	Diane Y. Meyer	28	F
5/13/1976	Maracella E. Buller	~55	F
5/20/1976	Warren D. Molthan		M
5/20/1976	Karl M. Kresge	44	M
5/23/1976	Nancy Rosemond Fields		F
6/6/1976	Barbara J. Greene	33	F
6/22/1976	Carol Simon	32	F
7/1/1976	Joanne A. Seal		F

Date	Name	Age	Sex
8/23/1976	Cynthia P. Williams	24	F
8/26/1976	Daniel Alexander		M
9/27/1976	Monica Duresne	20	F
10/4/1976	Diane L. Pratt (Hansen)	33	F
10/7/1976	Gary C. Bauer		M
10/24/1976	John A. Sealey	48	M
10/26/1976	Rory M. O'Mahar	30	M
11/18/1976	James Halligan	44	M
11/20/1976	George M. Stewart	55	M
1/5/1977 ·	Kenneth Pattison	19	M
1/21/1977	Patricia J. Wedertz	36	F
1/20/1977	Verna Mae Rogers	30	F
Unknown	Judith Mailander	34	F
1/31/1977	Stephen A. Riss	24	M
2/1/1977	Nicholas L. Bari		M
2/8/1977	Patricia M. Knecht	26	F
2/10/1977	Ronald E. Woodruff	28	M
2/10/1977	Marc Salinger	28	M
2/16/1977	Annabel B. Busse	50	F
2/20/1977	Tullia Tesaura		F
2/21/1977	Joseph D. Knowles		M
3/20/1977	Judith Mailander		F
4/9/1977	Deborah R. Lea	45	F
5/11/1977	Karen Ford		F
5/16/1977	Virgil Ward	42	M
5/25/1977	Scott W. Goldsmith	29	M
5/30/1977	Sharon Ungewitter	24	F
5/31/1977	Eugene Casey	27	M
6/2/1977	Judy R. Heitzman	37	F
6/8/1977	James E. Yates	63	M
6/10/1977	Richard B. Hubbell, Jr.	32	M
6/23/1977	Dorothy M. Ferguson	57	F
7/5/1977	Gordon Lee MacRae	22	M
7/13/1977	Stephen S. Luskow	26	M
7/16/1977	Friedhelm Will Bially	25	M
7/21/1977	Stephen S. Luskkow	26	M

Date	Name	Age	Sex
8/8/1977	Harold Keith	21	M
8/18/1977	Alfred Preston	65	M
9/1/1977	Margaret Macko	24	F
9/29/1977	Ingrid C. Stockstad	22	F
10/1/1977	Bayani L. Mariano	28	M
10/1/1977	Elizabeth M. Cocjin	23	F
10/2/1877	Robert Allen Fast	35	M
10/5/1977	Daniel Gridley		M
10/12/1977	Andrew R. Schoenstein	15	M
10/23/1977	Tom Wexman	25	M
12/9/1977	Robert A. Powers	28	M
1/4/1978	Linda Louise Ryner	33	F
2/27/1978	James R. Wagonis	21	M
3/20/1978	Lawrence McCarthy	65	M
4/17/1978	Wilfred Leary	57	M
5/18/1978	Thomas S. Davlin	19	M
5/19/1978	Brian C. Murphy	28	M
8/2/1978	Robert Escobar	34	M
8/16/1978	Polly M. Schmidt	31	F
10/9/1978	Lawrence Morrow	34	M
12/22/1978	John H. Browning		M
12/28/1978	Arthur Nightingale	64	M
Dec. 1978	Jeffrey S. Yates	34	M
1/9/1979	Ron Michael Martello	27	M
3/10/1079	Nicholas Samaras	38	M
3/16/1979	Wayne W. Stone	26	M
3/25/1979	Paul A. Ferguson	25	M
3/27/1979	Michael Joe Canepa	26	M
4/2/1979	James William McAleer	72	M
5/7/1979	Elliot Scott Helfer	33	M
5/26/1979	Josephine Solorzano		F
6/8/1979	Charles E. Howard	59	M
6/11/1979	Rosemary Flaherty	29	F
9/19/1979	Christiane S. Vismanis		F
9/24/1979	Scott W. Stalker	21	M
10/31/1979	Neal Anthony Zappa	24	M

Date	Name	Age	Sex
11/28/1979	Philip M. Blair	51	M
5/28/1980	Wendy Cochrane	28	F
6/13/1980	Gilbert R. Brunk	43	M
7/9/1980	Donna Lee Howe	33	F
7/20/1980	Menasse Lorber	52	M
8/26/1980	Wolfgang H.G. Kopke	34	M
9/1/1980	Juan Domedon	57	M
11/1/1980	Brian David Boykin	20	M
6/3/1981	Charles B. Porter	36	M
6/7/1981	Jennifer Estep	22	F
6/6/1981	Roy B. Pavia	38	M
6/11/1981	Charles Schlesinger	27	M
7/3/1981	Moses Kinoshita		M
7/26/1981	Janet Suzanne Hoch	18	F
8/21/1981	Patrick McCullough	42	M
8/31/1981	Michael J. Murray		M
9/16/1981	Louis Galland	46	M
10/6/1981	Elizabeth Yeats	44	F
10/8/1981	Daniel Robert Hogg	19	M
10/13/1981	Mary J. Stone	30	F
11/7/1981	Sandra K. Cohen	23	F
12/5/1981	Jerry R. Painter	22	M
12/11/1981	Michael D'Archambeau	31	M
12/24/1981	Thomas L. Boeninghausen	45	M
2/4/1982	Michael S. Cox	31	M
3/17/1982	Jeffrey Masic	30	M
4/3/1982	Clara Hiroko Shitanishi	37	F
4/12/1982	Ronald A. Gubi	29	M
4/20/1982	Janice White	31	F
4/29/1982	William H. Murphy	61	M
6/7/1982	Dianna M. Anderson	31	F
6/26/1982	Thomas Vincent LaCoste	62	M
7/21/1982	John Alfred Beyer	53	M
8/23/1982	Rita Frazier	37	F
8/28/1982	Robert F. Trifton	29	M
9/6/1982	Enrique Martinez	16	M

Date	Name	Age	Sex
9/9/1982	Carl Montgomery	23	M
10/23/1982	Jonathan Cramer	36	M
11/20/1982	Benjamin Blizzard		M
11/28/1982	David P. Branson	58	M
12/4/1982	Serge Boutourline, Jr.	50	M
12/27/1982	Frank T. Stager	26	M
2/21/1983	Joseph Francis Coogan	28	M
6/6/1983	Charlene Montaner	27	F
6/7/1983	Cheryl Ann Block	17	F
7/28/1983	Pieriett Chague	56	M
9/23/1983	Eveline Blumenstock	41	F
10/6/1983	Catherine M. Hafeez	33	F
10/17/1983	Richard Lowell Plumb	39	M
11/14/1983	William John Murphy	35	M
12/27/1983	Craig Cumming	27	M
2/13/1984	Eshai DeKaliata	70	M
2/22/1984	Edwin Deutsch	53	M
3/29/1984	Timothy Craig Stephens	38	M
5/2/1984	Michael Arnold Fuchs	31	M
6/18/1984	James J. Gavras	37	M
6/29/1984	Daniel Joseph Curly	46	M
8/1/1984	John R. Manwarren	36	M
9/14/1984	Lawrence Robert Heaton	36	M
9/23/1984	Mildred Minor	46	F
10/8/1984	Robert Gross	29	M
10/21/1984	Theadra Meraz	20	F
10/22/1984	James Mills	48	M
2/19/1985	Norman Thomas Luffman	34	M
3/27/1985	Michael John Casentini	71	M
5/22/1985	Peter Detula	65	M
6/28/1985	Jean M Erickson	49	F
9/12/1985	Bruce R. Beale	38	M
12/9/1985	Marianne Waldherr	35	F
12/11/985	Donald Reidhaar	52	M
12/17/185	Richard John Fisch	34	M
1/23/1986	John E. Lee	33	M

Date	Name	Age	Sex
1/25/1986	Ann L. Weinstock	43	F
1/29/1986	Randy Nickle	31	M
2/25/1986	Robert Unruh	69	M
5/8/1986	Ernest J. Zaplitny	56	M
6/11/1986	Robert S. Coleman	38	M
6/26/1986	Andrew L. Leung	33	M
7/9/1986	Daniel Mundy	31	M
7/10/1986	Joanne Nagasawa	33	F
7/15/1986	Carlos Grau	45	M
8/14/1986	John A. Throm	36	M
8/17/1986	Wolfram Lothar Fischer	23	M
2/19/1987	Gordon Bertsch	48	M
3/26/1987	Barbara Harper	34	F
3/30/1987	Lynn R. Catalano	41	F
4/21/1987	Dennis Pooler	46	M
5/6/1987	Rebecca Dewey	42	F
5/12/1987	Irene Rodriguez	39	F
6/15/1987	Mirtha Beale	34	F
7/14/1987	Catherine Chan		F
7/30/1987	Patricia Etta Beeson	38	F
8/11/1987	Donald J. Schinkel	56	M
9/14/1987	Karen Virginia Miller	44	F
9/15/1987	Corwin B. Cannon	29	M
9/15/1987	Marvin Smith	33	M
9/15/1987	Karen A. Miller	44	F
11/19/1987	Kenneth O. Mason	34	M
11/27/1987	Karen Sue Hoggatt	27	F
2/1/1988	Sarah Birnbaum	18	F
4/27/1988	Catherine M. Smith	21	F
5/30/1988	Cathleen Ann Hughes	30	F
6/27/1988	James Humphreys	55	M
7/27/1988	Wilhelmina Van der Gleyden	30	F
9/22/1988	Daniel McGee	41	M
10/1/1988	Rik Helmke	34	M
10/3/1988	William Johntz	65	M
10/13/1988	Christoper J. Stowe	23	M

Date	Name	Age	Sex
5/13/1989	Sergio Arreaga	23	M
6/24/1989	Janene L. Minnick	20	F
8/23/1989	David Schuster		M
9/26/1989	Bryan T. Kahl	34	M
10/18/1989	Richard S. Woodside	34	M
11/28/1989	Michael J. Distaso	40	M
11/29/1989	Keith Scott Orner	42	M
2/8/1990	Donald Benedetti		M
5/21/1990	Emmett Vincent McCourt, Jr.	35	M
7/3/1990	David Nelson	23	M
7/8/1990	David T. Keilty	30	M
8/13/1990	Mark Robert Meuer	40	M
8/27/1990	John Alan Stewart	29	M
8/30/1990	Edward J. Giza	37	M
1/29/1991	David Ferguson III	23	M
2/5/1991	Alex David Kaufman	29	M
3/27/1991	Sumein Amy Lee	31	F
4/1/1991	Maureen Elizabeth Smith	35	F
6/7/1991	Murray Davidson	38	M
6/23/1991	Ronald Ralph Berst	38	M
7/25/1991	Nancy Mary Wooldridge	33	F
9/26/1991	Alison Stowe Lett	32	F
10/1/1991	Scott Alan Herst	20	M
10/5/1991	Robert Myron Herrell	21	M
1/21/1992	Margaret Ernestine Suiter	50	F
2/9/1992	Jun Fen Tan Chun	34	F
2/10/1992	Yvonne Bonar	25	F
4/1/1992	David Chan	30	M
5/7/1992	Peter C. Sundar	36	M
6/10/1992	Brian Hulette	24	M
6/24/1992	Pablo Rivera Frias	36	M
7/14/1992	Nam Hee Lee	31	F
7/20/1992	Gerard Joseph Delaire	46	M
8/9/1992	Sachiko Collins	62	F
8/12/1992	Donald Herbert Sommer	56	M
9/3/1992	John C. Merillat	46	M

Date	Name	Age	Sex
9/16/1992	Christine Adriene Randle	19	F
10/29/1992	Thomas C. Volin	33	M
11/4/1992	Craig Michael Brodie	31	M
11/7/1992	Michael Glenn Crews	36	M
1/28/1993	Steven Bennett Page	32	M
2/12/1993	Joe Luis Espinoza	36	M
4/9/1993	Daniel James Lytle	40	M
4/21/1993	Paul Kempe Rasmussen	41	M
4/30/1993	Christopher M. Furay	32	M
5/14/1993	Yuet Lay Lew	44	F
6/9/1993	Anh Phuong Dao	29	F
6/12/1993	Stephen Francis Salvi	42	M
6/16/1993	Richard Flores	30	M
6/16/1993	Philip G. Koyl	46	M
7/6 /1993	Lois Betti Caprista	40	F
7/15/1993	James Michael Williamson	44	M
8/26/1993	Roy Larson Raymond	46	M
9/7 /1993	Phillip Padayhag	58	M
9/27/1993	Andrew Martin Siegel	33	M
10/5/1993	Alfred Lawrence Bernal	65	M
10/19/1993	Anh Kim Au	20	F
11/25/1993	Filomeno M. De La Cruz	37	M
11/26/1993	Kenneth John Elwood	36	M
12/3/1993	Ronda Karen Schaff	29	F
1/2/1994	Katy Perina		F
2/4/1994	Mary Yu	66	F
2/6/1994	Dawn Beth Williamson	34	F
2/21/1994	Jim R. Garcia	47	M
2/26/1994	Brian Patrick Timoney	43	M
3/15/1994	Dennis Lynn Million	43	M
3/27/1994	George Alexander Rankin	28	M
4/6/1994	Gretchen Jean Feiker	44	F
4/14/1994	Michael William Losh	22	M
6/2/1994	Michael Laurence Tognotti	31	M
6/24/1994	John Walter Lawler	44	M
7/5/1994	Dennis Lyle Benson	28	M

Date	Name	Age	Sex
7/8/1994	Camtuyen Thi Phan	20	F
8/5/1994	Thomas Michael Chavez	41	M
8/9/1994	Patricia Ruth Grim	63	F
9/12/1994	Robert Lee Harelson	47	M
9/13/1994	Gerald Alan Rush	39	M
9/13/1994	James Daniel MacDonald	30	M
9/14/1994	Kari Sutton	33	F
9/17/1994	Neil Minkin	51	M
9/29/1994	Josefina Gabales Miles	50	F
10/2/1994	Lawrence Walter Skinner	52	M
10/3/1994	Leonard William Rothschild	46	M
10/16/1994	Matt Burnich	83	M
10/19/1994	Bruce David Penman	44	M
11/5/1994	Nancy Carol McGee	45	F
11/19/1994	Greg Anthony Sanchez	47	M
12/25/1994	James D. Singer	46	M
12/31/1994	John Anthony Gulotta	41	M
1/12/1995	Kenneth Farrington Bishop	30	M
1/14/1995	Mark Finch	33	M
1/28/1995	Steven Fung Nar Cheung	24	M
2/6/1995	Henry Murrietta Salazar	68	M
3/19/1995	Raymond F. Voelker	19	M
4/1/1995	Thomas Michael Gaughan	38	M
4/19/1995	Gregory Gene Miller	30	M
5/1/1995	Mark Vaughan Davenport	31	M
5/13/1995	David Andrew Hanagan	34	M
5/23/1995	Paul Alan Duffy	31	M
5/26/1995	William Charles Hudner	22	M
6/5/1995	Paula Jean Hickey	35	F
6/28/1995	Gary L. Lindsey	48	M
7/8/1995	Kai Cheung Wan	63	M
7/26/1995	Duane Blackburn Garrett	48	M
7/27/1995	Monica De Las M. Burbano	36	F
7/30/1995	Nelson Omar Amaya	42	M
8/9/1995	Beverly L. Unangst	43	F
8/21/1995	Michael Joseph DeBono	41	M

Date	Name	Age	Sex
8/22/1995	Danilo Cendana Esperon	38	M
8/31/1995	Thomas F. McConnell	68	M
9/2/1995	Richard Buckingham-Clark	38	M
9/10/1995	Kenneth George Clennell	31	M
9/10/1995	Dorothy Kim King	40	F
9/21/1995	Dwight Earl Purdy	48	M
9/21/1995	Kenneth Cuong Lee	21	M
9/22/1995	Jason Saltzman	24	M
9/29/1995	Diana Louise Robbins	48	F
9/30/1995	Reginald Whealton	44	M
10/1/1995	Denise Lynn Atchison	41	F
10/7/1995	David Leon Flint	47	M
10/11/1995	Robert Andris Faltens	23	M
10/11/1995	Cau Huynh	71	M
10/17/1995	Geraldine Florence Rathbun	69	F
10/27/1995	Julian Foster Arntz Jr.	69	M
10/31/1995	Stephen Eugene Medlin	45	M
12/19/1995	Jeff O. McCall	23	M
12/19/1995	Eric Atkinson	25	M
1/25/1996	Steven D. Hawkins	45	M
2/19/1996	Robert Patrick Enders	55	M
3/6/1996	Andrew Piggott	63	M
3/17/1996	Robert Eric Jackson	46	M
4/6/1996	Doris Miriam Rotter	59	F
5/13/1996	David Dwayne Jones	37	M
7/15/1996	Kenneth Clayton Keiser	42	M
7/27/1996	Anthony Wayne Cunningham	24	M
8/14/1996	Donna MacFarlane	32	F
8/21/1996	Wayne A. Davies	54	M
8/29/1996	Robert Thomas Lowe	62	M
8/31/1996	Marie Anathin Keeling	58	F
9/19/1996	Louise Michele Solomon	34	F
9/20/1996	Elinore M. Smith	48	F
10/18/1996	Mark Horton	37	M
12/1/1996	Venesio Reis	21	M
12/29/1996	Bailey Ashley Anderson	23	F

Date	Name	Age	Sex
2/14/1997	William Gregory Sass	22	M
2/16/1997	Margaret Mary Ryan	59	F
3/12/1997	Shing Chu Ho	52	M
3/31/1997	Alexander Garfil Tuazon	32	M
4/12/1997	Joseph Henry Yingling	40	M
4/16/1997	Evan Llewellyn McLeod	44	M
5/10/1997	Roy William Buttle	40	M
6/4/1997	John Charles Rundstrom	47	M
6/5/1997	Jenny Anne Van Biljouw	34	F
6/9/1997	John Mark Baar	35	M
6 /9/1997	Brendan Michael Bray	21	M
6/28/1997	Michael Farley Kenigsberg	25	M
7/4/1997	Krzysztof Zajac	43	M
7/13/1997	Rick Ronald London	20	M
8/5/1997	John James Stead	30	M
8/17/1997	Oleg Sandler	47	M
8/21/1997	Wayne Alton Davies	54	M
8/25/1997	Wilson Junior Ortiz	32	M
8/26/1997	Markjolin Aaron Iacovini	26	M
9/4/1997	Timothy Christopher Utzman	21	M
9/9/1997	John Dominic Ewing	20	M
9/17/1997	Joseph M. Franjieh	23	M
9/22/1997	Ada Cristina Lescallett	39	F
9/30/1997	Donald James Newman	40	M
10/30/1997	Susan Jane Hess	54	F
11/4/1997	Bernard Glenn Miller	60	M
12/11/1997	Martin Walter Brown	39	M
12/22/1997	Jaqueline Alves	33	F
2/10/1998	Craig Allen Pancallo	35	M
2/20/1998	Michael Y. Nosov	19	M
4/4/1998	Susan Melony Fox	41	F
4/14/1998	Jean Lasher Gregory	57	F
4/23/1998	Santino Emilio Alotaya	23	M
4/24/1998	Vanessa Nicole Chapman	22	F
4/24/1998	Christine Yo Bepp	51	F
4/26/1998	Jill Marie Collins	29	F

Date	Name	Age	Sex
6/14/1998	Daniel Teague Hogan	24	M
6/20/1998	Bruce Glenn Marlowe	51	M
7/7/1998	Sheila Marie Lanier	30	F
7/10/1998	John Michael Drips	37	M
8/12/1998	Elaine Angela Martin Elli	33	F
8/14/1998	Carl Marshall Duncan	51	M
8/31/1998	Linda Anne Walden	52	F
9/25/1998	Anthony Paul Fitzpatrick	37	M
10/1/1998	Lee Joseph Santolucita	26	M
10/11/1998	Kenneth Thomas Casey	48	M
10/12/1998	Rahim Dawood Mussa	29	M
10/18/1998	Robert Thomas Ferguson	31	M
12/14/1998	Robert Paul Lewis	56	M
1/6/1999	Michael Graham	28	M
2/6/1999	Robert Warren Souders	37	M
3/13/1999	William Alan Lechner	45	M
3/16/1999	Richard Stone Sayre	53	M
3/25/1999	Mark Jon Pennington	30	M
3/29/1999	Leo Charles Moffet	49	M
4/4/1999	Jeremy Holden	46	M
5/8/1999	Edward James Morris	37	M
5/28/1999	Sanjay K. Lalwani	33	M
6/24/1999	Ronald Joseph Yoest	45	M
8/7/1999	Gayle Anita Hart	56	F
8/14/1999	Scott Patrick Galloway	34	M
8/24/1999	Wai Leong Lee	19	M
10/17/1999	Leonard Claude Allan	32	M
11/15/1999	Benjamin Curtis Page	27	M
12/7/1999	Olympia Isadore Monteleone	35	F
12/8/1999	Kacey Kurtis Chock	31	M
1/8/2000	Kenrick Ming Sung Young	29	M
1/22/2000	Mary Irene Webber	54	F
4/29/2000	Enrique Elwin Bonilla	20	M
5/17/2000	Brian Alexander Ward	39	M
5/24/2000	Charles Frederick Buck	56	M
7/8/2000	Richard Dyer Malonek	21	M

Date	Name	Age	Sex
7/19/2000	Randolph Kelley	46	M
7/30/2000	Takao Jack Suzuki	52	M
9/13/2000	William Kevin Walker	28	M
10/22/2000	Nadir Ali Mahmoud	24	M
11/7/2000	Harold Dean Cabiness	46	M
3/16/2001	Juan Miguel Moran	53	M
3/19/2001	Laura Hotchkiss Brown	43	F
4/16/2001	Dorothy Mae Merson	63	F
6/14/2001	Nancy Kay Ozod	58	F
6/17/2001	Sonny James Basilico	52	M
7/19/2001	Mark Gordon Markey	38	M
8/7/2001	Wesley Joon Kim	55	M
8/28/2001	Thomas Ray Kirby	49	M
9/6/2001	Michael John Enders	52	M
10/8/2001	Randy Clark Hoffman	49	M
11/20/2001	Anthony Moreno	21	M
12/9/2001	Charles John Walterscheid	58	M
12/17/2001	Marissa Renee Imrie	14	F
1/5/2002	Gary Brad Chinn	27	M
1/16/2002	Christopher D. Doumeng	32	M
2/26/2002	Embre Dashaw Steward	28	M
3/7/2002	Jason Singh Chahal	20	M
3/11/2002	Sarah Jeffrey	37	F
3/17/2002	Sandra Louise Mougeot	59	F
3/26/2002	Dante P. San Buenaventura	43	M
4/24/2002	Sylvia Ann Orkand	43	F
4/29/2002	Gary John Loesch	44	M
5/25/2002	Dennis Wayne Luce	59	M
5/27/2002	Floyd George Yost	69	M
6/8/2002	Christian Jesus Silva	23	M
7/8/2002	Robert Nelson Rowe	77	M
9/6/2002	Chris Domingo	50	F
9/14/2002	Gregory Benton Coiner	52	M
9/20/2002	Brett Norman Keeton	38	M
11/13/2002	Jolene Renate Cunningham	33	F
12/4/2002	Jack Stephen Conrad	49	M

Date	Name	Age	Sex
12/12/2002	James Deavours Loftin	45	M
1/24/2003	Tracy Lea Heineman	35	F
2/6/2003	Carol Catherine Powell	55	F
2/6/2003	Albert Ostroff	76	M
3/2/2003	Christina Anne Tunteri	27	F
3/12/2003	Sheldon Trumbull Hawk	58	M
3/19/2003	Paul Aladdin Alarab	44	M
5/18/2003	Kelly Glen Clizbe	40	M
6/5/2003	Emil Friedlander	34	M
6/6/2003	Gordon Brooke Thomas	35	M
6/19/2003	Michael George Meyer	53	M
6/21/2003	Hiromi Komoto	33	F
6/26/2003	Daryll Jay Dennis	32	M
7/7/2003	Roberto Oquias	72	M
7/11/2003	Donna Marie Marengo	54	F
8/30/2003	Victor Leinhardt Hanson	84	M
9/8/2003	Eric Luther Vermes	53	M
10/26/2003	Katherine Elizabeth Hull	26	F
11/13/2003	John P. Mikulak	38	M
12/21/2003	William Joe Watson	52	M
1/16/2004	Philip Joseph Manikow	21	M
2/6/2004	Frank Aldo Cuneo	38	M
2/20/2004	Donald David Congress	63	M
3/7/2004	Anya Alexandra Hausner	20	F
3/9/2004	James Lawrence Singer	55	M
4/11/2004	Elizabeth Ann Smith	44	F
4/28/2004	David Lawrence Paige	49	M
5/6/2004	Gregory Meighan Faulkner	49	M
5/10/2004	Deborah Chedel	35	F
5/11/2004	Gene Romal Allen Sprague	34	M
7/16/2004	Klaus Graser	41	M
8/2/2004	Dan Leslie Rubinstein	52	M
8/20/2004	Rachel Anne Lichtle	39	F
9/16/2004	Bernard Lynn Blackburn	55	M
9/28/2004	Lameda Ruth Camilli	40	F
10/26/2004	Phil Allen Holsten	33	M

Date	Name	Age	Sex
11/11/2004	Michael Raymond Barnard	40	M
12/16/2004	Ann Louise Noon	58	F
12/29/2004	Davin Salo	28	M
1/27/2005	Roger David Bradford	59	M
2/1/2005	Jonathan J.A. Zablotny	18	M
2/6/2005	Daniel John Pelton	37	M
2/18/2005	Jennifer Marie Oxford	26	F
2/22/2005	Annapurna Louise Bech	33	F
2/28/2005	Seyed Siamek N.M. Divan	46	M
3/31/2005	Osmon Ahmed Sukhera	27	M
4/14/2005	Theodore Henry Milikin	53	M
4/24/2005	Lois Anne Houston	75	F
5/6/2005	Alisha Esther Alexander	19	F
5/19/2005	Michael Scott O'Brien	42	M
5/24/2005	Moises David Frias Urbina	18	M
8/10/2005	Mary Elizabeth McKinzie	25	F
9/15/2005	Milton Rubin Van Sant	85	M
9/29/2005	Alexander L. Quisenberry	21	M
10/11/2005	Silas Paul Coats	34	M
10/14/2005	Catherine Marie Bickle	39	F
10/24/2005	Robert Joseph Garland	36	M
10/25/2005	Helena Marie Taylor	49	F
11/29/2005	John William Skinner	17	M
12/6/2005	Gita Catherine Jahn	54	F
2/13/2006	Kenneth Bruce Bostock	48	M
2/15/2006	Fua'autoa Uiva Te'o	48	M
3/2/2006	Lisa Michelle Aspromonte	44	F
3/11/2006	Jeremy Seth Hybloom	34	M
3/14/2006	Michael James Hullhorst	47	M
3/22/2006	Christopher Brozda	49	M
3/24/2006	Dennis Michael Collins	65	M
4/13/2006	Henry Harold Brown	54	M
5/15/2006	Richard Wallace Kanes	62	M
5/27/2006	Timothy Gene Cronin	48	M
6/1/2006	Clinton Edward Jeffrey	35	M
6/14/2006	Laura I. Conway	29	F

Date	Name	Age	Sex
6/30/2006	Eric Benjamin Fagan	35	M
7/7/2006	Lorraine Suzuko Ota	31	F
7/17/2006	Christopher J. Perkins	55	M
7/24/2006	Rickey A. Williams	28	M
7/25/2006	Patrick H.Y. Tom	42	M
8/22/2006	Barbara Lynn Dickinson	49	F
8/28/2006	John Gregory McMacken	51	M
9/1/2006	Dean Jon Larson	40	M
10/16/2006	Rachel Paige Wahl	32	F
10/21/2006	Robert Edward Pickus	60	M
12/9/2006	Lori Elise Dahm	37	F
12/10/2006	Thomas Edward Herman	49	M
12/20/2006	Mark Bernard McLean	50	M
12/22/2006	Katherine Kirkham Movius	65	F
12/23/2006	Suzanne Eileen Tanner	58	F
1/1/2007	David Stephen Papageorgiou	52	M
1/7/2007	Tad Steven Pethybridge	44	M
2/3/2007	Bryan Woot Loon Lee	44	M
2/14/2007	Kin Wah Chan	52	M
2/16/2007	Todd Alan Brooks	46	M
2/27/2007	John Burns Campbell	38	M
2/25/2007	Claudio Marcelo Katz	47	M
3/4/2007	Jakob Maxwell Heyer Elliott	36	M
3/4/2007	James Janna Wu	57	M
3/6/2007	Ross Alan Crabill	23	M
3/9/2007	Margaret Dawn Butz	64	F
3/13/2007	Jack Lloyd Packard	50	M
3/28/2007	Steven Frederick Glotzbach	53	M
4/4/2007	Diana Lynn Slade	39	F
4/9/2007	Chastity Marie Boerema	33	F
5/8/2007	Henry Lew	18	M
5/12/2007	Scott Keith Ferraiolo	55	M
5/19/2007	Christopher Lee Jurgensen	37	M
6/8/2007	Nicholas Kupka Bushnell	29	M
6/16/2007	Paul Derek Humphrey	39	M
6/25/2007	Kipard Fyler Pearson	40	M

Date	Name	Age	Sex
7/9/2007	Bret David Yonemura Nishida	22	M
7/22/2007	Amy Kathleen Villanueva	57	F
7/26/2007	Lawrence Craig Collins	40	M
8/7/2007	Thomas Eugene Haselwood	45	M
8/7/2007	Owein Morgan Sanders	27	M
9/9/2007	Ethel Anne Davis	59	F
9/25/2007	Cameron Huntley Travelli	31	M
9/26/2007	Brett Maurice Anderson	47	M
10/1/2007	Michael Christian Zulaybar	26	M
10/2/2007	Colin Matthew Reed	23	M
11/2/2007	George Walter Brick	37	M
11/11/2007	Jon Paul Taylor	35	M
11/18/2007	Debra Lee McClinton	39	F
11/19/2007	Dennis Jimenez Aranda	35	M
12/15/2007	Michael H. Wollenweber	46	M
2/13/2008	Donovan Shayne Barks	36	M
3/18/2008	Erik Steven Brown	39	M
4/16/2008	Halyna Karpa	23	F
5/25/2008	Zachary John Thurston	38	M
6/8/2008	John Francis Barniea	49	M
6/18/2008	Adam Quentin Saltzman	38	M
6/25/2008	Olivia Ann Crowther	23	F
8/1/2008	Renae Elizabeth Benson	47	F
8/13/2008	Michael John Tymchyshyn	37	M
9/8/2008	Dahlia B. Horowitz	37	F
9/16/2008	Paul A. Clevenger	23	M
9/26/2008	Matthew Pelham Freeman	21	M
10/3/2008	Laura Margaret White	19	F
10/21/2008	Alanna R. Olson	29	F
11/14/2008	Lisa Amber Gourley Osirio	23	F
11/23/2008	Aaron Michael White	30	M
11/25/2008	Russell Dean Jones	46	M
12/1/2008	Robert Allen Heller	59	M
12/15/2008	Francisca Schneider	72	F
12/30/2008	Robert Scott Timmons	30	M
1/26/2009	Anastasya A. Gogolitsyna	20	F

Date	Name	Age	Sex
2/13/2009	Robert James Bobier	37	M
2/24/2009	Marques Davon Battle	28	M
3/13/2009	Robert Tracy Fullerton	41	M
4/2/2009	Vincent David Mulroy	52	M
5/7/2009	Branden Bryce O'Tarrow	26	M
5/12/2009	Hillary Elyse Burton Bannister	25	F
6/4/2009	Theodore East Duren	22	M
7/23/2009	Rene Lee Ing	56	M
8/5/2009	Alexander Bray Baxter	20	M
8/13/2009	Shawn Michael Balla	44	M
8/19/2009	David Michael Ranzer	61	M
9/2/2009	Gary Charles Zanoni	59	M
9/2/2009	Christopher R.L. Skov	53	M
9/11/2009	Sandy Wei Hong Mai	35	F
9/17/2009	Sundeep Singh Sumal	31	M
9/17/2009	Erika Diano Legaspi	28	F
10/27/2009	Stephen John Stout	50	M
10/31/2009	Joseph Christopher Houk	40	M
12/9/2009	David Marshall Reeves	58	M
2/9/2010	Joseph Dandridge Bibb	54	M
2/15/2010	Gilbert Gutierrez	24	M
2/25/2010	Michael Deroyce Holmon	32	M
3/1/2010	Sean Patrick Maloney	29	M
3/21/2010	Ryan Michael Hallie	34	M
3/23/2010	Lisa Ann Bores	35	F
4/12/2010	Mia Denise Guerrette	40	F
5/7/2010	Branden Bryce O'Tarrow	26	M
5/12/2010	Hillary Elyse Burton Bannister	25	F
5/29/2010	Margot Chapman	61	F
6/23/2010	Richard Darrell Adams	61	M
6/26/2010	Daniel Michael Richards	53	M
7/8/2010	Nigad Mohamed Saladin	73	M
8/1/2010	Scott Allen Hopkins	52	M
8/16/2010	Martin Francis Brown	46	M
8/20/2010	Kelly Cathleen Slattery	42	F
9/1/2010	Kelly Cliff Moser	40	M

Date	Name	Age	Sex
9/13/2010	Kyle Bradley Markel	24	M
10/27/2010	Barry Andrew Beckman	45	M
10/28/2010	Michael Bernavage	55	M
11/7/2010	Frank Thomas Janes	51	M
11/23/2010	Jacob Ryan-Turpin Story	28	M

BIBLIOGRAPHY

INTERVIEWS

Most of the interviews for this book were conducted between September and December 2010. A few took place in March and April 2011. The majority were in person, sometimes followed up by a phone call or e-mail. The locations ranged from people's homes and offices to coffee shops and my office. Several interviews had to be done by phone for logistical reasons, and one was done by e-mail, at the person's request. Two individuals asked to see a draft of their comments, prepared for publication. This was provided, and both persons approved.

BOOKS

Alvarez, A. *A Savage God.* New York: W.W. Norton & Company, 1971.

Berman, Alan L., Jobes, David A., Silverman, Morton M. *Adolescent Suicide: Assessment and Intervention.* Washington, D.C.: American Psychological Association, 2006.

Brown, Allen. *Golden Gate: Biography of a Bridge.* New York: Doubleday, 1965.

Cimbolic, Peter, Jobes, David A. *Youth Suicide: Isues, Assessment, and Intervention.* Springfield: Charles C. Thomas, 1990.

Colt, George Howe. *November of the Soul: The Enigma of Suicide*. New York: Scribner, 2006.

Durkheim, Emile. *Suicide*. New York: The Free Press, 1951.

Dybel, Louise Nelson. *Paying the Toll*. Philadelphia: University of Pennsylvania Press, 2009.

Fedden, H.R. *Suicide: A Social and Historical Study*. New York: Benjamin Blim, 1972.

Heckler, Richard A.. *Waking Up, Alive*. New York: Ballantine Books, 1994.

Jamison, Kay Redfield. *An Unquiet Mind*. New York: Knopf, 1995.

———. *Night Falls Fast: Understanding Suicide*. New York: Alfred A. Knopf, 1999.

Jobes, David A, Shneidman, E.S. *Managing Suicidal Risk: A Collaborative Approach*. New York: Guilford Press, 2006.

Joiner, Thomas. *Why People Die by Suicide*. Cambridge: Harvard University Press, 2005.

———. *Myths about Suicide*. Cambridge: Harvard University Press, 2010.

Linde, Paul R.. *Danger to Self*. Berkeley: University of California Press, 2010.

MacDonald, Donald and Nadel, Ira. *Golden Gate Bridge: History and Design of an Icon*. San Francisco: Chronicle Books, 2008.

Marcus, Eric. *Why Suicide?* New York: HarperCollins, 2010.

Miller, John. *On Suicide*. San Francisco: Chronicle Books, 1992.

Mungo, Ray. *San Francisco Confidential: Tales of Scandal and Excess from the Town that's Seen Everything*. New York: Birch Lane Press, 1995.

Shea, Shawn C. *The Practical Art of Suicide Assessment*. Hoboken: John Wiley and Sons, 2002.

Sherwood, Ben. *The Survivor's Club*. New York: Grand Central Publishing, 2009.

Shneidman, Edwin S.. *A Commonsense Book of Death*. Lanham: Rowman & Littlefield, 2009.

———. "A*utopsy of a Suicidal Mind*. New York: Oxford University Press, 2004.

———, Farberow, N. *Clues to Suicide*. New York: Harper & Row, 1957.

———. *Definition of Suicide*. Lanham: Jason Aronson Inc., 1995.

———. *The Suicidal Mind*. New York: Oxford University Press, 1996.

———. *Suicide as Psyche*. Northvale: Jason Aronson, Inc., 1993.

Starr, Kevin. *Golden Gate: The Life and Times of America's Greatest Bridge.* New York: Bloomsbury Press, 2010.

van der Zee, John. *The Gate: The True Story of the Design and Construction of the Golden Gate Bridge.* New York: Simon & Schuster, 2000.

STUDIES

Beautrais, A. L. "Effectiveness of Barriers at Suicide Jumping Sites: A Case Study." *Australian and New Zealand Journal of Psychiatry,* 2001.

———. "Suicide by Jumping: A Review of Research and Prevention Strategies." *Crisis,* 2007.

Beautrais, A. L., Gibb S. D., Horwood, L. J., and Larkin, G. L. "Removing Bridge Barriers Stimulates Suicides." *Australian and New Zealand Journal of Psychiatry,* 2009.

Beck, A.T., Kovacs, M., Weissman, A. "Hopelessness and Suicidal Behavior." *Journal of the American Medical Association.* 1975,

———, Kovacs, M., Garrison, B. "Hopelessness and Eventual Suicide." *American Journal of Psychiatry,* 1985.

———, Steer, R.A., Carbin, M.G. "Psychometric Properties of the Beck Depression Inventory." *Elsevier Science.* 1988.

———, Brown, G., Berchick, R.J., Stewart, B.L, Steer, R.A. "Relationship Between Hopelessness and Ultimate Suicide." *American Psychiatric Association,* 2006.

Bennewith, O., Nowers, M., and Gunnell, D. "Effect of Barriers on the Clifton Suspension Bridge England, on Local Patterns of Suicide: Implications for Prevention." *British Journal of Psychiatry,* 2007.

Cantor, C. H., and Hill, M. A. "Suicide from River Bridges." *Australian and New Zealand Journal of Psychiatry,* 2007.

Daigle, M. S. "Suicide Prevention Through Means Restriction: Assessing the Risk of Substitution." *Accident Analysis and Prevention,* 2005.

Blaustein, M., and Fleming, A. "Suicide from the Golden Gate Bridge." *American Journal of Psychiatry,* 2009.

Breggin, P.R. "Suicidality, Violence, and Mania Caused by Selective Serotonin Reuptake Inhibitors (SSRIs)." *Internal Journal of Rick and Safety in Medicine.* 2003/2004.

California Department of Mental Health. "California Strategic Plan on Suicide Prevention." 2008.

Callanan, V.J., Davis, M.S. "A Comparison of Suicide Note Writers with Suicides Who Did Not Leave Notes." *Suicide and Life-Threatening Behavior,* 2009.

Curwen, T. "His Work Is Still Full of Life." *Los Angeles Times,* June 5, 2004.

Davidson, C. L., Wingate, L. R., Rasmussen, K. A., and Slish, M. L. "Hope as a Predictor of Interpersonal Suicide Risk." *Suicide and Life-Threatening Behavior,* 2009.

Draper, J. "Suicide Prevention on Bridges: The National Suicide Prevention Lifeline Position." 2008.

Ezzell, C. "Why? The Neuroscience of Suicide." *Scientific American,* 2003.

Florentine, J. B., and Crane, C. "Suicide Prevention by Limiting Access to Means: A Review of Theory and Practice." *Social Science & Medicine,* 2010.

Golden Gate Bridge District. "Golden Gate Bridge Physical Suicide Deterrent System Project." l2008.

Joiner, T.E., Brown, J.S., Wingate, L.R. "The Psychology and Neurobiology of Suicidal Behavior." *Annual Review of Psychology,* 2005.

———, Rudd, D.M. "Negative Attributional Style for Interpersonal Events and the Occurrence of Severe Interpersonal Disruptions as Predictors of Self-Reported Suicidal Ideation." *Suicide and Life-Threatening Behavior,* 1995.

———, Rudd, D.M., Rajab, M.H. "The Modified Scale for Suicidal Ideation." *Journal of Abnormal Psychology,* 1997.

———, Van Orden, K.A. "The Interpersonal-Psychological Theory of Suicidal Behavior Indicates Specific and Crucial Psychotherapeutic Targets." *Internal Journal of Cognitive Therapy,* 2008.

Lindqvist, P., Jonsson A., Eriksson A., Hedelin A., and Bjornstig U. "Are Suicides by Jumping Off Bridges Preventable? An Analysis of 50 Cases from Sweden." *Accident Analysis and Prevention,* 2004.

Lubin, G., Werberloff, N., Halperin, D. et al. "Decrease in Suicide Rates After a Change of Policy Reducing Access to Firearms in Adolescents." *Suicide and Life-Threatening Behavior,* 2010.

Marin County Coroners Office and the Bridge Rail Foundation. "A Ten-Year Report: Golden Gate Bridge Suicide Demographics." 2007.

———. "A Fifteen-Year Report: Golden Gate Bridge Suicide Demographics." 2009.

Miller, M., Azrael, D., and Hemenway, D. "Belief in the Inevitability of Suicide: Results from a National Survey." *Suicide and Life-Threatening Behavior*, 2006.

O'Carroll, P. W., and Silverman, M. M. "Community Suicide Prevention: The Effectiveness of Bridge Barriers." *Suicide and Life-Threatening Behavior*, 1994.

Pelletier, A. R. "Preventing Suicide by Jumping: The Effect of a Bridge Safety Fence." *Injury Prevention*, 2007.

Reisch, T., and Michel, K. "Securing a Suicide Hot Spot: Effects of a Safety Net at the Bern Muenster Terrace." *Suicide and Life-Threatening Behavior*, 2005.

Reisch, T., Schuster, U., and Michel, K. "Suicide by Jumping and Accessibility of Bridges: Results from a National Survey in Switzerland." *Suicide and Life-Threatening Behavior*, 2007.

Rosen, D. H. "Suicide Survivors." *Western Journal of Medicine*, 1975.

Seiden, R. H. "Can a Physical Barrier Prevent Suicides on the Golden Gate Bridge?" University of California School of Public Health, June 5, 1973.

———. "A Tale of Two Bridges: Comparative Suicide Incidence on the Golden Gate Bridge and San Francisco-Oakland Bay Bridges." *Omega*, 1983.

———. "Where Are They Now? A Follow-up Study of Suicide Attempters from the Golden Gate Bridge." *Suicide and Life-Threatening Behavior*, 1978.

———. and Tauber, R. K. "Pseudocides vs. Suicides." Fifth Annual Conference for Suicide Prevention (London), 1970.

Slovak, K., and Brewer, T. W. "Suicide and Firearm Means Restriction: Can Training Make a Difference?" *Suicide and Life-Threatening Behavior*, 2010.

Shneidman, E.S. "'Suicide' and 'Suicidology': A Brief Etymological Note." *Suicide and Life-Threatening Behavior*, 1971.

———. "Perturbation and Lethality as Precursors of Suicide in a Gifted group." *Suicide and Life-Threatening Behavior*, 1971.

———. "The Psychological Pain Assessment Scale," *Suicide and Life-Threatening Behavior*, 1999.

———. "Suicide" in *Encyclopedia Britannica*, Vol. 21, pp. 383-385. 1973.

———. "Suicide Notes Reconsidered." *Psychiatry*, 1973.

————. "Suicide on My Mind, *Britannica* on My Table." *American Scholar,* 1998.

Simon, T.R. Swann, A.C., Powell, K.E., Potter, L.B., Kresnow, M., O'Carroll, P.W. "Characteristics of Impulsive Suicide Attempts and Attempters. *Suicide and Life-Threatening Behavior,* 2002.

U.S. Department of Health and Human Services. "National Strategy for Suicide Prevention: Goals and Objectives for Action." 2001.

Weigel, Randolph R. "Suicide: What Leads People to Kill Themselves?" University of Wyoming, October 2007.

ARTICLES

ABC News. "The Bridge of Death." October 2006.

ABC News. "Man Survives Suicide Jump from Golden Gate Bridge." April 28, 2006.

Adamick, Mike. "Destination Suicide." *Contra Costa Times,* March 11, 2005.

Allen, Michael O. "Barriers May Buff Golden Gate's Taint." *New York Daily News,* June 1, 1997.

Allen, Teresa. "Debate Over Bridge Barrier Moves into its 50th Year." *Marin Independent Journal,* October 12, 1986.

Anderson, Scott. "The Urge to End It All." *New York Times Magazine,* July 6, 2008.

Ashley, Guy. "New Suicide Barrier Plan." *Marin Independent Journal,* March 7, 1997.

————. "Suicide Barrier Picks Up Momentum." *Marin Independent Journal,* December 14, 1996.

————. "Suicide Fence Delays Anger Bridge Board." *Marin Independent Journal,* September 6, 1997.

————. "Talks Reignite Over Suicide Barrier on Golden Gate." *Marin Independent Journal,* January 27, 1997.

Associated Press. "Advisor to Gore Is Found Dead in San Francisco." *Seattle Times,* July 28, 1995.

Augarten, Stan. " Subject: Suicide." *Columbia Journalism Review,* July/August, 1982.

Benson, Heidi. "Lethal Beauty: Saving a Life." *San Francisco Chronicle,* November 5, 2005.

Benefield, Kerry and Johnson, Julie. "Windsor Teen Survives Leap from Golden Gate Bridge." *Press Democrat*, March 11, 2011.

Berton, Justin. "Evidence Leads Police to Believe Danville Teenager Killer Herself.: *San Francisco Chronicle*, May 26, 2011.

Blum, Andrew. "Suicide Watch." *New York Times*, March 20, 2005.

Bower, Amanda. "A Survivor Talks About His Leap." *Time*, May 24, 2006.

Brazil, Eric. "Lawyer's Jump from Bridge Baffles Friends, Colleagues." *San Francisco Examiner*, October 5, 1994.

Breslau, Karen. "An Unblinking Look at Suicide." *Newsweek*, October 20, 2006.

Brenner, Keri. "Marin Joins Campaign for Barrier on Bridge." *Marin Independent Journal*, March 2, 2005.

Broom, Jack. "Work to Begin Next Week on Barrier Fence for Aurora Bridge." *Seattle Times*, April 14, 2010.

Brooks, John R. "A Bridge's Tragic Toll." *San Francisco Chronicle*, July 16, 2008.

Cabanatuan, Michael, "Bay Bridge Suicides Feared." *San Francisco Chronicle*, March 11, 2006.

———. "Big Plans to Mark Bridge's Milestone." *San Francisco Chronicle*, March 13, 2011.

———. "Bridge Directors Vote for Net to Deter Suicides." *San Francisco Chronicle*, October 11, 2008.

———. "The Great Barrier Debate." *San Francisco Chronicle*, July 9, 2008.

———. "Panel to Weigh Design Funds for Suicide Net." *San Francisco Chronicle*, July 18, 2010.

———. "Suicide Barrier, Carpool Toll Likelier." *San Francisco Chronicle*, February 13, 2010.

Cook, Gale. "A Marin Blueprint for a New Golden Gate Bridge Agency." *San Francisco Examiner and Chronicle*, February 19, 1978.

Cooper, Lara. "Landmark Bridges Around the World Employ Suicide Barriers." *Noozhawk*, May 4, 2010.

Craib, Ralph. "Tourists See Gate Suicide." *San Francisco Chronicle*, October 5, 1976,

Delgado, Ray. "GG Bridge Suicide Fence Has Dissenters." *San Francisco Examiner*, June 10, 1998.

Dicke, William. "Edwin Shneidman, Authority on Suicide, Dies at 91." *New York Times*, May 21, 2009.

Dougan, Michael. "Bridge Suicide Barrier Plan Has Air of Urgency." *San Francisco Examiner*, November 7, 1998.

Doyle, Jim. "Suicide Patrol for Golden Gate Bridge." *San Francisco Chronicle*, February 24, 1996.

Dunn, Mark, and Dowsley, Anthony. "Anti-Suicide Barrier Urged for West Gate Bridge." *Herald Sun*, June 14, 2008.

Evans, Mark. "Bridge Suicides Hot Record 45 in '95." *Marin Independent Journal*, February 11, 1996.

Fagan, Kevin. "Golden Gate's Typical Jumper is Single, Male." *San Francisco Chronicle*, September 10, 2009.

———. "Windsor Teen Survives Usually Fatal Plunge." *San Frqncisco Chronicle*, March 11, 2011.

Fields-Meyer, Thomas. "The Jumper Who Lived." *People Magazine*, September 5, 2005.

Fimrite, Peter. "A Step Toward Suicide Barrier on Famous Span." *San Francisco Chronicle*, March 12, 2005.

———. "Anti-Suicide Fence Sample on Display." *San Francisco Chronicle*, June 10, 1998.

———. "The Great Barrier Debate." *San Francisco Chronicle*, March 10, 2005.

———. "Mourner's Emotional Plea for Bridge Suicide Barrier." *San Francisco Chronicle*, February 25, 2005.

———. "Students Design 3 Barriers." *San Francisco Chronicle*, May 26, 2005.

Foster, Lee. "The Bridge Is Their Beat." *California Living*, March 1975.

Frazier, Colby. "Caltrans to Begin Suicide Barrier Construction." *Daily Sound*, June 22, 2010.

Friend, Tad. "Jumpers." *New Yorker*, October 13, 2003.

Gallagher, Nora. "Bridge Jumpers Who Have Lived." *San Francisco Magazine*, April 1975.

Gelineau, Kristen. "Neighbor Saves Scores of Lives at Suicide Spot." *San Francisco Chronicle*, June 14, 2010.

Gerhard, Susan. "Over Troubled Waters." *Bay Guardian*, April 20-26, 2005.

Glionna, John M. "Bridge's Deadly Allure Lingers." *Los Angeles Times/Modest Bee*, June 5, 2005.

———. "Survivor Battles Golden Gate's Suicidal Lure." *Seattle Times*, June 4, 2005.

————. "Renewed Focus on a Bridge's Deadly Allure." *Los Angeles Times*, July 31, 2007.

Gordon, Rachel. "Golden Gate Bridge Chief Moving On." *San Francisco Chronicle*, June 16, 2010.

————. "Public Prefers Net as Bridge Suicide Barrier, Survey Says." *San Francisco Chronicle*, July 29, 2008.

————. "Suicide Barrier: Emotions High." *San Francisco Chronicle*, July 23, 2008.

Gumbel, Andrew. "Bridge to Nowhere." *Independent*, October 2006.

Guthmann, Edward. "Lethal Beauty: The Allure." *San Francisco Chronicle*, October 30, 2005.

Halstead, Richard. "Bizarre Day on Bridge." *Marin Independent Journal*, June 29, 1997.

Hamlin, Jesse. "Lethal Beauty: Family Grief." *San Francisco Chronicle*, October 31, 2005.

Harris, Art. "A Hard Look." *San Francisco Examiner*, August 10, 1977.

————. "Public Prescriptions for Golden Gate's 'Epidemic.'" *San Francisco Examiner*, March 16, 1977.

————. "Stopping Suicides." *San Francisco Examiner*, March 3, 1977.

————. "Suicide: The View from the Bridge." *San Francisco Examiner*, March 2, 1977.

————. "Would a Barrier Stop Suicides?" *San Francisco Examiner*, March 13, 1977.

Harvey, Mike. "The Golden Gate to Heaven: Suicides Go on as Bridge Still Waits for Safety Net." *New York Times*, November 7, 2009.

Hines, John Kevin. "A Suicide Survived." *San Francisco Medicine*, November/December 2005.

Ho, Patricia. "Analysis of Caltrain Death Patterns Begins Long-term Study of Railroad Suicides." *Stanford Daily*, November 19, 2010.

Horowitz, Donna. "Wire Fence Eyed for GG Bridge." *San Francisco Examiner*, March 8, 1007.

Hurd, Rick. "Family of Missing Teen Thanks the Community." *Contra Costa Times*, May 28, 2011.

————, and Kazmi, Sophia. "S.F. Search Mission Becomes a Recovery." *San Francisco Chronicle*, May 26, 2011.

Jacobson, David. "A Leap of Despair." *Detroit News*, January 17, 1995.

Jastrow, Doug. "Classmates Grieve Over Girl's Death." *Contra Costa Times,* February 21, 2010.

Jindrich, Dr. Ervin J. "Golden Gate's Suicides Are Preventable." *Marin Independent Journal,* November 16, 1998.

Kahn, Bob. "Manslaughter on the Golden Gate Bridge." *The Montclarion,* April 12, 1972.

Kazmi, Sophia. "Search for Danville Student Centers on S.F." *Contra Costa Times,* May 25, 2011.

King, John. "Lethal Beauty: The Engineering Challenge." *San Francisco Chronicle,* November 4, 2005.

———. "Safe, Slick Suicide Barrier Sounds Simple—But It's Not." *San Francisco Chronicle,* March 10, 2005.

Kirst, Sean. "Suicide-Prevention Counselor Says Barriers to Jumping Should Be Considered." *Post-Standard,* April 5, 2002.

Koopman, John. "Lethal Beauty: No Easy Death." *San Francisco Chronicle,* November 2, 2005.

———. "Lethal Beauty: The Talkers." *San Francisco Chronicle,* November 2, 2005.

Krauss, Clifford. "A Veil of Deterrence for a Bridge with a Dark Side." *New York Times,* February 11, 2003.

Krieger, Lisa M. "On Tarcks Lives Are Lost But Also Saved." *San Jose Mercury News,* September 6, 2009.

———. "Preventing Suicides at the Tracks." *San Jose Mercury News,* October 24, 2009.

KTVU. "Suicide Documentary Angers Golden Gate Bridge Officials." January 19, 2005.

Lagos, Marisa. "'Dismally Normal' Suicide Rate for Golden Gate in 2005." *San Francisco Examiner,* January 7-8, 2006.

———. "Fatal Jumps from Bridge Rise Sharply." *San Francisco Chronicle,* January 18, 2007.

———. "Golden Gate Bridge." *San Francisco Chronicle,* January 27, 2007.

Langreth, Robert, and Ruiz, Rebecca. "The Forgotten Patients." *Forbes,* September 13, 2010.

Lee, Henry K. "Missing Danville Teen's Bike Found Near GG Bridge." *San Francisco Chronicle,* May 24, 2011.

Leenaars, Antoon A. "Lives and Deaths: Biographical Notes on Selections of the Works of Edwin S. Shneidman." *Suicide and Life-Threatening Behavior,* November 2010.

Lelchuk, Ilene, and Allday, Erin. "Parents Reflect, Schools Mobilize to Curb Suicide." *San Francisco Chronicle,* January 22, 2007.

Maddan, Heather. "Lethal Beauty: Nine Suicides." *San Francisco Chronicle.* November 1, 2005.

Mahoney, J. Michael. "If Suicide Barriers Are 'Ugly,' Suicides Are Uglier." *Marin Independent Journal,* December 15, 1996.

Marech, Rona. "Armed with Kind Words and a Helping Hand, Golden Gate Bridge Patrol Watches for Hints of Despair Amid the Crowd." *San Francisco Chronicle,* March 13, 2005.

Marin Independent Journal. "Two Jump off Golden Gate Bridge." June 2, 1996.

Matier, Phillip, and Ross, Andrew. "Baffling Rise in Bridge Suicides." *San Francisco Chronicle,* October 5, 1994.

———. "Caltrain to Use Camera as Suicides Rise." *San Francisco Chronicle,* July 4, 2011.

———. "Film Captures Suicides on Golden Gate Bridge." *San Francisco Chronicle,* January 19, 2005.

———. "Suicide Film Renews Call for Golden Gate Bridge Barriers." *San Francisco Chronicle,* January 24, 2005.

McCandless, Brittany. "City Firefighter a Hero in Documentary on Golden Gate Bridge." *Pittsburgh Post-Dispatch,* January 11, 2007.

McKinley, Jesse. "Golden Gate Managers Vote to Build Suicide Net." *New York Times,* October 11, 2008.

———. "San Franciscans Try Again to Suicide-Proof the Golden Gate Bridge." *New York Times,* August 11, 2006.

Moran, Mark. "Suicide Barrier Sought for Golden Gate Bridge." *Psychiatric News,* April 1, 2005.

Muller, Paul. "The Students Deliver a Lesson." *San Francisco Chronicle,* May 26, 2005.

Murphy, Jeffrey G. "Everyday Heroes." *The Beacon,* April 1997.

Nardi, Elisabeth, and Fischer, Karl. "Missing Danville Girl's Bike in S.F." *Contra Costa Times,* May 24, 2011.

National Public Radio. "In Suicide Prevention, It's Method, Not Madness." July 8, 2008.

NBC11. "Coroner: Golden Gate Bridge Suicide Numbers Up." January 9, 2008.

Norberg, Bob. "Engineers Will Study Who Really Designed Bridge." *Marin Press Democrat,* June 19, 1992.

O'Brien, Tia. "Gone." *San Francisco Magazine,* December 2008.

Olson, Jenni. "Power Over Life and Death." *San Francisco Chronicle,* January 14, 2005.

Omer, Haim, and Elitzur, Avshalom C. "What Would You Say to the Person on the Roof? A Suicide Prevention Text." *Suicide and Life-Threatening Behavior,* Summer 2001.

Ostler, Scott. "Journey to the Bridge—and Back." *San Francisco Chronicle,* November 10, 1999.

———. "Saving Lives Just Part of the Job." *San Francisco Chronicle,* January 10, 2001.

Ostrom, Mary Anne. "Momentum Grows for Barrier on Golden Gate." *San Jose Mercury News,* May 24, 2007.

Paterniti, Michael. "The Suicide Catcher." *GQ,* May 2010.

Payne, Paul. "Bridge District Extends Suicide Barrier Study." *Press Democrat,* March 11, 2006.

———. "Bridge Suicides Increase Again." *Press Democrat,* January 3, 2008.

———. "Golden Gate Suicide Barrier Considered Again." *Press Democrat,* February 25, 2005.

———. "Teen Bridge Jumper Did It 'For Kicks'." *Press Democrat,* March 11, 2011.

Penaloza, David Carrillo. "Ex-Tar Mulroy Believed to Have Jumped to His Death." *Daily Pilot,* April 6, 2009.

Pestian, John. "A Conversation with Edwin Shneidman." *Suicide and Life-Threatening Behavior,* November 2010.

Petit, Charles. "Bridge Jumpers Say They Were 'Reborn' as They Fell." *San Francisco Chronicle,* April 19, 1975.

Philp, Catherine. "I Jumped, and Lived." *Times Online,* February 8, 2007.

Prado, Mark. "Barrier Study Finds Support." *Marin Independent Journal,* February 25, 2006.

———. "Behind the Push for a Suicide Barrier." *Marin Independent Journal,* February 27, 2005.

————. "Bridge Suicide Barrier Stalled." *Marin Independent Journal*, October 22, 2005.

————. "Crossover Accident on Golden Gate Bridge Highlights Barrier Issue." *Marin Independent Journal*, August 17, 2010.

————. "Fence's Price Tag Could Reach $25 Million." *Marin Independent Journal*, March 12, 2005.

————. "Film an Emotional Wrench for Families." *Marin Independent Journal*, May 1, 2006.

————. "Golden Gate Bridge Chief Eyes Return to Reno." *Marin Independent Journal*, July 29, 2009.

————. "Golden Gate Bridge Barrier." *Marin Independent Journal*, August 24, 2009.

————. "Golden Gate Bridge Gets Ready for 75th Birthday. *Marin Independent Journal*, May 30, 2011.

————. "Golden Gate Bridge Suicide Barrier Debate." *Marin Independent Journal*, December 17, 2007.

————. "Marin Coroner Pushes for Bridge Suicide Barrier." *Marin Independent Journal*, December 17, 2007.

————. "Panel OKs $5 Million for Barrier Design." *Marin Independent Journal*, July 16, 2010.

————. "Patrols, Emergency Phones Stop Some, But Not All." *Marin Independent Journal*, February 27, 2005.

————. "Report: 31 Jumped from Golden Gate Bridge in 2009." *Marin Independent Journal*, January 24, 2010.

————. "Study OK'd for Suicide Barrier on GG Bridge." *Marin Independent Journal*, September 22, 2006.

————. "Suicide Barrier Could Withstand 100 MPH Winds." *Marin Independent Journal*, June 13, 2007.

————. "Suicide Barrier Study Endorsed." *Marin Independent Journal*, March 25, 2006.

————. "Suicide Net Just Needs Cash." *Marin Independent Journal*, February 13, 2010.

————. "Teen Suicides from Golden Gate Bridge Churn Barrier Debate." *Marin Independent Journal*, August 23, 2008.

Prado, Mark, and Breithaupt, Bard. "Bridge Barrier Could Be Up by 2010." *Marin Independent Journal*, September 28, 2007.

Preuitt, Lori. "Not Again: Caltrain Investigates Palo Alto Suicide." *NBC Bay Area*, October 20, 2009.

Reed, Susan. "Patrols Help Reduce Golden Gate Suicide Rate." *CNN*, December 30, 1996.

Rego, Nilda. "Bridge Project Spans Imaginations." *Contra Costa Times*, October 19, 2008.

―――. "From Dream to Golden Reality." *Contra Costa Times*, October 26, 2008.

―――. "Golden Gate Bridge Plan is Built Step by Step." *Contra Costa Times*, October 12, 2008.

Reiten, Mary B., and Jung, David J. "Civil Liability for Suicide Barriers." Public Law Research Institute, May 22, 1998.

Resiman, Will. "Bridge Suicides Exceed Yearly Average." *San Francisco Examiner*, January 22, 2010.

―――. "Funding for Golden Gate Bridge Suicide Net Proves Elusive." *San Francisco Examiner*, August 6, 2009.

―――. "Surviving Bridge Plunge Nearly Impossible." *San Francisco Examiner*, March 20, 2008.

Reuters. "Suicide Risks Shared Across Borders." February 1, 2008.

Ritter, John. "Suicides Tarnish the Golden Gate." *USA Today*, January 31, 2005.

Roach, Mary. "Don't Jump!" *Salon*, February 9, 2001.

Robertson, Michael. "Legends of the Fall." *San Francisco Focus*, January 1997.

Rosenfeld, Jordan E. "The Bridge." *Pacific Sun*, October 2006.

Ross, Martha. "Would a Suicide Barrier on the Golden Gate Save Lives?" *Walnut Creek Patch*, May 27, 2011.

Ryan, Joan. "Room of Grief." *San Francisco Chronicle*, February 25, 2005.

―――. "Teen Grieves, Writes After Pal's Suicide." *San Francisco Chronicle*, February 20, 2005.

Salkeid, Luke. "British Graduate Jumped from Golden Gate Bridge After Studying Websites." *Daily Mail*, May 28, 2009.

Saracevic, Alan. "Suicide City." *Bay Guardian*, May 17, 1995.

Saunders, Debra J. "Do Not Romanticize This Death." *San Francisco Chronicle*, August 2, 1995.

Savlov, Marc. "The Gate Escape." *Austin Chronicle*, January 26, 2007.

Scheide, R.V. "Death Throws." *Metroactive*, March 24, 2004.

Seiden, Richard H. "Reverend Jones on Suicide." *Suicide and Life-Threatening Behavior*, Summer 1979.

Simon, Robert I. "Just a Smile and a Hello on the Golden Gate Bridge." *American Journal of Psychiatry*, May 2007.

Speich, Don. "Media Suicide Coverage Debated." *Marin Independent Journal*, January 21, 2007.

————. "Today I Am Committing Suicide." *Marin Independent Journal*, January 12, 2007.

Stovall, Jeffrey, and Domino, Frank J. "Approaching the Suicidal Patient." *American Family Physician*, November 1, 2003.

Stryker, Jeff. "Publicizing a Magnet for Suicide." *San Francisco Chronicle*, February 6, 2005.

Taylor, Michael. "Golden Gate Bridge's Fatal Attraction." *San Francisco Chronicle*, July 14, 1995.

Torres, Stephen. "A Life of Death." *Bay Guardian*, August 8, 2007.

Trumbull, Todd. "Lethal Beauty: The Allure." *San Francisco Chronicle*, October 30, 2005.

USA Today. "Golden Gate Tries Wires to Keep Suicides at Bay." June 12, 1998.

Vick, Karl. "The Golden Gate: A Bridge Too Deadly?" *Washington Post*, March 3, 2008.

Walker, Thaal. "New Talk of Bridge Suicide Barrier." *San Francisco Chronicle*, January 30, 1993.

Walsh, Jason. "Bridge Jumpers leave Coast Guard Rescuers Saddened, Annoyed." *Pacific Sun*, June 17, 1983.

Weiss, Mike. "Lethal Beauty: A Survivor's Story." *San Francisco Chronicle*, November 1, 2005.

Welch, William M. "'Suicide Bridge' Sours Feud." *USA Today*, October 12, 2009.

Welte, Jim. "Grim Portrait of Bridge Suicides." *Marin Independent Journal* September 10, 2009.

Wilkes, Jim. "Bridge a 'Veil' of Hope." *Toronto Star*, January 21, 2003.

Wollan, Malia. "Funding for Golden Gate Bridge Barrier OK'd." *New York Times*, July 29, 2010.

Zemora, Jim Herron. "Bridge Suicide No. 987." *San Francisco Examiner*, March 26, 1995.

Zinko, Carolyne. "Ammiano Pushing to Get Started on Bridge Suicide Barrier Study." *San Francisco Chronicle*, February 8, 2006.

———. "Gate Bridge District to Start Study of Barriers." *San Francisco Chronicle*, March 11, 2006.

———. "Golden Gate Star of Dark Documentary." *San Francisco Chronicle*, April 29, 2006.

———. "Lethal Beauty: The Advocate." *San Francisco Chronicle*, November 3, 2005.

———. "Lethal Beauty: An Inside Look at Who Jumps." *San Francisco Chronicle*, July 31, 2007.

———. "Lethal Beauty: The Barrier Debate." *San Francisco Chronicle*, November 3, 2005.

———. "Lethal Beauty: The Bureaucracy Barrier." *San Francisco Chronicle*, November 3, 2005.

———. "Lethal Beauty: The Toronto Example." *San Francisco Chronicle*, November 3, 2005.

———. "35 Jumped to Their Deaths Last Year." *San Francisco Chronicle*, January 11, 2008.

———. "Three Options Offered for Bridge Suicide Barrier." *San Francisco Chronicle*, May 24, 2007.

———. "Suicide Barrier Is Called Feasible." *San Francisco Chronicle*, May 25, 2007.

———. "Suicide Barrier Study Gets Push." *San Francisco Chronicle*, February 25, 2006.

———. "Shoes Memorialize Bridge Jumpers." *San Francisco Chronicle*, September 28, 2008.

MOVIES

Olson, Jenni. *The Joy of Life*. San Francisco, 2005.

Steel, Eric. *The Bridge*. New York, 2005.

MISCELLANEOUS

Abstract: "Suicide and the Bridge: A Search for Solutions." November 19, 1969 suicide symposium.

Lawsuit: Claim of death of Leonard Branzuela by Maria Martinez, filed September 5, 1995.

Lawsuit: Petition for review after final decision of the Court of Appeal, November 6, 1995.

Minutes: Golden Gate Bridge District board of directors meetings, 1940 to 2010.

Minutes: Golden Gate Bridge District building and operating committee, 1970 to the present.

Pamphlet: "A Bridge Suicide is Suspected: What Do You Do Now?" The Bridge Rail Foundation, 2008.

Report: Public safety patrol twelve-month evaluation, April 1, 1996 through March 24, 1997.

Speech: "The Critical Relationship Between Suicides and Publicity." Dale W. Luehring, Golden Gate Bridge District General Manager, at the November 19, 1969, suicide symposium.

WEB SITES

www.suicidology.org (American Association of Suicidology)

www.afsp.org (American Foundation for Suicide Prevention)

www.bridgerail.org (Bridge Rail Foundation)

www.suicideprevention@dmh.ca.gov (California Strategic Plan on Suicide Prevention)

www.ggbsuicidebarrier.org (Golden Gate Bridge District)

http://goldengatebridge.org (Golden Gate Bridge District)

http://goldengatebridgesuicides.com (Dayna Whitmer's Web site in memory of her son)

www.ilovecasey.com (John Brooks's Web site in memory of his daughter)

www.suicidepreventionlifeline.org (National Suicide Prevention Lifeline)

www.pfnc.org (Psychiatric Foundation of Northern California)

www.samhsa.gov (Substance Abuse and Mental Health Services Administration)

www.sprc.org (Suicide Prevention Resource Center)

INDEX

Text: 10/14 Palatino

Display: Univers Condensed Light 47 and Bauer Bodoni

Compositor: Westchester Book Group

Printer and binder: Maple-Vail Book Manufacturing Group